John Keay's recent books include *of the Middle East 1900–1960* and *L East*. He lives in Scotland and is married to the author Julia Keay. Together they edited the *Collins Encyclopaedia of Scotland* and are now revising the *London Encyclopaedia*. John's earlier books include standard histories of India and the English East India Company. His latest is *Mad About the Mekong: Exploration and Empire in South East Asia*.

The Spice Route

A History

JOHN KEAY

JOHN MURRAY

© John Keay 2005

First published in Great Britain in 2005 by John Murray (Publishers)
A division of Hodder Headline

Paperback edition 2006

The right of John Keay to be identified as the Author of the Work has been asserted by him in
accordance with the Copyright, Designs and Patents Act 1988.

1

A CIP catalogue record for this title is available from the British Library

ISBN 0 7195 6199 X

Typeset in Monotype Bembo by Servis Filmsetting Ltd, Manchester

Printed and bound by
Clays Ltd, St Ives plc

Hodder Headline policy is to use papers that are natural, renewable and recyclable products and
made from wood grown in sustainable forests. The logging and manufacturing processes are
expected to conform to the environmental regulations of the country of origin.

John Murray (Publishers)
338 Euston Road
London NW1 3BH

Contents

List of Illustrations

Section Two

Preface

Until the tsunami of late 2004, the Sri Lankan fishing-port of Hambantota had changed little since Leonard Woolf, the soon-to-be husband of Virginia, was posted there in 1908. The shop nearest to Woolf's residence was still an ironmongery-cum-grocery, and in its dark interior the proprietor still perched behind a wide wooden counter of odd but traditional design. Across the counter's surface, narrow strips of plywood had been criss-crossed and glued to create a honeycomb of small square receptacles. There were maybe a hundred of these compartments, and each contained an item of withered woodland detritus – roots, seeds, twigs, nuts. The plastic jars and old tobacco tins ranged alongside held more of the same but with a preference for leaves, buds and viscous essences. All were dispensed with great precision, pared if necessary with a scalpel, weighed in jeweller's scales, and then carefully wrapped in twists of yesterday's newspaper. For all were spices. Though not much to look at, their smell announced them, its clashing aromas rasping the sinuses with the olfactory equivalent of an aural assault by massed brass bands attuning their instruments. It seemed scarcely credible that to obtain these same noisome and unprepossessing substances mankind had first ventured into the unknown and aspired to mastery over his global environment.

History loves a paradox, and there can be none greater than a taste for spices being responsible for the exploration of our planet. Sovereigns pledged their prestige, and navigators risked their lives, not in the quest for gold or the thirst for power but to redirect the distribution of a few inessential and today almost irrelevant vegetable products. Whether eastward-bound like Vasco da Gama or westward like Christopher Columbus and Ferdinand Magellan, the great Renaissance pioneers invariably sailed in search of spices. The discovery of the Americas, of a sea-route round Africa and of that missing link in the world's circumference that was the Pacific were all incidental to this quest for pungency and flavour. So, by extension, were the developments in shipbuilding, navigational science and ballistics that eventually gave the maritime powers of western Europe superiority over other nations and led on to dominion and empire.

But the lure of spices was no novelty, nor was it narrowly conducted. It began with the dawn of history and would extend to the ends of the earth. Ages before da Gama weighed anchor, a whiff of spices enticed into unknown waters Pharaonic and Phoenician seafarers, Graeco-Roman traders, Indo-Arab merchants, Muslim scholars, Venetian fortune-seekers, African adventurers and Chinese emissaries. Just about every maritime pioneer from before the age of Alexander the Great almost to that of Napoleon had a nose for pungent substances. Thanks to the challenge of sourcing and redirecting these exotic commodities, mankind learned to overcome his fear of the world's briny wastes, to master their navigation, discover their remotest shores and so, as it were, 'grow into' the fullness of his planet.

The story of Europe's great age of expansion and empire has often been told. The origins and economics of the spice trade both before and after Europe's Renaissance intervention have also been studied. But less has been made of the geographical progression of this usually east–west trade and far too little is known of the non-European element in its history. In tracing the spice route's ancient articulation, its gradual exploration and its continual realignment, this account may be the first to set Europe's post-1400 endeavours within the context of a wider, older quest.

No vital industry depended on spices, and with the exception of medicine, no branch of the arts or sciences could not have managed without them. The human body needs minerals, notably salt; but pepper, the most substantially traded of all spices, is a dietary irrelevance. One might live a perfectly healthy life without ever ingesting, inhaling or otherwise being exposed to any one of the desiccated bits of vegetation that have traditionally been considered spices. Nor are they addictive in any physiological sense. The withdrawal symptoms that might be evinced at times of scarcity were purely social and economic.

That, though, was the point. In ages past, when utility was paramount, the allure of spices lay precisely in their glorious irrelevance. Rare enough to imply distinction and distinctive enough to be unmistakable, spices unashamedly announced themselves as luxuries. Some had curative or stimulative properties, but mostly their pungent aromas and piquant flavours were deployed simply to advertise the consumer's extravagance and excite the envy of others. They flattered and caressed, confounding the coarse, enhancing the commonplace. To the nose and the palate they acted as silk to the touch or as music to the ear.

Silk, once exclusively the product of the Chinese empire, enjoyed a similar distinction. The Greeks and Romans were seduced by its feel and dazzled by its sheen long before they understood how it was made or where it came from. Such mysteries only enhanced its appeal. Demand in western Asia and Europe generated a whole nexus of trade routes by which, in the form of yarn, cloth and apparel, it travelled laboriously overland from China. But the romance of these routes, later dubbed collectively 'the Silk Road', was a purely European conceit. Other silk routes to India and south-east Asia were ignored. Only the long caravan trails across the desert to Samarkand and the Mediterranean were celebrated, studied and eventually explored. To Europeans, it was this 'Silk Road', their 'Silk Road', that was seen as a challenge and deemed worthy of a name.

The same was true of spices. Logically the concept of a single spice route is almost indefensible. Spices grew, and still do, in warm but widespread locations, and they reached markets even more widespread by a whole web of routes. Some spices scarcely travelled at all. India was probably the world's largest consumer as well as its largest producer; China, too, was both an importer and an exporter. There cannot therefore be said to have been a single trading corridor linking the world's spice gardens to its spice kitchens. Nor was the direction of the trade-flow consistent. Saffron, for example, anciently travelled west to east, then east to west, and may now be about to go into reverse again.

The notion of a single spice route arose simply because Europeans assumed the primacy of their own consumer-region and supposed the existence of a definable producer-region. Between these two must run 'the spice route', although unlike the Silk Road it apparently crossed more water than land and so lent itself to frequent realignment. As navigators grew bolder, ships more seaworthy and instruments more sophisticated, the route edged away from the shoreline, and the short cuts across open water were extended.

The producer-region was known vaguely as 'The Indies'; but it became more specific as individual spices were correctly sourced. By the later Middle Ages, only three of the finest culinary additives still eluded geographical identification. Among commodities whose remote provenance amounted to a defining characteristic, these three were evidently the remotest. Almost in despair, and before their native habitat was actually discovered, they were allocated their own producer entity – the so-called 'Spice Islands'. Like 'the Silk Road', this name too provoked speculation, excited adventurers and was perceived as a challenge.

The muddled ideas of the ancients led to spectacular misapprehensions and some strikingly relevant deductions. Later, medieval Christendom, agog at the maritime sagas of the Muslim world, explored the wilder shores of invention to concoct tales so tall they elevated the Spice Islands into a veritable paradise. Less charming were the casual atrocities proudly perpetrated by the bearded sea-dogs of Renaissance and Reformation Europe. Their triumphs were thereby tainted, and ultimately paradise itself was plundered. Whole societies were destroyed, and the mystique of the world's most romantic trade was hopelessly debased. The promise of the spice route, cherished for millennia, evaporated within a couple of centuries.

It is not in the end a pretty story. Nor is it one richly endowed with archaeological or artefactual remains. Indeed one could retrace the entire spice route without ever consciously encountering any solid evidence of its existence. Like spices themselves, the romance of the route lingers on in less tangible form, in the delinquent breeze that leaves untroubled an atmosphere thicker than soup, or in the swish of breakers busily reducing coral to powdered sand and so obliterating the tide-lines of the past, its forgotten perils and its uninvited landfalls.

In Mattancheri near the mouth of Cochin's great harbour, a small bazaar largely dedicated to wholesaling spices still scents the inshore

wind, so lending a exotic tang to what was once one of the spice
routes great entrepôts. Inland the pepper vines of Kerala's tangled
woods still trail from any convenient host; and across the Palk Strait
the grocers of Sri Lanka may yet refill the compartments of their spice
counters by simply growing their own. But cinnamon, Sri Lanka's
most famous spice, is now more widely produced in the uplands of
west Sumatra where the dainty trees line the irrigated rice fields like
willows in the English Fens.

Further east, Surabaya, the maritime metropolis of east Java, still has
a harbour exclusively reserved for sail. Here more than anywhere the
spice route lives on not just in exotic odours but in a way of trade and
a means of travel. The quay is over a mile long and devoid of either
gantries or containers. Cargoes consist of sacks and crates. The dock-
side is jammed with pick-ups, handcarts and gangplanks, all backing
like excited harvesters into a forest of shipping. Vaguely termed *pinisi*
or *prahus*, the ships are hand-built of teak, mostly in Sulawesi or
Borneo; single or twin-masted – but nowadays with an engine as
well – they may displace up to 250 tons. Da Gama and Columbus used
vessels of a comparable size. The *pinisi* are moored not alongside the
quay but end-on to it and so close together that the enfilade of their
projecting bows and bowsprits forms a rakish avenue. They look like
tethered swordfish, their colour a bleached shade of whalebone.

Rice, copra, sugar and sago now form the mainstay of their trade;
spices are incidental. But once clear of the river and out into the haze-
laden Java Sea, their seasonal routings still faithfully replicate those of
the spice age. To Ambon and Timor, Makassar and Melaka,
Palembang and Padang the *pinisi* sail with the same winds, buoyed by
the same promise and fearful of the same dangers. A reef off the coast
of Sulawesi might be the very one on which Drake's *Golden Hind* ran
aground; of the hulks reported by divers in a bay at Tidore one could
be the *Trinidad*, Magellan's flagship; and on a Moluccan hilltop the
overgrown ramparts are those of Fort Belgica, whose Dutch masters
superintended the demise of the traditional trade. Little imagination
is needed in such places; but to recreate the romance of the spice
route, a lot of history may be helpful.

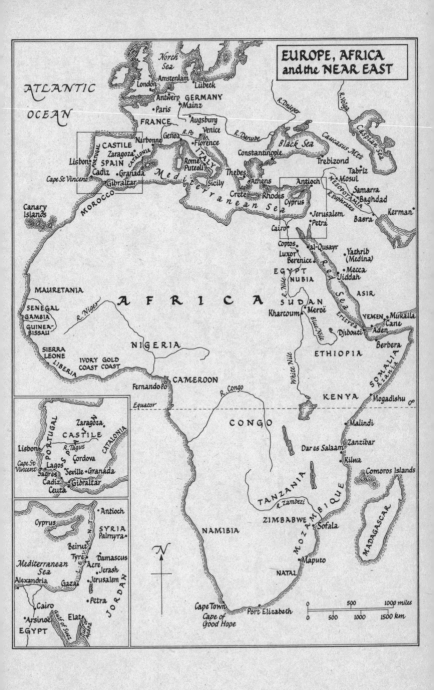

EUROPE, AFRICA
and the NEAR EAST

ATLANTIC
OCEAN

North
Sea
Amsterdam
London   Antwerp Lübeck
•Paris   GERMANY
         Mainz
FRANCE   Augsburg
         Venice   R. Danube
Narbonne Genoa   R. Po
CASTILE   •Florence   Black Sea   Caucasus Mts
SPAIN CATALONIA Rome Constantinople   Caspian Sea
Lisbon Zaragoza ITALY Puteoli   Trebizond   R. Volga
  Cadiz •Granada Mediterranean Thebes Athens   Tabriz
Cape St Vincent Gibraltar   Sicily Crete Rhodes Antioch Mosul Samarra
                                   Sea   Cyprus MESOPOTAMIA Baghdad
Canary   Cairo •Jerusalem R. Euphrates Kerman
Islands   MOROCCO   Petra   Basra

MAURETANIA   Coptos   al-Qusayr
                                  Luxor• Berenice   Yathrib
SENEGAL   EGYPT NUBIA   (Medina)
GAMBIA   •Mecca
GUINEA-   A F R I C A   R. Nile Jiddah
BISSAU   ASIR
                          NIGERIA   SUDAN   YEMEN •Mukalla
SIERRA   Khartoum •Meroë   Eritrea Cane
LEONE IVORY GOLD   Blue Nile Djibouti Aden
LIBERIA COAST COAST   Berbera
              Fernando Po CAMEROON   ETHIOPIA SOMALIA Azania
                          R. Congo   White Nile KENYA Mogadishu 0°
Equator
              CONGO   •Malindi

              PORTUGAL   Dar es Salaam Zanzibar
Zaragoza   Kilwa
CASTILE
Lisbon R. Tagus CATALONIA   TANZANIA Comoros Islands
Cape St Córdova   R. Zambezi
Vincent Lagos •Seville •Granada ZIMBABWE MOZAMBIQUE Sofala
Sagres Cadiz •Gibraltar NAMIBIA   MADAGASCAR
        Ceuta   Maputo
                                         NATAL
        •Antioch
Cyprus SYRIA
        Palmyra•
Beirut   N
Tyre •Damascus
Mediterranean Acre Jerash   Cape Town Port Elizabeth
Sea Gaza •Jerusalem JORDAN   Cape of
Alexandria   Good Hope
        •Petra   500   1000 miles
•Cairo
•Arsinoë Elat   0 500 1000 1500 km
EGYPT Gulf of Suez

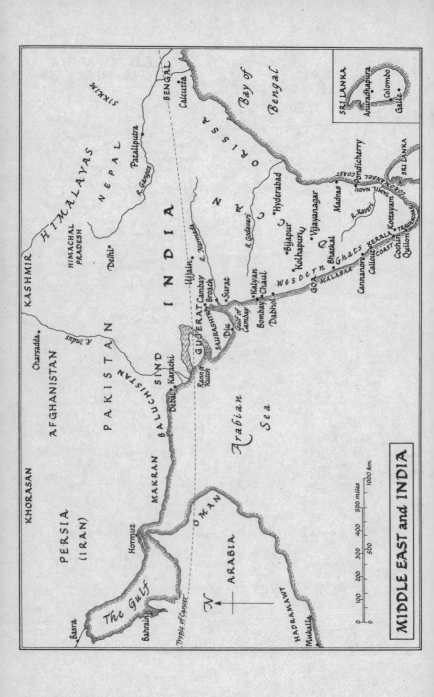

MIDDLE EAST and INDIA

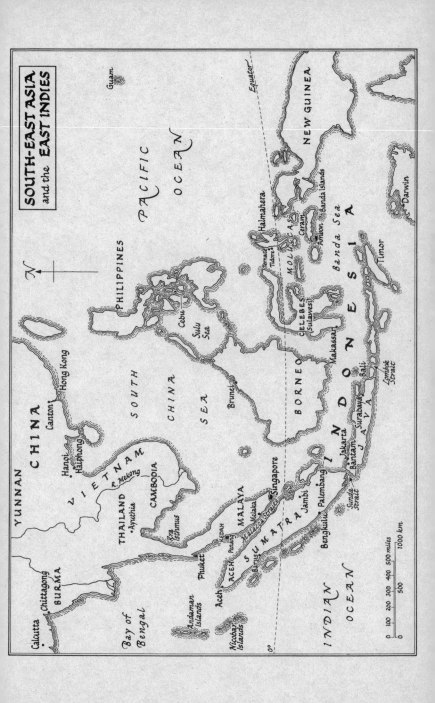

SOUTH-EAST ASIA and the EAST INDIES

I

Before the Fall

The Malay merchants say that God made Timor for sandalwood
and Banda for mace and the Moluccas for cloves, and that this
merchandise is not known anywhere else in the world except in
these places; and I asked and enquired very diligently whether
they had this merchandise anywhere else and everyone said not.

Tome Pires, *The Suma Oriental*, 1515[1]

HIGH IN A handsome tree, on an island in the middle of nowhere,
a limb of foliage gyrates. Perhaps it is shaken by the clumsy flir-
tations of the island's outsize pigeons, or perhaps the waxy leaves of
the *myristica fragrans* are simply set astir by an equatorial breeze. The
branch bucks, a twig snags, and a ripe fruit is detached. Globular and
peach-like, the fruit drops towards the forest floor and so embarks on
an odyssey beyond the dreams of Odysseus. For this descent, though
obscure and unremarked, is as pregnant with consequence as the flap
of a butterfly's wing to subscribers to the chaos theory. Thanks to
amorous pigeons or freak zephyrs, one of those commodities that we
call spices has begun the longest journey accorded by history to any
of nature's products.

Transported to the other side of the world, bits of the fruit of *myristica fragrans* once tamed rough Attic wines, immobilised the bowels of
dysenteric Egyptian sailors, and lent a lip-smacking distinction to
frothy steins of Augsburg ale. Today essences from the same fruit scent
bars of cosmetic soap, add zest to Christmas puddings, and supposedly
constitute one of the top-secret ingredients in such proprietary brands
as Vicks VapoRub and Coca-Cola.

The island growers are not unaware of all this downstream activity and have ever sought to profit from it. When a harvest is decreed, they gather up the fallen fruit and dislodge what more they can by nudging the trees with long poles to which baskets are lashed. Carted home, the flesh of the fruit is then immediately detached from the stone. Sometimes they make an unexciting jam with it. In the sixteenth century the Portuguese thought highly of this preserve and found the expense of transporting such a comparatively heavy commodity to be well worth while. Garcia da Orta, a Goa-based physician whose *Colloquies on the Simples and Drugs of India* first faithfully revealed the botanical provenance of many spices, reckoned the jam a sovereign tonic. Good for both the brain and the nervous system, it was also a useful *digestif* and invaluable in combating 'disorders of the womb'.

> The thick outer rind is very good made into a conserve and it has a pleasant taste. It comes from Banda in jars of vinegar, and some people eat it in a salad. But all that comes to this land [i.e. India] is in the form of a conserve with sugar, a very beautiful fruit leaving an agreeable scent in the mouth.[2]

The jam, however, was an incidental by-product; demand for it was, and is, variable, and the pulpy flesh had often deteriorated by the time it was collected. The spice lies within the fruit, like the pearl in the oyster. There, encasing the stone, nestles the aril, a soft and lace-like membrane. Carmine in colour but, when dried in the sun, turning scarlet, orange and then a brownish gold, this fragile substance the world knows as mace. And as for the stone itself, the small round kernel of this fruit from an island in the middle of nowhere, it is nutmeg. Mace and nutmeg come from the same fruit; and for most of history, that fruit came only and exclusively from one of the remotest locations imaginable.

There are actually ten small islands to which the *myristica fragrans* is native. Known collectively as the Bandas, they cluster in the middle of the Banda Sea which, famed for its fishing grounds, is located just below the equator about 500 miles (800 km) north of Darwin in Australia and may belong to either the west Pacific or the Indian Ocean. The largest of the Banda Islands measures 12 square miles (30 sq. km), the smallest just a few cramped acres, and one of them consists entirely of an active volcano. From Ambon, the earthquake-prone capital of the Moluccas (or Malaku province in eastern Indonesia), it takes up to eighteen hours to reach them by boat or thirty minutes in a minuscule aeroplane. Either way, a clear day and a calm sea are essential. The Bandas are not to be found except on the best of maps and it is easy to miss them.

Green and unkempt stacks looming from a hazy horizon announce both anchorage and airstrip. In a sea of halogen clarity, turquoise depths shade to the milky ramparts of a sub-aqua wonderland where liveried fish glide and dart through fretted coral palaces. Ferns and palms tumble down from the hills to lean out over the shoreline as if for a better view of these candy-coloured shallows. From the flanks of Gunung Api (literally 'the fire mountain') the lava-flows slither straight into the sea, there to dribble down the coral like dirty candle wax. And all the while, high in the forest canopy, the pigeons drum up their special welcome. 'Of birds,' wrote the naturalist Alfred Russel Wallace during his 1861 visit, 'the most remarkable is a fine and very handsome fruit-pigeon (*Carpophaga concinna*), which feeds upon the nutmegs, or rather on the mace, and whose loud booming note is to be continually heard.'[3] While lesser doves bill and coo, the Blue-tailed Imperial Pigeons of the Bandas bill and boom. Their call resonates round the islands and lends to the stillness of an impeccable tropical morning an ominously martial rhythm. Unease afflicts the visitor, and it has nothing to do with the smoking vents of Gunung Api. In fact, the occasional shower of volcanic ash is a necessary benison, replenishing the nutrients and minerals on which the islands' unique ecology depends. That the setting is palpably soured is due to other eruptions. The taint of human greed hangs in the heavy air like the after-thud of a cannon shot. Islands so favoured invited close attention. As well as attracting traders, they excited monopolists, fired patriots, and unhinged empire builders. Geography ordained a paradise; history made it a killing field. If Eden springs readily to the mind of the modern visitor, it is an Eden after the Fall.

Yet the Fall was a long time coming. For over a thousand years the bakers and brewers of Europe, the apothecaries, vintners, embalmers and perfumers, crumbled their mace and grated their nutmeg in profound ignorance of where these fragrant substances came from. Not till the fifteenth century did the Bandas appear on any extant chart and not till the sixteenth did a European vessel venture within sight of them. The same was true of the thousands of other islands in the Moluccas, including those whence came the clove. Efficacious for almost every known ailment, and the most desirable of culinary spices, cloves were as prized in China as in Europe. Pound for pound they often outpriced nutmeg, if not mace, and for centuries they too were of uncertain origin.

Rarity of itself commanded a hefty premium; so did the pungency, variety and utility of the myriad different spices. But for most of history, what endowed spices with their unique appeal was the mystery of where they came from. They were not just exotic but, in most cases, of quite unfathomably remote origin. Supply seemed as providential and precarious as the weather; like the manna that rained down on the Israelites, they partook of the supernatural. Tantalisingly, here were fragrances, flavours and tinctures in everyday use yet of whose origins men knew no more than they did of the ambrosia on which Olympian gods royally dined or the *soma* on which India's deities became so gloriously drunk.

Ignorance bred superstition. Wondrous tales were generated of the perils of spice culture and the rites necessary to overcome them. Herodotus, the fifth-century BC Greek historian, made the cutting of cassia, a kind of cinnamon, sound decidedly perilous. The shrubs grew in the middle of a lake and the harvest was contested by 'winged creatures like bats, which screech horribly and are very fierce'. They attacked especially the eyes, which had to be carefully protected, presumably by screening them behind wickerwork spectacles.

For collecting cinnamon proper, continues Herodotus, the procedure 'is even stranger'.

> The Arabians say that large birds bring those dry sticks called cinnamon for their nests, which are built with clay on precipitous mountains that no man can scale. To surmount this difficulty, they have invented the following artifice: having cut up into large pieces the limbs of dead oxen and other beasts of burden, they lay them near the nests and retire to a distance. The birds fly down and carry off the joints to their nests, which are not strong enough to support the weight of the meat and fall to the ground. Then the men come up and gather the cinnamon, and in this manner it reaches other countries.[4]

Seemingly Herodotus had heard rumours about the edibility of certain birds' nests. The idea that they might be built of cinnamon, one of the few spices that came in nest-size sticks, provided an explanation for both the edibility of the nests and the provenance of the spice. In fact, neither the birds' nests nor the cinnamon orginated in Arabia or anywhere near it. They could, though, be sourced in southeast Asia; and both owed something to the always discriminating Chinese.

The mystique of spices weathered the enquiries of classical scholarship, ran riot in the credulous Dark Ages, and blossomed in medieval times. In the 'Lond of Lomb...growethe the peper', says Sir John Maundevile, a popular but pseudonymous and thoroughly unreliable knight-of-the-quill whose geography is as errant as his fourteenth-century spelling.

> And it growethe no where ell[s]e in alle the World but in that Forest ... in that Contree be manye manere of Serpentes and of other Vermyn, [because of] the great he[a]te of the Contree and the Peper. And sume men seyn that whan thei will gadre [gather] the Peper, thei maken Fuyr [fire], and brennen [burn] aboute, to make the Serpentes and Cokedrilles to flee.

Maundevile rightly thought this nonsense; for if they were to 'brennen aboute', would not the pepper itself be 'brent'? So what in fact they did, he says, was to rub on a good snake-and-crocodile repellent. (In Maundevile's day, the 'cokedrille' was reckoned but another kind of 'Serpente', despite its four short legs and 'grete Nayles, like Clees or Talouns'.)

> Thei anoynten [t]here Hondes and [t]here Feete with a juyce made of Snayles and of othere thinges of the whiche the Serpentes and the venymous Bestes haten and dreaden the Savour; and that maketh [t]hem flee before [t]hem, because of the smelle; and then thei gadren it seurly ynow [i.e. they gather it – the pepper – safely enough].[5]

Maundevile placed this pepper-producing 'Lond of Lomb' somewhere off the coast of 'Ynde', or India, and he attributed cloves, nutmegs and mace to the 'Yle of Java'. Though wrong about all of them, he erred in the right direction. By common consent most spices came from 'the Indies', a term that comprehended all the tropical regions of the East. And by the fourteenth century guesswork was giving way to report. Travellers like Marco Polo had already reached south-east Asia from India and China, while Arab, Persian and Indian navigators had long since reached China from India and south-east Asia. The West was getting warm in its search for the 'Spice Islands'. Their long-forbidden fruit would soon be delighting bearded sea-dogs and filling foreign holds. Time was running out for the Eden that was the Banda Islands.

For speculation, while generating much misunderstanding and myth, also roused endeavour and excited invention. Against formidable odds the transport of spices would steadily expand throughout recorded history. It prompted a succession of important innovations in navigation and nautical design; it enticed Greek sailors into the Indian Ocean, Indian merchants to Arabia and Africa, and Arab merchants to Indonesia and China; and ultimately it persuaded Europeans to undertake those voyages of exploration that resulted in the discovery of the Americas and the circumnavigation of the globe. For Christopher Columbus and Ferdinand Magellan, as for Vasco da Gama and Francis Drake, the long-sought prize was neither territory nor gold but the spices of the Indies. Spices provided the major incentive for voyaging into the unknown; and the profits to be made from them guaranteed the necessary funding and political support for such voyages.

The same motivation would drive English and Dutch navigators to brave the pack-ice of the Arctic in their search for a north-east passage round Russia or a north-west one round Canada; in both directions the short polar 'passage' was supposed to open out onto the sun-drenched promise of the Spice Islands. When it failed to do so, the English and the Dutch turned to the sub-equatorial spice routes pioneered by the Portuguese and the Spanish. No other trade was so hotly contested, and no other group of commodities so exercised nations or so changed the course of history. Thanks to, among other spices, the pepper, cinnamon, sandalwood and camphor of the Indies, the cloves of the north Moluccas and the mace and nutmegs of the Bandas, man first acquired a comprehensive understanding of the geography of his planet.

A taste for mastery over it would quickly follow. Atrocities would be freely committed, wars fitfully fought, states toppled, peoples uprooted, hundreds of ships lost, thousands of lives squandered – and all for limited quantities of various desiccated barks, shrivelled berries, knobbly roots, dead buds, crumpled membranes, sticky gums and old fruit stones, none of them exactly indispensable and most of them quite irrelevant to the generality of mankind. Just such a collection of fibrous matter might well have constituted the nesting material of some large and voracious Arabian birds. All that distinguished it from any other collection of vegetable bric-à-brac was its piquancy and its pungency, properties detectable only by the two most underrated of the human senses, taste and smell.

Credulity is still challenged by almost every aspect of the spice trade. One should not be too hard on Herodotus, Maundevile and practically every intervening writer for allowing their imaginations to run away with them. They are not the only ones. In the same way as they heartily endorsed the value of spices without having much idea of where they came from, modern scholarship concedes the antiquity of the trade without having much idea of when it began. It certainly pre-dated the Roman Empire, and if, as seems likely, spices were being transported over prodigious distances as early as 3000 BC, the spice route may be said to pre-exist recorded history.

In global terms, the trade thus defies the commercial norm. Unlike China's tea, South America's rubber or the Middle East's oil – all of which were first 'discovered', then tapped, cultivated, traded and processed – spices were first tapped, cultivated, traded and processed, then 'discovered'. The dynamic of the spice story is therefore peculiarly that of unravelling a geographical mystery, of sourcing certain existing commodities by exploration and enquiry while simultaneously trying to reroute them. As a definable quest for certain reward, it is as much about the route as the commodities. Like the search for the Holy Grail, it attracted dedicated seekers rather than casual prospectors and entailed textual scrutiny as well as adventurous travel.

As will become all too apparent, the term 'spices' covers a multitude of products from many different parts of the world. But it was the Moluccas in eastern Indonesia that would prove to be the most remote and improbable of these producer-regions, and to them would ultimately be reserved the name of the 'Spice Islands'. The most remote of the Moluccas were the mace- and nutmeg-producing Banda Islands. From there the spice route may be said to originate; and since most of south-east Asia is either island or coastline backed by impenetrable rain forest, the only outlet was by sea. The story of the spice route is essentially one of maritime activity.

Yet it was not always so. If a straight line from the Banda Islands to Paris or London were to be drawn on a map, or better still round a globe, it would in fact bisect as much land as water. The most direct route for a Europe-bound consignment of cloves or nutmegs entailed no interminable oceanic crossings; and in the days before sailors cared to lose sight of the coastline, the amphibious character of this routing may have been decisive. Cargoes needed only to be shipped between the peninsulas – Malaya, India, Arabia, Africa – that so obligingly dangled from the underside of the Eurasian land mass. In between these comparatively short voyages – which might be further broken down by island stopovers *en route* – the spices could be moved overland by river or road. Merchants may have preferred such landward routes because they passed through more of Asia's usually inland cities and so increased the sales options. Merchandise could either be sold off for local consumption – the demand for spices in the East always exceeded that in the West – or sold on for further westward and northward movement.

Ideally the story of the spice route might be told in terms of how, over the centuries, these land portages were one by one eliminated as the trade gradually became emancipated from *terra firma*. Naturally, circumventing the peninsular stepping-stones meant a much longer journey. Instead of the 10,000 miles (16,000 km) of a direct amphibious routing to western Europe, by the sixteenth century a nutmeg from the Bandas faced a voyage of nearly 20,000 miles (over 30,000 km). When performed in a single vessel, it was nevertheless quicker and substantially cheaper. Bulk shipments meant economies all round. They eliminated the exactions of innumerable middlemen – carters, cameleers, customs posts. Likewise, direct maritime access, together with naval superiority, eliminated less bellicose competitors and so ensured the lowest possible purchase price and the highest possible resale value.

A few spices had traditionally travelled west almost entirely over-land. They would continue to do so. Musk, rhubarb and cassia ori-ginated in or near the Chinese empire and were often exported, along with silk, brick-tea and other Chinese products, by camel and cart through the trans-Asian trade corridors known collectively (and retrospectively) as 'the Silk Road'. Cloves, mace and nutmegs may anciently have reached the cities of central Asia by the same route, after having first travelled as far by sea to China as they must by land to, say, Bukhara.

But these were exceptions, and until the second millennium AD spices from the Spice Islands generally travelled west along the skirts of Asia in a series of sea strides interspersed with land portages. Assessing the evidence relating to south-east Asia, one authority has called this phase of east–west trade 'the Isthmian Age'.[6] The isthmus under consideration was that of the Malay peninsula; and throughout discernible history, ports on and about this pendant of land between the South China Sea and the Bay of Bengal were much engaged in the transshipment of spices.

Obviously nutmegs and mace from the Banda Islands, and cloves from the north Moluccan islands of Ternate, Tidore, Bachian and Halmahera, had first to be uplifted and shipped the length of the Indonesian archipelago before they reached the Malay peninsula. This collection service seems to have been performed entirely by local shipping. There is no convincing evidence of Chinese, Indians, Persians or Arabs, let alone Europeans, frequenting the Moluccan ports before the fourteenth century; nor do foreigners appear to have reached the island of Timor, a principal source of the boudoir-scented sandalwood.

These first 2,000 miles (3,000 km) of the spice route were probably controlled from the steamy ports on the north coast of Java, or from Makassar (sometimes called Ujung Pandung) on the west coast of 'the spider-like island'[7] of Sulawesi (sometimes called Celebes). Various seafaring peoples of the archipelago are thought to have been involved at different times, including the Bandanese themselves, the Javanese, the proto-Malay Celates and other ancestors of today's Malay *orang laut* ('sea-folk', 'sea-gypsies') and Makassar's Bugis people.

By foreigners – Asian or European – seeking to usurp control of this most obscure extremity of the spice route, all such indigenous operators would be termed 'pirates', a pejorative freely applied to any rivals and especially to local seafarers who attempted to defend what they considered their own territorial waters and maritime rights. The Bugis of Makassar, in particular, invited obloquy. Master-shipwrights and excellent navigators who were supposed to be able to detect a reef purely by smell, they darted in their rakish *prahus* (sailing vessels, sometimes with outriggers) from unsuspected anchorages on the coasts of Borneo and Sulawesi to challenge all rivals. Against monopolistic Europeans the Bugis would continue to wage a rearguard action well into the nineteenth century, by which time the term 'bogey' or 'bogy' was entering common English usage. This may have been a coincidence; but allusion to the spice trade being not uncommon in nursery rhymes, those who as children were hush-hushed to bed by 'here comes the Bogey-man' may well originally have been threatened by a 'Bugis-man' who, at the helm of a piratical *prahu*, would certainly 'catch you if he can'.

In an earlier and less alarmist age the Bugis and other Indonesian carriers made for ports on the east coast of the Malay isthmus to dispose of their spices. Here consignments purchased for the always important markets of the Chinese empire would be transferred to other vessels that often included towering junks from China itself. What we know of this trade and of the east coast Malay ports prior to the fifteenth century is largely derived from Chinese sources. They refer to the peoples of both the south-east Asian mainland and western Indonesia as *K'un Lun*, and commonly credit these *K'un Lun* with the cultivation of the nutmegs and cloves that in fact came from the far Moluccas.

Ascribing producer status to somewhere that was really only a place of purchase or transshipment was a common error which would bedevil conjecture about the spice trade. When Herodotus located his cinnamon-scavenging birds in Arabia, he made the same mistake. Just as in China cloves and nutmegs were supposed to come from Malaya, Sumatra or Java, so in the West many spices were thought to originate in Arabia or adjacent parts of east Africa. Some did, but many others were awarded to Arabia or Africa simply because it was from there that these strange commodities finally emerged over the horizon of ascertainable account to enter well-known conduits, like that up the Red Sea to Egypt and the Mediterranean.

In the East during the Isthmian Age (prior to about AD 1000), spices destined for western markets crossed the Malay peninsula by land. A number of likely portage routes have been tentatively identified; and through time, these seem to have slipped south from the narrow Kra isthmus in what is now southern Thailand towards the Malacca Strait off what is now Singapore. By about the sixth century AD shipping was beginning to use the strait itself, but still with a stopover for trans-shipment at one of the ports in its vicinity. The difference between the prevailing winds in the South China Sea and those of the Bay of Bengal often necessitated a halt, as did the limits of local nautical knowledge and the emergence in about the seventh century AD of Srivijaya, a considerable maritime power noticed in both Indian and Chinese sources, that was based on Palembang in eastern Sumatra.

Writing in the twelth century Chou K'u-fei, a minor Chinese offi-cial, reckoned Palembang 'the most important port-of-call on the sea-routes of the foreigners from the countries of Java [Sho-p'o] in the east and from the countries of the Arabs [Ta-shi] and Quilon [Ku-lin, on India's Malabar coast] in the west'. 'They all pass through [Palembang] on their way to China,' says Chou K'u-fei.[8] His obser-vations were expanded in the next century in a compendious *Description of the Barbarous Peoples* (*Chu-fan-chi*) by Chau Ju-Kua, a senior customs officer.

> San-fo-ts'i [Srivijaya], lying in the ocean and controlling the strait through which the foreigner's ship and cart traffic must pass, anciently employed an iron chain as a barrier to keep the pirates of other coun-tries in check. It could be raised or lowered by a cunning device... [but] after some years of peace it has been removed and now lies coiled up on the shore. The natives reverence it like a Buddha, and vessels coming there sacrifice to it. When rubbed with oil it shines as new. Crocodiles do not dare to pass over it to make mischief.[9]

Like Herodotus, Chau Ju-Kua here seems to have confused two quite distinct pieces of information. In the process of collating various reports, he evidently mistook the cross-river chain commonly used as a defence by estuarine ports in south-east Asia for something altogether more ambitious which, spanning the Malacca Strait itself, might explain Srivijaya's supremacy over it. Clearly, though, Palembang and its successors did exercise an effective control of the strait, and they probably owed their prosperity to this stranglehold. After an uncertain interlude, command of the strait would in the fourteenth century be usurped by the eponymous Malay port of 'Melaka' (as the town, if not the strait, of Malacca is now spelled) and in the nineteenth century by Singapore, Melaka's neighbour.

The Malay peninsula, along with the Malacca Strait and the various ports that flanked it, thus consituted both a bottle-neck and an entre-pôt of the spice route. Throughout most of history, those spices that originated either in the Spice Islands themselves or elsewhere in what is now Indonesia passed through this node of commerce. So did large quantities of Arabia's and India's spices on their reverse journey to China. The Chinese reckoned the Malay Peninsula crucial as both a source and a supplier of exotic produce, and the Portuguese would later confirm its importance by making the capture of Melaka and the control of its strait one of their priorities in the Far East. The bottle-neck would not be bypassed until in the sixteenth century Spanish, English and Dutch navigaors challenged the Portuguese monopoly by opening a new route that outflanked the Malacca Strait by way of the Sunda Strait between Sumatra and Java.

A route map of the spice trade consists, then, not of a single line but of looping skeins of itineraries that arc through numerous inter-mediate points-of-call but converge into a solid mass at various major hubs or nodes – rather like airline routings as represented on the maps in in-flight magazines. Heading west from the Malacca Strait, the next such node was to be found near the tip of the Indian peninsula. Here too there was once an Isthmian Age when Indonesian spices, instead of being carried round Cape Comorin or Sri Lanka, were landed on India's east (or Coromandel) coast and then transported overland to ports on its west (or Malabar) coast.

A trail of Roman coin-finds across the peninsula between Madras and Calicut attests the early popularity of this overland 'short cut', and textual sources appear to confirm it. In the first century BC Strabo, the greatest of classical geographers, was able to demonstrate some know-ledge of India – 'a nation greater and more flourishing than any other' – and he knew of Egypt's trade with the Malabar ports. But of Cape Comorin, India's southernmost extremity, and of the Coromandel coast and the Bay of Bengal, he had no knowledge other than the wholly erroneous notion that 'the confines [of India] extend as far as the Eastern Sea and the southern part of the Atlantic'.[10] For Strabo, in other words, south India converged with south Africa; the Indian Ocean was thereby cut in two and the Arabian Sea as nearly land-locked as the Mediterranean.

In the first century BC Roman knowledge extended little beyond India's west coast because that was as far as those who traded under Rome's auspices ventured. Spices from further afield, like the cloves and nutmegs of the Moluccas or the sandalwood of Timor and the camphor of Sumatra, entered the purview of the Roman world through India's west coast ports. Yet the attraction of these ports for the Roman Empire, as for all later visitors from the West, lay not in their role as entrepôts for the exotic produce of Indonesia but as producer-outlets for the better-known spices of southern India itself. These included ginger, cardamom, turmeric and above all black pepper, the mainstay of the spice trade and its only bulk commodity.

Harvested in the hill-forests of south India, loose pepper was shipped from the adjacent Malabar ports in such vast quantities that a cargo of nutmegs and cloves from the Moluccas might literally be submerged in it. In the sixteenth century as much as eighty per cent of all Portuguese spice imports would consist of peppercorns, and in the early seventeenth century Dutch and English shipments would show a like preference. Back in the Middle Ages, Arab and Indian carriers also concentrated on pepper, shipping it both west and east; indeed if Marco Polo may be believed, in the thirteenth century for every vessel despatched with pepper for the European market, there sailed ten similarly laden for China.

Earlier still, classical sources are unanimous in making black pepper the principal Oriental import of the Roman Empire. So many ships sailed every summer from the Red Sea to the Malabar coast for pepper that it ceased to be regarded as an inessential luxury and by the fourth century AD may have been a staple of Roman life. Such, at least, is the explanation usually given for its omission from the Alexandria Manifest, a listing of dutiable commodities imported into the Roman

Empire via the Egyptian port-city of Alexandria where the spice route debouched into the Mediterranean. The inclusion of white pepper, but not of black, is taken to mean that black pepper was too mundane to attract duty.

Deep-packed in Indian peppercorns in another ship's hold, a notional cargo of nutmegs and cloves from the Moluccas now embarked on the Arabian Sea. Though already 4,000 miles (6,000km) into their odyssey, the spices were not yet half-way to their ultimate destination. Ahead lay another voyage to another maw-like node of the trade, either at the entrance to the Persian/Arabian Gulf or at that to the Red Sea. Access to the Gulf meant passing through the Hormuz/Oman Strait, that to the Red Sea meant the Bab el-Mandeb Strait between Aden and the 'horn of Africa'.

The African 'horn' itself, otherwise Cape Guardafui on the Somali coast, was long known as the 'Cape of Spices'. This was in recognition of its importance as a crucial landfall for vessels coming from the Malabar coast. As of the first century BC such vessels might have cut straight across the Arabian Sea on the longest sea-leg of the entire spice route. Weeks without sight of land led men to hail the Cape of Spices with jubilation. Though rocky and dangerous, it promised imminent shelter and the eagerly awaited amenities of a Red Sea port.

In marked contrast, vessels heading for the Gulf rather than the Red Sea were more likely to loop up the Indian coastline from Malabar to Gujerat and then Sind in what is now Pakistan. Cargoes of pepper and the now smothered cloves and nutmegs might here be supplemented with other spices from northern India and the Himalayas. Indigo, ginger and long pepper might be uplifted at the Gujerati ports, spike-nard and bdellium at the Sindi ports.

Which of the two routings was preferred – via the Gulf or the Red Sea – depended on political conditions as well as on the state of navigational knowledge. Of the dangling peninsulas that formed the stepping-stones of the ancient spice route, Arabia was the first to be eliminated. Herodotus records that the Persian emperor Darius (521–486 BC) sent an expedition from what is now Afghanistan down the Indus and round the Arabian coast into the Red Sea. Alexander the Great was evidently contemplating something similar at the time of his death in 323 BC. Coasting round the Arabian peninsula was therefore an option from at least the third century BC, although the Gulf seems to have remained the more popular route for another two hundred years.

The situation changed with the arrival of Roman rule in Egypt following Mark Antony's short-lived alliance with Cleopatra in the mid-first century BC. Rome's acquisition of Ptolemaic Egypt led to tighter control over the Red Sea coast and was followed by an unexpected 'discovery', as momentous in its day as Vasco da Gama's of the sea-route round Africa. For the winds of the Arabian Sea, it was learned, conformed to a consistent and extremely congenial pattern. According to the season, or monsoon, in summer they would propel a sailing ship from the Red Sea straight to the Malabar coast and in winter they would propel it back again. A voyage that along the coast had taken months now took a matter of weeks. Traffic increased dramatically. Spices became big business, and for the next two centuries the Red Sea was the West's undisputed gateway to the East. Meanwhile hostilities between Rome and the Parthian and then Sassanid rulers of Persia made the Gulf route unsafe. But in the fourth century, as Rome itself succumbed to invasion while the eastern half of its empire based on Byzantium waxed glorious, the situation was reversed. Now the Red Sea became unsafe and the greater purchasing power of Constantinople wrenched the spice route north and so back towards the Gulf.

Whether approaching Europe from the Gulf or the Red Sea, all cargoes from the East faced another long overland haul. In Roman times spices arriving in the Red Sea were landed at a port on its African coast for conveyance by camel to the upper Nile and then by boat down-river to the Mediterranean and Alexandria. For cargoes landed in the Gulf, this order of desert and river was reversed. Consignments reaching the head of the Gulf usually proceeded first by boat up the Tigris or Euphrates rivers and then by camel across the Syrian desert. Mediterranean ports like Antioch, Tyre or Alexandria were again the destination.

These desert stages across the Middle East spawned powerful kingdoms whose hold over the landward trade routes may be compared to that of Srivijaya over the sea-lanes of south-east Asia. The wealth generated by east–west exchange brought luxury and power to otherwise isolated oases like Petra in Jordan and Palmyra in Syria. Both challenged the might of Rome, Petra until the first century AD and Palmyra in the second and third centuries AD; under the formidable Queen Zenobia, Palmyra actually invaded Egypt. The rock-cut façades and classical colonnades of their once gracious cities still testify to an otherwise barely explicable prominence.

On to Europe, and still the spice route skipped amphibiously from sea to land whenever the geography permitted. From Egypt or the Levant, eastern imports were shipped to Italy. Those destined for further afield might then be reshipped to Narbonne in the south of France, then repacked for river and road carriage to Flanders, and perhaps reshipped again to Britain or the Baltic. In its heyday Rome, of course, was the major beneficiary, but as of about the tenth century Venice and other Italian city-states would grow as rich and powerful on the proceeds of the spice trade in Europe as had Palmyra and Petra in the Middle East, or Srivijaya in the Far East.

Because navigation in medieval Europe was, if anything, less advanced than in contemporary Asia, the overland haul through France would long outlast its Isthmian equivalents in India and southeast Asia. Not until the fourteenth century would Venetian galleys brave the Straits of Gibraltar and sail round the Iberian peninsula to deliver pepper and other spices direct to Antwerp and London. Another long portage was thus eliminated; but the advantage would be short-lived. For only two centuries later, this route would itself be rendered largely redundant when Vasco da Gama doubled the Cape of Good Hope in 1497 and so circumvented the last and the most formidable of all the peninsular obstructions between the Spice Islands and Europe, namely Africa.

The entire route between the Banda Islands and Europe's Atlantic seaboard was finally emancipated from the Isthmian Age. But contrary to classroom opinion, the Portuguese (and later the Dutch and the English) did not revolutionise the routing of the spice trade. They simply completed the process of its liberation from the physical, economic and political obstructions inherent in overland travel. The spice route's conversion into an exclusively blue-water sea-way was the result of a cumulative process stretching back at least two millennia.

A narrative constructed around some such progression from the staccato voyaging of the ancients to the uninterrupted open-sea routing of the early modern period would undoubtedly serve well. But in all accounts of the spice trade such an essentially geographical approach defers to a more historical and partisan treatment. Some navigators and nations being better at recording their commercial and maritime activities than others, the story is commonly divided into eras corresponding to the supposed dominance enjoyed by the most articulate participants. Hence the accepted chronology of Graeco-Roman, Indo-Arab, Portuguese-Spanish and Anglo-Dutch periods.

The source materials dictate such an approach, yet their detail often denies it. Greek merchants are found sailing on Indian vessels, and Arab navigators assisting Portuguese mariners. A host of other peoples – Chinese, Malay, Persian and African – emerge as major participants. Any global exchange depended on the collaboration of many parties; so did the development of nautical science and navigational aids. The story of the spice route embraces not just exploration, endeavour and empire but a host of less obvious developments, not the least of which concerns the cargoes themselves. Over time, requirements changed, prices fluctuated, fashion took its fickle course, and the nature of spices was itself redefined. For the nutmeg farmers of the Banda Islands it was a combination of all these things, along with the emergence of European sea-power, that would spell disaster.

2

On the Origin of *Species*

INDIAN PICKLE (very Superior)
Ingredients: To each gallon of vinegar allow 6 cloves of garlic, 12
shalots, 2 sticks of sliced horseradish, ¼lb of bruised ginger, 2oz
of whole black pepper, 1oz of long pepper, 1oz of allspice, 12
cloves, ¼oz of cayenne, 2oz of mustard seed, ¼lb of mustard,
1oz of turmeric; a white cabbage, cauliflowers, radish-pods,
French beans, gherkins, small round pickling onions, nastur-
tiums, capsicums, chilies, etc.

Mrs Beeton's Book of Household Management, 1859–61[1]

GIVEN THE DIFFICULTIES of obtaining spices, it is perhaps surprising that there was a spice trade at all. Why not simply collect
seeds of the relevant plants and establish them somewhere more convenient? Instead of trundling all that vegetable bric-à-brac half-way
round the world, and having to repeat the process year after year to
ensure a steady supply, the spiceries could have been relocated. As
experimentation would eventually prove, suitable combinations of
soil and climate were not exclusive to the East; many were replicated
in parts of Africa, the Americas and Australasia; and in some of these
locations the conditions would be found so favourable as to improve
yields.

For better or worse, the naturalisation of eastern spices in the
West – plus that of western, mainly American, spices in the East – would
ultimately undermine the whole mystique of the trade. With the diffu-
sion of spice cultivation in the eighteenth century, the myths would be
demolished, the markets glutted, and demand diverted to other stimulants. In effect it was globalisation that would consign the jewels of the
vegetable kingdom to the indignity of being shrink-wrapped in super-

market sachets and then paraded on dinky racks in kitchens where nobody cooks.

Yet naturalisation was not new and had occasionally transformed aspects of even the ancient world. Writing in the first century AD, Pliny the Elder noted with disgust the progress of 'a tree which has been procured from a foreign clime merely for the sake of its shade'. This was the plane tree, the same as still lines European roads and takes a heavy toll of incautious motorists. From Asia Minor it had been introduced to the Ionian Islands and then, says Pliny, 'it crossed from there to Sicily, became one of the first trees introduced into Italy, and has now travelled as far as Belgium'.[2]

Spices, too, were transplanted. Some, especially those that consisted of roots or rhizomes, had a natural inclination towards it; if not thoroughly dried, they might start putting out shoots while still in transit. Ginger, for instance, was an incorrigible colonist. Ibn Batuta, the Arab Marco Polo, noticed that in the fourteenth century Chinese ships visiting India's Malabar ports were festooned with anti-scorbutic greenery including 'herbs, vegetables and ginger planted in wooden troughs'. Originally native to south-east Asia, *Zingiber officinale* (the name, with subtle adjustments, travelled with the root) had achieved a wide distribution throughout the East and the Pacific in prehistoric times and would repeat this process in Africa and the Americas.

Over the centuries, then, spice production had a tendency to shift around. The restriction of, say, nutmeg cultivation to the tiny Banda Islands, though not exceptional, was by no means the rule. Nor was it always necessary actually to transplant anything. Many spice-yielding plants grew wild in the forests of south and south-east Asia but were not commercially harvested or taken into cultivation until exceptional demand provided some encouragement. Thus black pepper, which until the thirteenth century was supplied almost entirely from south India, would have emerged as a major cash crop on the islands of Sumatra and Java by the early seventeenth century when Dutch and English ships came calling.

Obviously all this movement in the sources of supply introduces another variable into the history of the spice route. More crucially, though, it raises a query about how exotic or pungent a plant must be in order to qualify as a spice. Saffron, for example, was once less regarded than it is today because the purple crocus from which it was extracted was not particularly mysterious. It flourished in European locations extending from Asia Minor, whence it originated, to Saffron Walden in England, where it was naturalised. Only subsequently, when its labour-intensive cultivation became largely centred in Kashmir, did it seem sufficiently exotic to qualify as one of the most precious of spices.

All of which raises the even more difficult question of what actually constitutes a spice. The matter admits of no simple answer, there being many definitions but none that commands universal acceptance. If, for instance, ginger can be grown on deck, or on someone's window-sill, it loses the exoticism associated with spices. From a lack of sun or a change of soil, it may also lose its spicy properties. And if it is being grown for the leaf rather than the root, it scarcely differs from, say, parsley or coriander. In effect it has become a herb.

One school of thought holds that the distinction between herbs and spices has nothing to do with provenance and everything to do with substance. Herbs are green and leafy, spices dried and leafless; nothing could be simpler. But what then of dried herbs? In *The Oxford Companion to Food*, Alan Davidson, while addressing the problem with the utmost circumspection, introduces a further category in the shape of condiments, or 'spices or other flavourings added to food at the table'. He elaborates on the appearance-based criteria for distinguishing herbs and spices – leafy-undried versus unleafy-dried – and, by way of a litmus test, applies them to the decidedy unexotic mustard plant. 'Thus mustard greens would be a herb, mustard seeds a spice, while mustard in a mustard pot, at table, would be a condiment. This would be a convenient set of definitions, and has the merit of being as close to common usage as any rational definition could be expected to come.'[3]

The trouble with such a definition is that 'common usage' tends to mean 'current usage' and to exclude 'traditional usage'. Today the English term 'spices' connotes only edible – and mostly culinary – aromatics, flavourings and tinctures. Historically, and especially in the context of an ancient trade and an extensive trade route, it was used in a much less restricted sense. This recognised the importance of spices in the preparation of not just food and drink but medicines, ointments, cosmetics, air-fresheners, aphrodisiacs, fumigants and dyes. Other exotic ingredients used in these trades, though unwelcome in the kitchen and not necessarily even of vegetable origin – the foul-smelling musk, for instance, which came from a gland in the Himalayan musk deer – might also be reckoned spices. So might high-value imports of exotic origin that were used in none of these trades and had no discernible fragrance or taste but were yet highly desirable and so – a crucial criterion – eminently dutiable. Under this catch-all definition even manufactured goods like Indian cottons and Chinese silks could be lumped into the spice trade.

The culprit in all this is the Latin noun *species*. From it the English language derives a whole family of words – 'special', 'specification', 'species', 'especially' and so on – as well as 'spice'. Originally the Latin word meant simply 'type' or 'kind', a meaning that survives in English in the word 'specie' as reserved for cash 'in kind', that is 'coinage'. In Roman usage *species* quite often implied value, and in time it acquired an even more 'specific' meaning. The word came to be used to denote the 'type' or 'kind' of article on which import duty was payable; and it seems to have been in this context that it gave rise to the French *épice* and the English 'spice'. Reference has already been made to the 'Alexandria Manifest', a fifth-century tariff of Justinian's reign listing those goods that were liable to duty at the great port of Alexandria. The manifest is headed *species pertinentes ad vectigal*. This may be translated as 'the types [of items] subject to import duty'. Alternatively, because many of them are recognisably what we now call spices and because *species* is elsewhere often used to designate spices, the heading may be rendered as 'the spices subject to duty'.

The Alexandria Manifest lists fifty-four of these *species*. Not all are identifiable but about half might be considered spices by the cooks of today. These include several forms of cinnamon and cassia, ginger, white pepper, long pepper, two sorts of cardamom, and asafoetida. Conspicuously absent are nutmeg, mace, cloves, turmeric and black pepper. The last, as already noted, may have been omitted because it was already being shipped in such quantity that it could no longer be considered a dutiable luxury; but the others, all known to the later Roman world, were definitely prized fare and their omission from the customs' schedule is a mystery, though not the only one.

In all classical inventories of exotic imports there appears a bewildering variety of aromatic extracts obtained from the wood of trees and shrubs in the form of oils, resins, gums or simply combustible sticks and shavings. They were used mainly in the perfume and incense businesses and often in conjunction with what we now call spices – which, to the ancient world, they were too. In value, if not in bulk, imports of these arboreal products probably exceeded those of culinary spices; the spice route may in fact have owed its genesis to them, as will be seen.

In the Alexandria Manifest several such products feature, including spikenard (an unguent), aloes-wood (a wood) and myrrh (a resin). Yet of the equally prized camphor oil, sandalwood and frankincense the Manifest contains no mention at all. Conceivably some interruption of the spice route in the Far East, perhaps at that isthmian portage over the Malay peninsula, had temporarily halted supply in the fifth century. This would account for the absence of Indonesia's camphor and sandalwood, along with the Moluccan contingent of nutmeg, mace and cloves.

But the omission of frankincense, a product of Arabia, cannot be so easily explained. Myrrh's near-neighbour and inseparable companion since long before the Three Wise Men set off for Bethlehem, frankincense was the quintessential *species*. Its value may be judged from Pliny's reference to its processing, an operation which was attended with the sort of security now reserved for the enrichment of uranium.

> Great Scot! [literally 'Hercules!'] At Alexandria, where the frankincense is prepared for sale, no amount of vigilance is sufficient to guard the factories. A seal is put upon the workmen's aprons, they have to wear a mask or a fine-mesh net over their heads, and before they are allowed to leave the premises they have to strip off all their clothes.[4]

Sailors arriving back in Lisbon in the sixteenth century would be subjected to similar scrutiny, including the body search; seemingly nothing was more tempting than to stuff a handful of peppercorns down one's hose. In the same century the sultan of Bengal's chamberlain reportedly derived an income of 2,000 *cruzados* a year from selling the particles of masticated camphor retrieved from the contents of his master's golden spittoon.[5] Frankincense, though seldom ingested, was in Roman times just as sought after, just as valuable. And since it is not in the nature of governments to overlook any source of income, let alone one so rewarding, it may be assumed that it did indeed attract duty. The Alexandria Manifest therefore looks to be incomplete. Perhaps the only form in which, thanks to some medieval copyist, it survives represents merely a précis of the original or a selection from it.

Other items included in the Manifest can scarcely be accommodated under any definition of spices, however attentuated: 'lions', 'leopards' and 'panthers', for instance; or 'ivory', 'tortoiseshell' and numerous named gems. All are listed simply because, as rank extravagances or outrageous status symbols, they merited punitive taxation. Likewise presumably 'Indian eunuchs' and, the last in the list, 'Indian hair', which then as now was prized by wig-makers. But if panthers were dutiable, why not tigers? And if Indian eunuchs, why not African slaves? Both passed through Alexandria, the slaves in considerable numbers. The Manifest seems concerned only with the 'types' of goods liable to duty; it is not a comprehensive catalogue.

For a more thorough listing, indeed the ultimate inventory of spices, one must look much later and to an altogether more meticulous and reliable catalogue. It was compiled about 1320 by a merchant of Florence called Francesco di Balducci Pegolotti, who included it in his exhaustive book *The Principles of Commerce*. Here the number of separate entries runs to an impressive 289. To a trader like Pegolotti, all were unquestionably spices, although the most desirable were highlighted 'to indicate specifically those wares which were sold in minute quantities at high prices'. These were known as 'minute spices'.[6]

Again the list includes a few apparent impostors. 'Fresh oranges', 'dates' and 'rice from Syria' sound like the antitheses of spices if only because of a value-to-weight ratio that must have had Pegolotti's business partners tearing their hair out. Portability was what made conventional spices the perfect long-distance cargo. Comparatively low in bulk and light in weight, largely imperishable and easily broken down into smaller loads, they could be bagged, shipped, stored, transshipped, wholesaled, retailed and shelved almost indefinitely. Indeed these characteristics were so important as to suggest another possible definition of spices.

Items from Pegolotti's list like 'white lead', 'tin plate' and 'old copper' also seem to challenge this definition. They are not, though, to be understood as industrial shipments but as small consignments for mainly pharmaceutical and decorative use. Likewise his inclusion of 'waste paper', surely the least likely of all priceless commodities. At the time the making of paper from pulped rags was in its expensive infancy in Europe. Wastage was kept to a minimum, and any material that could be recycled would have commanded a ready sale.

Like Justinian's Alexandria Manifest, Pegolotti's list also includes numerous items that may not be very familiar today. 'Skink' and 'scammony', 'squinanth' and 'sinoper', 'turbith', 'tabasheer' and 'turquoise of Tyre' were probably not on everyone's shopping list even in the fourteenth century. But they are mentioned in other sources; they were undoubtedly of high value; and worked into rollicking verse, no muse could possibly take exception to them.

Other exotica which, though no longer 'in common usage', can readily be identified, serve just as well to evoke the mystique of the trade. Like the spices they denote, their names have an unfamiliar tang, while in their crumpled syllables one might just detect the musty odour of a precious antiquity. 'Amomum', for instance, could be a love philtre, or perhaps a powerful mantra; it was in fact a form of cardamom. More suitably, the gelatinous-sounding 'bdellium' was Pegolotti's preferred term for gum guggul, another desert resin like frankincense, though in this case from Afghanistan and Pakistan. 'Dragon's Blood', naturally, was a fiery-red pigment; sometimes called cinnabar, it was found in Somalia and on the neighbouring island of Socotra.

From Socotra, a botanical treasure-chest of outlandish shrubbery, also came 'aloes', a runny substance with a suitable name in that, though apparently a plural, it was grammatically dispensed in the singular. As the inspissated juice of the agalloch plant, aloes was valued as a purgative throughout the constipated East and was on no account to be confused with 'aloes-wood'. Sometimes called lign(um) aloes, eagle-wood or gharu-wood, aloes-wood came from a lofty tree native to the Mekong basin whose timber famously sank in water and whose root, when dried and ground, cured just about everything. On the evidence of Dioscorides, a first-century AD physician and pharmacologist, a dose of aloes-wood would have been just the antidote to an overdose of aloes.

> One dram of the root, made up as a potion, is prescribed for fluidity and weakness of the stomach and for heartburn: drunk with water it helps those with liver or kidney pain, or dysentery or colic... Crumbled and boiled in water [the trunk-wood] makes a mouthwash for sweet breath and a paste to be applied to the whole body [to keep out the cold]. It is also burnt like frankincense.[7]

In China aloes-wood was used almost exclusively for incense, though some was pulped to produce a strongly scented paper. Chau Ju-Kua distinguished no less than five different qualities of the wood. In the West it was very expensive, in fact 'right dere-worth', as Sir John Maundevile puts it. He understood that the wood was fished out of the Nile having 'comethe out of Paradys terrestre'.[8] This was wrong if you believed the Nile to have its source in Africa; but if, like many from Alexander the Great onwards, you thought it shared a source with the Ganges in a 'terrestrial paradise' among mountains higher than the moon on the far side of India, then it was a good guess.

The gums and resins of Pegolotti's list are supplemented by a wide range of nards and balsams (or balms). Both being oily shrub or plant essences, they too were used more for perfumes, for funerary embalming and for medicinal concoctions than for food. Pegolotti's 'balsam' is highlighted and so was probably 'balsam of Mecca' (otherwise 'balm of Gilead'), the product of another Arabian shrub but one which had been successfully naturalised in Palestine before the first century AD. 'Every other scent ranks below balsam,' says Pliny. It too was extremely expensive, though rather easily adulterated; and in recognition of its fame, following the Roman conquest of Judaea leafy saplings of balsam were carried in triumph through the streets of Rome. 'Even trees figure among the captives in our triumphal processions,' noted the disapproving Pliny.[9]

Of Pegolotti's nards, the queen was undoubtedly 'spikenard', the 'very expensive' pomade with which, according to St John, 'Mary

[Magdalene] anointed the feet of Jesus'.[10] This gesture is usually inter-preted as a foot-bath, though a foot-massage would be more in keeping with spikenard's reputation. Mary then famously 'wiped' the Saviour's feet with her hair in an act of humility that might also rate as one of coquetry combined with understandable economy. Spikenard had all sorts of lascivious connotations, perhaps because it was extracted from the erect 'spike', or flower-head, of *Nardostachys jatamansi*, a native of the high Himalayas although it was later grown in Spain.

From the Himalayas came also the costly 'costus', another of Pegolotti's significant spices; a root that is known as putchuk in English and as *cuth* in Hindi, costus is still dug (under licence) in parts of Himachal Pradesh and Kashmir but today goes exclusively to the Chinese market for medicinal use. It may be practically the only spice that has never been naturalised outside its native sward. 'Myrobalan', which was not to be mistaken for 'malabathron' (otherwise tejpat, another kind of cinnamon), was a small green Indian fruit, while 'colocynth' was the juice of the bitter-apple, actually a gourd. 'Cubeb' was a kind of pepper; the gum 'tragacanth' came from the astragalus plant; 'galangal', or galingale, was a ginger-like root originally from Vietnam; and 'ladanaum' was another sticky Arabian resin (often with goats' hairs adhering to it, according to Pliny).

Of pigments, 'mandrake' or mandragon (mandragore) had emetic properties, 'realgar' or red orpiment was downright poisonous, 'verdi-gris' then as now came from mould on copper, and 'ambergris' was not a vegetable at all but a yellow or grey secretion given off by sperm whales. From 'agaric' (a cathartic) to 'zedoary' (an anaphylactic) Pegolotti ranges through the alphabet to produce as exotic a vocabu-lary as any in literature.

In such strange and often mystifying company it comes as no small relief to meet those spices that have withstood the test of time. Changing fashions, toppling empires and scientific scrutiny have taken a heavy toll of the balsams, nards and gums, but the culinary spices have largely held their own. Pegolotti's various cinnamons, cassias, cumins, cardamoms, cloves, gingers, peppers, saffron, mace and nutmeg still feature in favourite cookbooks and flavour, often uncred-ited, many commercial food products. Thanks to restaurateurs and ready-meal makers of Asian descent, they have staged a comeback – so much so that 'spices' and 'spicy' are now often taken to be defining characteristics of exclusively Indian cooking.

Even the myths are not totally discredited. Though the origins of Pegolotti's edible spices – to which should be added turmeric – are no longer a mystery, we still credit their employment with wondrous effects, some of which are neither medicinal nor aphrodisiac. A case in point would seem to be the long-held belief that spices were essential in the preservation of butchered meat. Europe's interest in the spice trade, and its designs on the spice route, are so confidently predicated on this assumption that historians almost blush to repeat it. As J. H. Parry writes, in a standard work on European exploration and expension:

> It is a commonplace of economic history that the farming commu-
> nities of Europe, down to the late seventeenth century at least, suffered
> from a chronic shortage of winter feed for cattle. Large numbers of
> beasts had to be slaughtered every autumn, and the meat preserved for
> winter consumption by being salted or pickled...Apart from salt, the
> preservative spices were all produced in tropical countries: pepper...
> cinnamon...nutmeg and mace...[and] the most valuable preservative
> spice [of all] – cloves.[11]

To redress the unfair distribution of nature's wherewithal for preserv-ing dead carcasses, it is suggested that Europeans were practically obliged to engage in the spice trade. In a world ignorant of the freezer and the hermetically sealed can, it was the only way to fend off winter starvation. Like oil to today's industrialised economies, spices had sup-posedly become essential to the then agricultural economies of western Europe. In the fifteenth century the extension of Muslim control from the spice route to the producer regions themselves had only emphasised Christendom's vulnerability to a hostile embargo of these necessary commodities. Hence for good Catholic monarchs like those of Spain and Portugal it became imperative to seek the spices at source.

Yet whilst this is all so glaringly obvious to historians, it is not at all obvious to food scientists. Spices certainly transform boring food into something more appetising; but of themselves they apparently have

very few preservative properties. Preservation is effected by the generous application of salt, by drying or smoking, or by immersion in
various liquids (especially brines, oils, vinegars, spirits and even
syrups). The addition of spices to this process may improve the taste
and smell of the meat but it does not preserve it. Peppering a haunch
of meat, rubbing it with ground cinnamon or sticking it with cloves is
unlikely to produce any noticeable delay in its natural tendency to rot.

So say the chemists; and the food writers seem to agree. Mrs Beeton
treats of both preservatives and spices but she does so quite separately
and without so much as a hint that they may be identical. With apparent approval she quotes a 'Dr Paris in his work on Diet' to the effect
that foreign spices were not just inessential but undesirable since
they 'were not intended by nature for the inhabitants of temperate
climes'...'The best quality of spices is to stimulate the appetite, and
their worst to destroy, by sensible degrees, the tone of the stomach.
The intrinsic goodness of meats should always be suspected when they
require spicy seasonings to compensate for their natural want of sapid-
ity.'[12] Frederick Rosengarten, a modern-day spice-trader and an
eminent writer on the subject, sounds a similar note of caution. Oil
obtained from cloves and cinnamon may, like other oils, have some
germicidal properties, but 'research implies that spices were more
likely used in ages past to disguise the flavour of spoiled or deteriorat-
ing foodstuffs than for their preservative qualities.'[13]

Rosengarten was writing in the late 1960s, since when the suggestion that spices make rotten meat more palatable has also been challenged. 'It used to be said that spices were needed to disguise the off
flavour of spoiled meat,' says the Oxford Companion to Food, 'but this
was a piece of culinary mythology.'[14] In fact experimentation suggests
that, far from disguising the disgusting, spices may actually exaggerate
it. Our ancestors seemingly had no economic excuse for their pursuit
of exotic foodstuffs. They, like we, craved edible spices simply because
they made food more enticing and implied cosmopolitan tastes. Spicy
aromas stimulated the appetite, spicy flavours excited the palate, and
perhaps most important of all, spicy extravagance impressed the
neighbours.

This prestige function of spices can scarcely be exaggerated. Like
fine silks and acknowledged works of art, exotic fragrances and

flavours lent to aspiring households an air of superior refinement and enviable opulence. They conferred distinction. It had always been so and, for as long as spices remained rare and expensive, it would remain so. From earliest times they had been largely reserved for devotional and ceremonial purposes in the form of perfumes and incenses. Burnt or sprinkled, they were deemed especially gratifying by those least easy to appease, like the gods, the mighty and the dead. To acts of worship, divination and interment their swirling aromas lent a heady aura of sanctity, and their elusive savour could be taken to symbolise the reverence of devotees. Even Christianity, though initially opposed to the use of incense as a pagan totem, eventually sanctioned it on the grounds that it mimicked the prayers of the faithful rising up to heaven.

In an ever upwardly mobile world, the offertories and oblations once reserved exclusively for gods and ancestors were eagerly appropriated by others – first Pharaohs and Caesars, then generals and senators, priestesses, epicures, consorts, concubines and all who aspired to be especially worthy of consideration. As spices percolated down into society, they were also diverted to more utilitarian use. The sacred ointments and incenses had to compete for raw materials with toiletries, love-potions, laxatives, fumigants, air-fresheners and of course food additives.

On the scatter-gun principle, maximum efficacy in medicaments and perfumery, as in cooking, was thought to lie in combining the greatest possible variety of spices. For the poison-paranoid King Mithridates the Great of Pontus (d. 63 BC), a famous antidote was prepared that included thirty-six ingredients, nearly all of them recognisable as spices. Though too long to quote, it bore a worrying resemblance to a 'royal perfume' mentioned by Pliny a century later that was compounded of 'myrobalan, costus, amomum, Syrian cinnamon, cardamom, spikenard, cat-thyme, myrrh, cinnamon-bark, styrax-tree gum, ladanaum, balm, Syrian flag and rush, wild grape, cinnamon leaf, serichatum, cypress, camel's thorn, all-heal, saffron, gladiolus, marjoram, lotus, honey and wine'. And of these, moans Pliny, apart from the last few, 'not one is grown here in Italy, the conqueror of the world, or indeed in Europe'. All had to be imported at enormous cost; and for what? To gratify a taste 'for the most superfluous of all forms of luxury', which was also the most unrewarding 'since the person wearing the scent does not smell it himself'.[15] Pliny, a distinguished public servant as well the author of a comprehensive *Natural History* of the entire known world, was so scandalised that he waxed quite apoplectic on the whole subject.

> Moreover we have heard that someone of private station gave orders for the walls of his bathroom to be sprinkled with ointment, and that the emperor Caligula had the bath-tubs themselves scented; and so also did later one of Nero's slaves – so that this must not be considered a privilege of princes. Yet what is most surprising is that this indulgence has found its way into the camp [that is, the army]; at all events the eagles and standards...are anointed on holidays...no doubt it was for this reward that they were enticed into conquering the world! Indeed we look to such examples to sanction our own vices and so justify wearing hair-oil under a helmet. Great Scot, some people nowadays actually put scent in their drink.[16]

The only redeeming consideration was that nard-smeared ne'er-do-wells occasionally got their come-uppance. Lucius Plotius, a consul on the run, had been given away when his pursuers picked up his scent-trail and followed it to his secret hiding-place. Pliny thought Plotius' subsequent conviction unsound; but it was no worse than any scented dandy deserved, 'for who would not consider that people of that sort deserve to die?'[17]

Though Rome's import bill would decline markedly as the empire itself declined, it was no thanks to such fulminations. In what would become a constant refrain to the spice trade, Pliny complained that Rome was beggaring itself by having to export hard currency in order to import worthless exotica. When in the early Middle Ages the West's demand for spices escalated, it would be the returning Crusaders who were accused of squandering Christendom's wealth on oriental luxuries, then the Venetians who prospered from actually handling the spice trade in Europe, then the Portuguese crown which sought a blue-water monopoly of it. Meanwhile, on much the same grounds, the Chinese empire had completely withdrawn from a trade that it had looked poised to monopolise.

Back in Europe, in the seventeenth and eighteenth centuries the East India companies of London and the Netherlands would face a veritable barrage of identical censure. Contemporary economists simply could not conceive how exchanging the sheen of specie for the stench of spices could possibly be in the national interest. That it was nevertheless so would be handsomely demonstrated in the spicy genesis of two empires. Value and the potential for profit depended not on need but on demand; and in the creation of demand there were few more insistent imperatives than personal vanity and the human obsession with social prestige.

3

Frankincense and Cinnamon

> Oft at sea north-east winds blow
> Sabaean odours from the spicy shore
> Of Araby the blest.
>
> John Milton, *Paradise Lost*, bk IV

ACCORDING TO PLINY, incenses were not much used in the Mediterraean world until the fourth century BC, and 'at the time of the Trojan war they did not exist'.[1] Homeric gods were treated to nothing more spice-laden than eye-watering clouds of smouldering juniper and 'thyine wood' by way of an accompaniment to the libations of the faithful. Not until the eastern conquests of Alexander the Great in 333–323 BC was there any Western demand for spices to create either perfumes or incenses, says Pliny.

Yet casual references from well before Alexander's time suggest otherwise. In the sixth century BC the poet Sappho wrote of myrrh, cassia and frankincense being burnt at nuptial ceremonies. And among several Old Testament references which, in the form we now know them, may also date from the sixth century BC, there is the invitation to her lover by an eager temptress in Proverbs: 'I have perfumed my bed with myrrh, aloes [wood] and cinnamon,' she whispers after some perfunctory foreplay, 'Come, let us take our fill of love until the morning; let us solace ourselves with loves.'[2]

This apparent contradiction as to the antiquity of spice use in the Mediterranean world could be explained by Pliny's drawing a distinction between fragrances obtained from individual aromatics and those obtained from compounds that consisted of several concentrated essences. 'The various products [of nature] were not sufficiently remarkable by themselves,' he says, 'so luxury took pleasure in mixing them all up together and making a single scent out of the combination.'[3]

In the East aromatic compounds were the norm and seem to have been employed as devotional aids, personal perfumes, culinary additives (the later equivalent would be *garam masala*) and medicinal elixirs since very ancient times. It was these concentrated fragrances and fiery flavours, so much more pungent than a sprinkling of cinnamon, let alone a bonfire of juniper, that awaited Alexander's Macedonian troops in Iran and the Panjab. Despite initial caution, the invaders experimented with them, duly succumbed, and then took the tastes and habits thus learned back home with them. Pliny makes it sound as if they had contracted some sexually transferable disease and then become its carriers, a slighting inference that would later be levelled against both perfumed Crusaders returning from the Levant and curry-loving Englishmen homeward-bound from the Indies.

Where it all began, though, is hard to say. Pliny thought the Persians deserved the credit for the invention of spice-based perfume as a personal fragrance; they applied it more liberally than anyone else, indeed so drenched themselves in it as 'by its adventitious attraction to extinguish the stench of ingrown dirt'. To India, on the other hand, may belong the credit for the first systematised use of spices as medicaments; Sanskrit texts on the curative properties of many home-grown plants are thought to represent oral traditions going back to at least 1000 BC. But nowhere is it recorded which deity, for instance, was first favoured with incense, nor how the peppercorn, a small and unattractive berry 'with nothing obvious to recommend it', found its way into the cooking-pot. We can only wonder, like Pliny, 'who was the first person game enough to try it on his viands, or who was so greedy as to crave an appetite greater than that which mere hunger could excite?'[4]

In matters of early invention the Chinese are often a good bet. Archaeological and literary evidence suggests that pepper and cinnamon were in regular culinary use by, and probably before, the time of the western Han dynasty (second century BC). Both these spices appear to have been locally grown varieties; Chinese cuisine, like Indian, benefited from a wide range of indigenous spices and already evinced the catholicism and invention for which it is famed. By the fourth century AD aloes-wood and cardamom were being imported into China from Cambodia and Vietnam; cloves and nutmeg from the Moluccas were known, although their origins remained a mystery; and from northern India came long pepper (which bears no botanical resemblance to black pepper, being the seed-head of a short shrub more akin to the American chilli plant than to the straggling south Indian pepper vine).

It is thought that long pepper reached China overland from Bengal, and by the first century BC frankincense may have found its way to the Celestial Empire by the same route, having first been imported into India either by sea direct from Arabia or via the Gulf and along the emerging Silk Road. The stunted trees and shrubs from which both frankincense and myrrh were extracted grew exclusively in the arid lands about the mouth of the Red Sea. Frankincense, a gum-resin from several species of the genus *Boswellia*, was found mainly on the Arabian side; myrrh, a gum-resin (and also an oil) from several species of the genus *Commiphora*, mainly on the Somali side. Separated only by the narrow strait of Bab el-Mandeb, both locations were within 1,500 miles (2,500 km) of the monumental excesses of Egypt's ancient dynasties; and in the Pharaohs' desire to exact tribute and open trade with this southern hinterland lies a prime contender for the genesis of the spice route.

In the long pillared temple of Dayr al-Bahri at Thebes (near Luxor) a famous series of relief frescos dating from about 1480 BC narrates the story of one of these southern forays by the Pharaohs of the Middle Kingdom. According to the accompanying text, the expedition had been despatched by Queen Hatshepsut to somewhere called 'Punt'. It had travelled by both sea and land, had reached the 'incense terraces', and had then returned safely with much incense plus incense-trees (which were duly planted beside the Dayr al-Bahri temple), ebony, gold, cinnamon, monkeys, leopard-skins and live human specimens of all ages. It was in fact a typical explorer's haul and, but for incense instead of pepper, could have been the lading accumulated, three thousand years later, by Vasco da Gama.

'Never was brought the like of this for any king who has been since the beginning,' claims the Dayr al-Bahri inscription, adding that such commodities had formerly been obtained only via numerous middle-men and carriers and 'in return for many payments'.[5] The records contradict this with mention of several previous expeditions to Punt dating from as far back as 2800 BC; but it would appear that Hatshepsut's inititative put these contacts on a new footing and that thereafter they became sufficiently frequent to constitute a regular exchange. Certainly, too, this is the best documented of the Pharaonic expeditions. If the reliefs are accurate, we know that there were five ships and thirty-one incense trees, that the ships could be both rowed and sailed, that the people of Punt included negroes and Hamitic-looking persons, that their king had rings on his legs and a dumpy little wife, and that his country possessed giraffes, lions, tame cheetahs, baboons and what might be either hippos or rhinos (the relief is too worn to tell which).

Largely on the assumption that the incense was frankincense, Punt has been located in the Hadramawt, the region of southern Arabia bordering the Indian Ocean that accounted for most frankincense production. The Pharaonic expeditions have therefore been hailed as opening the entire Red Sea to navigation, and so in effect pioneering this sector of the spice route. But while the mention of cinnamon has led some authorities to look much further afield for Punt, the people and fauna depicted in the reliefs are more suggestive of an African location than an Arabian one. From later mentions of Punt in con-nection with Egypt's relations with Nubia, it seems that it may in fact have bordered the Red Sea on the Ethiopian, not the Arabian, side in what is now Eritrea. There too incense, though not frankincense, would have been obtainable; and to reach it the rather frail-looking Egyptian ships would not have had to brave the straits of Bab el-Mandeb, let alone any part of the ocean beyond. Remarkable as these voyages were, and although they certainly anticipated the later spice route, if they terminated in Eritrea they traversed no more than half of the Red Sea.

Enormous problems beset the reconstruction of geographical knowledge in the ancient world. Quite apart from the scarcity and unreliability of the sources, grave uncertainty often surrounds the translation of the most crucial terms. Allowance must be made for meanings having changed in the course of the centuries and for different peoples having different interpretations of them. The Egyptian word for 'incense' might indicate frankincense, myrrh, bdellium or any of the other gum-resins used for devotional purposes. 'Cinnamon' as understood in second-millennium BC Egypt could be the same as 'cinnamon' as understood in Europe two thousand years later, or something quite different. Perhaps it could even have grown, as in Herodotus' story of the birds' nests, in Arabia or east Africa. If not, then its availability in Punt could be evidence of an already extant trade from the Far East, where cinnamon originated. Or perhaps Punt was itself in the Far East. Anything seems possible, and exciting hypotheses have been constructed on the strength of such extrapolation from the most fragmentary evidence.

Geographical names can be even more misleading. As late as medieval times terms like 'India', 'Asia' and 'Ethiopia' were as airily invoked as are 'outer space', 'the universe' and 'the stratosphere' today. Such words are often used without regard to their proper meanings in order to indicate anywhere beyond the map-makers' reach and the layman's limited comprehension. In the same way the ancients sometimes used 'India' for Africa, while the words used for Africa – 'Libya', 'Ethiopia' and 'Trogodytica' (which does not, apparently, mean 'land of the cave-dwellers') – might be used for India or the Far East. No doubt Strabo's idea that India extended to the Atlantic contributed to this confusion. ('Africa' itself, incidentally, was much more precise; it meant just north Africa, that is the Mediterranean littoral stretching from Carthage to Mauretania and later known in Arabic as the Maghrib.) Like 'Punt', such place-names often have to be interpreted in terms of the context in which they appear or the products and characteristics awarded to them. The confidence with which we locate, say, 'Ethiopia' today can lead to misunderstanding.

If 'Punt' has kept the Egyptologists busy, two other terms – 'Ophir' and 'Sheba' – have exercised the biblical exegesists. In the First Book of Kings, while in the process of endowing and furnishing his temple, King Solomon is described as building a navy at a place near Elat, the now Israeli beach-resort at the head of the Gulf of Aqaba (one of the northern extremities of the Red Sea). King Hiram of Tyre furnished Phoenician sailors for this fleet, the Phoenicians of the Levant being the undisputed master mariners of their day. The fleet then sailed to

Ophir and returned with vast quantities of gold. This seems to have prompted the queen of somewhere called Sheba to pay a visit to Solomon in Jerusalem; she had heard of his fame, presumably from the Ophir-bound fleet, and, wanting 'to prove him with hard questions', travelled to Jerusalem accompanied by 'a very great train, with camels that bare spices, and very much gold and precious stones'.

Living up to his reputation for exceptional wisdom, Solomon indulged the queen's whim and emerged in triumph from her searching scrutiny. To universal admiration, he then took delivery of her presents. 'There came no more such abundancy of spices as those which the queen of Sheba gave to Solomon,' we are told, though it appears that 'Hiram's navy' supplemented them substantially with the gold and precious stones from Ophir plus 'great plenty of almug trees'. In a single year Solomon's receipts from these foreign contacts came to 666 talents of gold, as well as 'what he had of the merchantmen, and of the traffic of the spice merchants, and all the kings of Arabia, and of the governors of the country'.[6] It was a massive windfall and it enabled him to gild and furnish the temple in spectacular fashion.

King Solomon is thought to have reigned around 950 BC, so nearly six centuries after Queen Hatshepsut. But if his fleet sailed from Elat, it too must have headed south down the Red Sea, and so Ophir and presumably Sheba lay in that direction. Gold, gems and 'spices', rather than specifically incense, were the most prized products of these places, along with the 'almug trees' (from which Solomon caused to be made pillars, harps and 'psalteries for singers') and possibly 'silver, ivory, apes and peacocks' as credited to nearby 'Tharshish' in a later verse of Kings.

Like Punt's produce, this combination of commodities offers no easy solution to the mystery of Ophir's and Sheba's whereabouts. Nor are later references to these places more helpful. Fifteen hundred years after Solomon, and a thousand after canonical status was awarded to the Book of Kings, the Quran would recycle the biblical account and embellish it from Arabic tradition. In the process 'Sheba' was for the first time identified with 'Saba' or 'Sabae', a south Arabian kingdom famed for its wealth since pre-Roman times. Future archaeologists would thereby be sent scurrying to the uplands of Yemen on what has turned out to be a rewarding quest for Arabia's first great civilisation, but which has yet to prove more than a wild goose chase in respect of 'Sheba'.

The Sabaeans of Yemen would indeed be participants in the incense trade; perhaps as early as 750 BC Assyrian sources notice the presence of Sabaean camel caravans bringing, among other things, myrrh to the upper Euphrates region. But in Solomon's day, with no mention of incense in connection with Sheba/Saba's biblical queen, no evidence of an overland incense route then being in existence, grave doubts about whether, with camels barely domesticated at the time, such a route was even feasible, no known deposits of either gold or gems in Sabaean Yemen, no mention in the Sabaean king-lists of there actually being a kingdom in the tenth century BC, and no mention whatsoever of reigning queens, the identification of Sheba with Saba seems a long shot.

The kingdom of 'Sheba' whose queen had business with Solomon is now supposed to have been located in the opposite, north-eastern, half of the Arabian peninsula, perhaps near the Gulf; and Sheba's spices, although they may have included incense, are thought more likely to have been of Indian provenance and to have reached the head of the Gulf either by sea or overland. In other words, the biblical Sheba probably owed its wealth not to south–north incense exports but to an east–west trans-Arabian trade, typical of the Isthmian Age and involving all manner of commodities. Sheba therefore grew rich in much the same way as Palmyra of later fame. Its queen, in quizzing Solomon so closely, was probably negotiating transit rights for her 'merchantmen' and for that 'traffic of the spice merchants' through the land of Israel to the Phoenician ports on the Mediterranean coast.

'Ophir', where Solomon's Phoenician allies obtained the gold and almug trees, is even more of a problem. In a recent and balanced summary of the case, Nigel Groom discounts more fanciful claimants and again plumps for Eritrea, or perhaps Asir (a region on the Arabian side of the Red Sea north of Yemen that did once yield gold). Others have looked much further afield for Ophir. On etymological grounds 'almug' has been identified as sandalwood, the peacocks and ivory have been sourced in India or south-east Asia, and Ophir located any-where from the mouth of the Indus to the Malay peninsula or Indonesia. Another possible contender is Oman, near the mouth of the Gulf, where such Indian products may already have been available and where the modern Zuhar is supposed to have some linguistic affinity to 'Ophir'.

In all these versions, special significance is attached to Herodotus' mention of a Phoenician voyage right round the African continent in about 600 BC. It took the Phoenicians three years, and although Herodotus was sceptical, it struck him as curious because, in the course of long stopovers to grow food, the Phoenicians found the seasons reversed and the sun to the north of them. If Phoenician sailors were capable of such a feat, or had at least ventured south of the equator, they might well on an earlier occasion have reached India or even Malaya.

Against this, it is argued that if Herodotus knew of the African voyage, he would surely have heard of one to the other side of the Indian Ocean and have reported on it. The Phoenician ships, with their double rows of oars, were designed for the Mediterranean and would have been wretched craft in which to work along the desert coasts of Arabia, Iran and India – or Africa. In regard to the 'almug-trees', if they were indeed sandalwood it seems an odd material out of which to fashion musical instruments. And as for the spices, had they in fact been incense (whether from south Arabia or east Africa), it is decidedly strange that the Bible does not actually say so. As connoisseurs of thurification the Jews were in a league of their own; if the spices, like the gold and the almug-wood, were intended for the temple and 'the greater glory of the Lord', this would surely have been recorded.

'There is then nothing in the Old Testament story of the Queen of Sheba to connect her positively with south Arabia,' concludes Groom;[7] nor, one might add, is there sufficient evidence to assume that her spices were gum-resins or that the Egypto-Phoenician navy ever left the Red Sea. Like Hatshepsut's expedition, the naval initiative of Solomon and the commercial overtures (if that is what they were) from Sheba added little to the development of the spice route beyond associating Red Sea adventures, for the first time, specifically with 'spices'.

In respect of these Red Sea forays from ancient Egypt and Israel, the sources are more confusing than disappointing. It is the other way round in respect of the second major contender for the genesis of the spice route, namely early commercial overtures emanating from India and the Far East; here so little is known that even transparent invention would be gratefully scrutinised. Yet the existence of such activity – of regular intercourse between the earliest civilisations in India and Mesopotamia (Iraq), and of maritime contacts between Indonesia/Malaya and east Africa – can scarcely be doubted. Not surprisingly, since most spices apart from gum-resins originated in the East, it is probably in the East that the shoots of what would grow into the globe-encircling spice route first sprouted.

From archaeology we know that as far back as the third millennium BC the Mesopotamian civilisations of Sumer and Akkad used some spices. These included cardamom, which had probably been introduced into the country. Although the edible part of the plant is the scrunchy seed-pod, *Elettaria Cardomum* is botanically related to ginger and has a similarly robust rooting arrangement that lends itself to being transplanted. From the hills of southern India, in fact the still so called 'Cardamom Hills' of Kerala and Tamil Nadu, it had probably already spread to suitable parts of south-east Asia and to the Himalayas, where by hill-roads in Sikkim its aspidistra-like clumps of long pointy leaves still flourish. Removal to Mesopotamia would have required only transport, which might have been overland but was probably by sea.

The existence of maritime links between Mesopotamia at the head of the Gulf and the vast but enigmatic Harappan (or Indus Valley) civilisation of western India and Pakistan may nowadays be taken as established. Harappan terracottas and seals have been found in Mesopotamian sites of around 2000 BC, while Mesopotamian texts make mention of voyages to 'Dilmun' (Bahrein), 'Magan' (either Oman or the Makran/Baluchistan coast) and 'Meluhha' (which is thought to have been the Harappan state itself, or perhaps one of its ports like that excavated at Lothal on the Gujerat coast). The nature of this intercourse is uncertain and may have to await the long promised deciphering of the Harappan script. It would seem, though, a safe bet that if the Sumerians appreciated spices, any exchange with Indian ports would have included them. And if so, this leg of the future spice route between the Indus and the Gulf may pre-date, and certainly exceeds in length, even those Pharaonic forays down the Red Sea.

As for the suggested links between the islands of the Indonesian archipelago and those of east Africa, specifically Madagascar, the case for an early trade in anything, let alone the aromatic accoutrements associated with gracious living and elaborate ritual, is of a different order – as well as being inherently unlikely. Prior to the establishment of Hindu–Buddhist kingdoms in Sumatra in the fourth to fifth centuries AD, these places boasted no monumental civilisations and no literary traditions. They seem improbable candidates for pioneering what would have to rate as one of the most ambitious trade routes of the pre-Columbian age.

Yet there was indeed some transoceanic contact and perhaps population movement between Indonesia and Madagascar. Philologists detect many words in Malagasy that are evidently borrowed from Sanskrit via the languages of Indonesia; ethnologists detect racial similarities between the two peoples; and social anthropologists point to various shared technologies, especially in boat-building and design, none of which is found anywhere else in Africa other than Madagascar, Zanzibar and neighbouring parts of the mainland. If Pacific island groups, like Hawaii, were colonised from south-east Asia, there is no reason to doubt that peoples from Indonesia also strayed west and, with the help of the north-east monsoon, fetched up in and around Madagascar.

But the dating of these voyages is highly problematic, with suggestions ranging from the fifth century BC to the fifteenth century AD; and whether they ever attained that regular and reciprocal character essential to a trade route is still more doubtful. The evidence for commercial activity relies heavily on what Innes Miller, a passionate advocate of these contacts, calls 'the Cinnamon Route'.[8] Most classical sources, from Herodotus' *History* to Strabo's *Geography*, Pliny's *Natural History* and the anonymous *Periplus of the Erythraean Sea*, insist that cinnamon (and usually cassia as well) reached Egypt and the Mediterranean from a 'cinnamon country' located in either southern Arabia or east Africa. But because neither of these places in fact produces anything like cinnamon, which anciently grew only in the Far East, an explanation has been proposed in terms of the Indonesia–Madagascar connection. Cinnamon, and possibly other spices like the Moluccan nutmeg/mace and cloves, are supposed to have first reached the West by taking a southerly route to south-east Africa across the widest expanse of the Indian Ocean, a routing more adventurous even than that followed by the Portuguese although identical to that pioneered by the Spanish, English and Dutch in the sixteenth century.

A 4,000-mile voyage (over 6,000 km) from the coast of, say, Sumatra to that of Madagascar – and then nearly the same again northward by way of Mozambique, Tanzania, Kenya and Somalia to the Red Sea – seems unnecessarily circuitous. Yet, according to Miller and others, it is the only explanation that accords with the evidence of contemporaries. Strabo firmly locates 'the Cinnamom country' south of Egypt, and Pliny, in a surprisingly detailed account, confirms this. Pliny knew of Herodotus' story about the Arabian birds building nests of cinnamon twigs and quite rightly discounted it.

> These tales have been invented by the natives to raise the price of their commodities...[and] are false inasmuch as cinnamomum, which is the same thing as cinnamon, grows in Ethiopia, which is linked by intermarriage with the 'Trogodytae'. The latter buy it from their neighbours and convey it over the wide seas in ships [or 'rafts'] that are neither steered by rudders nor propelled by oars or drawn by sails, nor assisted by any design of art; in those regions only man and man's boldness stands in place of these things [or in those regions, they rely instead on the spirit of man and human courage, as Miller prefers].
>
> Moreover they choose the winter seas about the time of the shortest day, as an east wind is then chiefly blowing. This carries them on a straight course through the bays, and after rounding a cape a west-north-west wind brings them to the harbour of the Gebbanitae called Ocelia [otherwise Ocelis in the Bab el-Mandab straits near Aden].[9]

So for Pliny too, cinnamon came from Africa, or 'Ethiopia'. But it came from a particularly remote part of it that involved intrepid sailors undertaking a long sea voyage across several 'bays' in unusual craft propelled, for the most part, by easterly winds. Such winds would not have been helpful in working up the east African coast and so are taken to be those which carried the cinnamon traders from Indonesia. Their boats, or rafts, so lacking in any means of propulsion or steerage, are assumed to be larger versions of the outrigged canoes found in both

Indonesia and Madagascar. And in marked contrast to Pliny's withering comments on Herodotus, we are to understand that the enthusiasm which informs Pliny's conclusion about the spirit of man and human courage is compelling.[10]

Pliny says nothing about cinnamon originating anywhere other than Africa. But in the earlier references to be found in Strabo's *Geography* there is at least one mention of *kinamomophorou indikes*, or the 'Indian cinnamon-producing [country]'. This appears to contradict the geographer's earlier insistence that cinnamon came exclusively from somewhere south of Egypt; and on that basis his English translator firmly omits the adjective 'Indian'. Calling it 'a slip of the pen', he explains that 'Strabo certainly never supposed the Cinnamon country to be anywhere in India'.[11] Yet this is precisely what the text says, and given that Strabo thought India extended into the Atlantic, it is probably what its author meant.

None of which proves that this most precious of spices, or something like it, did not indeed once grow somewhere in Africa; overexploitation, especially when it entailed removing the bark of a tender tree, might simply have led to its subsequent extinction there. Nor does it prove that cinnamon was not once shipped direct from Indonesia to Madagascar, or to somewhere nearby on the east African coast itself. Given the ideas of the leading geographer of the day on the shape of India and of the Indian Ocean, a voyage from Indonesia might well have been supposed to involve crossing several 'bays', not to mention India itself. All this really indicates is the extreme caution with which geographical data of the period must be handled. Pliny's 'Ethiopia' could have abutted Indonesia just as Strabo's 'India' abutted Africa.

Both men were right in supposing that the Cinnamon country was somewhere very remote, indeed so remote that gross imprecision as to its whereabouts was excusable. It lay 'on the edge of the habitable world', says Strabo, beyond which the earth was too hot for humans, but it also lay 'opposite to', and shared a latitude with, 'Taprobane'. Although now reserved for a minuscule island off the south coast of Sri Lanka, all agree that in classical times 'Taprobane' was the term for the whole of Sri Lanka. Whether Sri Lanka was then, as subsequently, a major exporter of spices and especially cinnamon cannot be established. Strabo admits that in the first century BC little was known of the place except that it supplied Indian markets with ivory, tortoiseshell and 'other things in large quantities'.[12]

However, if simple plausibility be admitted to the debate, these 'other things' would have been spices, including cinnamon; and some of them, mostly cinnamon, must have bypassed the Indian markets and been carried straight from Sri Lanka to east Africa. There the Somali coast seems a more probable destination than Madagascar or Mozambique. Paralleling the 'pepper route' later taken by ships from the Malabar coast heading for a landfall at the Cape of Spices (Cape Guardafui), cinnamon shipments from Sri Lanka might have struck the Somali coast south of this cape and then been forwarded by local traders to the Red Sea.

If there was indeed a specific 'cinnamon route', this one seems consistent with the sources, although decidedly premature in respect of long-distance voyaging and wholly unreported. But then secrecy was part of the mystique of spices. As Pliny rightly notes, it was in a merchant's interest to make his sources of supply sound as improbable and unattainable as possible. It encouraged demand and boosted prices. Sometimes charging up to 1,000 denarii per pound (according to Pliny), the cinnamon traders would appear to have protected their monopoly as effectively by obfuscation as would any European power by superior gunnery.

Alexander the Great's march to India had introduced his soldiery to new lands, new spices, new combinations of spices and new uses for them. Additionally, the various accounts of his expedition confronted the scientific world with a substantial task of geographical identification and botanical classification. The geography exercised a succession of distinguished scholars from Eratosthenes, 'the father of geography', in the third century BC to Strabo in the first century BC and Ptolemy (Claudius Ptolemaeus) in the second AD. Meanwhile the botany was taken up in *An Enquiry into Plants* and a pithy little work *On Odours*, both by Theophrastus (d. 288 BC), the most distinguished of Aristotle's pupils and the acknowledged 'father of botanical studies'. Much later Dioscorides provided a pharmacological classification in his *Materia Medica* of about 65 AD.

A trickle of unfamiliar names, many of them derived from the Sanskritic words by which the various spices were known in India, thus entered Greek and Latin usage. Alchemists and quacks found themselves with an extended repertoire of mystifying ingredients, and men of letters with a deliciously abstruse vocabulary. The Roman playwright Plautus (d. *c.* 184 BC) went so far as to parody this craze for outlandish spice names by coining some of his own: *hapalosis, cataractria, cepolindrum* and *cicimandrum* sound so convincing that it is a wonder they were not subjected to import duty. As further evidence of the liberal use of spices in literature, Innes Miller cites the eulogy directed by a raddled slave-woman to her favourite tipple in one of Plautus' comedies;

> My beauty of Bacchus! You're old and so am I, and how I need you! Compared to you every other essence is as bilge-water! You are my myrrh, my cinnamon, my ointment of roses, my saffron, my cassia, my rarest of perfumes! Where you are poured there would I fain be buried![13]

The last sentence may imply that a liquor-soaked interment would be preferable to the conventional anointment with aromatics. In the early days of the Roman republic spices were much used for funerary purposes. The practice extended back to the embalming procedures of the Pharaohs and would be adopted to excess for state funerals under the Roman Empire.

While savants and writers embraced the new fashion for spices, others addressed the challenge of how to obtain a supply of these exotica. In this respect the trail of Alexander's conquests from the Mediterranean to the Panjab in northern India appeared to provide a corridor for overland trade. By overthrowing the Achaemenid, or Persian, empire (once ruled by Cyrus, Darius and Xerxes) Alexander had brought Egypt, the Middle East, Iran and Afghanistan under the single aegis of Macedonian rule.

But when he died, aged thirty-two and without an obvious heir, the empire of 'the world conqueror' promptly disintegrated into a number of jealous satrapies. Most were ruled by former comrades-in-arms who knew more of war than peace. Seleucus and his Seleucid successors established their sway in Syria, Mesopotamia, Iran and

beyond. Bactria in Afghanistan broke away and was swept by a succession of India-bound incursors from central Asia – Scythian,
Parthian and Kushan. Seleucid power was itself overthrown by
Scythians and Parthians, the latter constructing an empire against
which the forces of Rome would eventually be pitched. When
Roman generals like Pompey and Lucullus returned from the East,
their armies would bring back to Italy, just like Alexander's to Greece,
a keen new taste for spices.

East–west trade and diplomacy flourished as and when conditions
permitted. Official contacts with India were probably closest in the
fourth to third centuries BC. A Seleucid ambassador called
Megasthenes served at the court of India's great Mauryan empire at
Pataliputra (Patna in Bihar) during the reign of Chandragupta
(c.321–297 BC); and Ashoka (c.268–233 BC), his grandson, reciprocated with an initiative directed at several of Alexander's successors,
including the Seleucids in Asia and the Ptolemies in Egypt. Although
Megasthenes' account of Mauryan rule does not survive, several classical writers would draw on it for firsthand information about India;
and of their writings some do survive. Inevitably Megasthenes had a
north Indian bias, but he included mention of unspecified spices,
along with pearls, being imported into Bihar from the southern kingdoms – those of the Cheras, Pandyas and Cholas – at the tip of the
Indian peninsula. Within India, spices were already being traded over
the length and breadth of the subcontinent. Their onward movement
to west Asia has been inferred from the high level of Hellenistic
contact evident in the coinage, statuary and architecture of Bactria
and the Panjab during the last centuries BC and the first AD. In Iran
the Parthians, in particular, seem to have appreciated the value of
east–west trade and to have lent notable encouragement to the transit
of silk from China. No doubt this overland commerce included consignments of the more sought-after spices obtainable in north-west
India.

But as early as the third century BC maritime developments may
already have been rendering the landward carriage of such items
redundant. Moreover, the traffic in spices being as much south–north
as east–west – between the exotic abundance of the tropics and the
limited agricultural potential of chillier climes – it was better served

by a more meridional axis. Such was the route across the Arabian and Red Seas which debouched into the south-east Mediterranean through the populous lands of the Nile delta in Egypt.

Here Alexander's successors were the Ptolemies, that is Ptolemaeus I 'Soter' and his descendants (the much later geographer was unrelated to them). As Macedonian Greeks like Alexander himself, the Ptolemies fared rather better than their Seleucid counterparts in Asia. In addition to Egypt, a country then synonymous with wealth as the erstwhile land of the Pharaohs and the granary of the eastern Mediterranean, they commanded much of the trade-rich southern Levant (Palestine, Israel, Lebanon) plus the exotic resources of Nubia (Sudan). Unaffected by the ceaseless poundings of central Asian migration that buffeted the Seleucids, the Ptolemies would gloriously flourish in their adopted land for nearly three centuries, in fact until the unfortunate Cleopatra became the last of the line when she yielded her favours to Mark Antony and then her kingdom to the Romans.

True to their Hellenic origins, the Ptolemies established their capital at Alexandria on a site that faced towards the Aegean on Egypt's Mediterranean frontage. Built of white marble and spectacularly endowed with colonnades, monuments and palaces, the city was to achieve a magnificence that survived for seven hundred years and a commercial prominence, especially in the spice trade, that would endure for seventeen hundred years. It became by far the noblest of Alexander's many urban foundations; it was also, and designedly, his final resting-place, the Ptolemies having hijacked the emperor's funeral cortège as it made its way circuitously west from Babylon. With the sarcophagus installed within a mighty mausoleum of chastest classicism, no one could doubt the Ptolemies' claim to be the true successors of the Macedonian conqueror.

As well as being the guardians of Alexander's cult, the Ptolemies presumed to be the patrons of all that was finest in Greek civilisation. At the crossroads of three continents, they consciously gathered together the accumulated wisdom of the region, scouring the eastern Mediterranean for texts to fill the massive Alexandria library, for artefacts and performers to grace the great museum, and for scholars to live and study in both. The library, in particular, became the clearing-house of Hellenistic science and scholarship with perhaps one hundred thousand manuscripts and an army of copyists. Here geographers and astronomers like Eratosthenes, Strabo and Ptolemy laboured to construct their maps, their gazetteers and their new models of the heavens and the earth without ever straying from the marble halls and the shady walks. At a time when Athens was entering the autumn of its days and Rome scarcely roused by its martial spring, Alexandria basked in an all-year summer of Hellenistic pre-eminence.

Yet the Ptolemies also identified closely with their adopted land and saw themselves as the successors not just of Macedon but of Memphis and the many dynasties of ancient Egypt. They aspired to the same autocratic rule and the same luxurious style of living as the Pharaohs. The dead Alexander was co-opted into the pantheon of Egyptian deities; and in buildings like the Sarapion temple and the colossal Pharos – Alexandria's 'wonder of the world' lighthouse – the aesthetics of the Acropolis were married to the monumental skills of the Pyramids.

True to this legacy, the Ptolemies resumed the Pharaonic hunt for exotica and immediately revived the commercial enterprise of rulers like Hatshepsut. They opened trading stations down the Red Sea, dealt directly with the frankincense-producing regions of Yemen, and – a first for any Mediterranean kingdom – enjoyed some of the novelties provided by maritime trade with India. Until the fourteenth century AD the spice route as understood in Europe remained substantially that familiar to the Ptolemies – just as their erstwhile capital of Alexandria remained the trade's Mediterranean entrepôt.

Initially Ptolemaic interest seems to have been less in Asia's botanical products than in Africa's zoological wonders. To the pleasure gardens and parks of Alexandria were hauled a procession of trussed giraffes and caged baboons, of thrashing ostriches, hamstrung hippos and knotted pythons. Elephants were especially sought; hunting stations were established on the coast of Ethiopia, and special ships were designed to transport the elephants up the Red Sea. Although idle curiosity must have been quickly satisfied, the bounty offered for elephants was maintained; for behind their acquisition lay the momentum of an arms race.

The potential of elephants in warfare had been another discovery of Alexander's Indian campaign. The Seleucids had followed it up by forming their own elephant corps; and the Ptolemies, being at a geographical disadvantage in obtaining mahouts and elephants from India, sought to redress this imbalance by training African elephants. The programme, though a psychological success, ultimately failed when the pachyderms of Africa proved no match for their better-drilled Indian counterparts. Yet it was largely thanks to this initiative that the Red Sea was opened to trade from Egypt. Ptolemy II established Arsinoë, near Suez, as a forward base for operations and revived Pharaonic efforts to construct a canal which, linking the Nile with Arsinoë and the Gulf of Suez, would permit through traffic between the Mediterranean and the Red Sea. Further south, ports were established at Myos Hormos (near al-Qusayr) and later Berenice (still further south). Both were on Egypt's Red Sea coast and both were linked to the Nile at Coptos (near Luxor) by carefully maintained roads supplied with wells and caravanserais.

As the Ptolemaic merchant fleet fanned out down the Red Sea, it mastered its always tricky navigation and explored the potential of its Arabian and Ethiopian coastlines. Far-flung settlements were established for mineral extraction as well as for hunting, and many strange peoples on the Ethiopian and Somali coasts – 'Fish-Eaters', 'Root-Eaters', 'Turtle-Eaters' – were catalogued according to their diet and carefully described. They included tribes of 'Hulophagoi', or 'Fibre-Eaters', who foraged in the trees in family groups, lived 'entirely off tender shoots', displayed quite exceptional agility, never wore clothes and 'had sexual relations with their women in common';[14] indeed the description of the 'Fibre-Eaters' given by Agatharchides of Cnidos in a work on the Red Sea compiled about 150 BC is so detailed as to leave little doubt that these people were in fact chimpanzees. Between monkeys and men, as between Africa and Asia, the lines of demarcation were still blurred.

More significantly, these voyages led to the first certain opening of a maritime trade with the coast of Yemen. Whether or not it was frankincense that Punt had yielded to Hatshepsut or that Sheba had gifted to Solomon, the overland trade in incense to elsewhere in Asia already had a long, if little noticed, history. The ancient Sumerians may have burned Arabian resin, the Assyrians evidently coveted it, and by about 500 BC some form of frankincense had found favour with the Persian Achaemenids. Darius is said to have received an improbable 24.5 tons of it as an annual tribute from the Arabian tribes. For once Herodotus, who was born at about the time of Darius' death, well knew the facts of its provenance, though still disinclined to forgo the chance of embellishing them.

> When they gather frankincense they burn storax (the gum of which is brought to Greece by the Phoenicians) in order to raise a smoke to drive off the flying snakes; these snakes...are small in size and of various colours, and great numbers of them keep guard over all the trees which bear frankincense, and the only way to get rid of them is by smoking them out with storax.[15]

As usual there was a smut of truth here. Deadly 'snakes', notably the horned viper, may once have been common in southern Arabia, although the creatures that flew in swarms were surely locusts; and of the various rituals associated with the incising of frankincense trees and the collection of the 'tears' of gum-resin, one was certainly some kind of fumigatory thurification. Two centuries after Herodotus, and perhaps on the basis of information provided by a scouting expedition to the Red Sea despatched by Alexander himself, Theophrastus correctly identified Saba, Hadramawt and Qataban among the producer regions. Thereafter more intimate knowledge of these places awaited Ptolemaic initiative and the expertise in the storing and processing of geographic data provided by the Alexandria library.

This bore fruit before the end of the third century BC when Eratosthenes, the geographer then in charge of the library, by working from the reports there accumulated, offered a whole new list of place-names and much information on them. The capital of the Sabaeans, he reported, was 'Mariaba' (Marib), Qataban extended down to the straits (of Bab el-Mandeb), and from there and from Hadramawt came the frankincense and myrrh. Consignments for export were bartered to merchants from Minaea (Ma'in) in north Yemen, from which place the Minaean caravans took seventy days to traverse the length of Arabia and reach 'Aelana', or Elat, at the head of the Aqaba Gulf. Thence the incense was carried to Gaza on the Mediterranean.

In effect, Eratosthenes was describing the great 'Incense Route' of much subsequent fame and not a little fable. With the participation of other peoples, notably the Nabataeans of Petra in Jordan, this all-desert route sandwiched between the wastes of the Empty Quarter and the coastal ranges of western Arabia would witness the passage of interminable camel trains throughout the Roman period. In the first century AD it has been estimated that the annual export of frankincense along it stood at about 1,675 tons, requiring up to eleven thousand camels; and this did not include the traffic in myrrh and other goods.[16] Petra itself had a population of perhaps thirty thousand, and though the Nabataeans themselves seem not have served as caravanners, their capital provisioned, watered and taxed the trade to monumental effect. Little is known of the Nabataean pantheon but there seems to have been a 'patron deity of caravans, comparable perhaps with the Christian St Christopher'.[17] Despite persuasive attempts to prove differently, the Incense Route must have contributed to the prosperity of other Arabian societies, especially in mercantile centres like Yathrib, the al-Madina of later centuries, concerning which the testimony of the Quran and of Islamic tradition can scarcely be ignored, however 'tendentious'.[18]

Agatharchides, writing in Alexandria a century after Eratosthenes, also told of the overland route from Yemen but added evidence of a flourishing maritime trade under Sabaean control. He calls the region 'Eudaimon Arabia', the Greek form of 'Arabia Felix' or 'Fortunate Arabia'; and most fortunate it certainly was, since 'it bears most of the products considered valuable by us'. In fact so plentiful were the gum-resins of Sabaea that their scent pervaded the whole land.

> For the fragrance appears as something divine and greater than the power of speech to describe since it strikes and stimulates the senses of everyone. As for persons sailing along the coast, although they be far from land, that does not prevent them from sharing this kind of pleasure for in summer, when there is an off-shore breeze, it happens that the fragrance given off by the myrrh and other such trees reaches the nearby parts of the sea.[19]

Lest such good fortune be taken for granted, says Agatharchides, and men thereby forget the gods, this abundance had its drawbacks. As well as the snakes (which though unable to fly yet 'leap as they bite') there was menace in the heady air itself. Apparently it so congested the pores that the entire population was in constant danger of fainting. There was only one way to deal with this. In a novel variation on the 'hair of the dog' principle, Agatharchides notes that 'a brief fumigation with resin and the beard of a goat' worked wonders. It 'removed the stimulus of the excessively sweet odour' and, 'by the admixture of something that seems to cause discomfort', counteracted its effect.[20]

Saba, or Sabaea, which held sway over all the south Arabian kingdoms, was undoubtedly the most beautiful of cities. The royal palace, says Agatharchides, was a wonder of workmanship in gold and silver encrusted with ivory and gems, and the Sabaeans were the wealthiest people in the world; 'for they are the ones who distribute everything from Asia and Europe that is considered valuable.' Assuming that Agatharchides was referring to Marib, the Sabaean capital, this was a misconception. The city's prosperity, like that of Petra, depended heavily on an agricultural yield made possible by massive irrigation works including the great Marib dam, which would rise to 50 feet (15m) and stretch to over 550 yards (500m). Sabaean profits from the export of gum-resins may have been expended on the import of foreign goods, only a fraction of which may have been re-exported. But that in the mid-second century BC this trade existed at all, and with both 'Asia and Europe', gives pause for thought. One wonders whose were the ships plying between the Sabaean ports and 'Asia', how long they had been doing so and what was their route.

A hint of sorts comes in Agatharchides' next paragraph. Writing of Eudaimon Arabia's offshore islands, by which he almost certainly meant Socotra, he tells of 'white cattle' and 'walled cities' before which 'merchant vessels ride at anchor from many neighbouring countries...Most of those [ships] encountered are from the port that Alexander built by the Indus river. Not a few however come from Persia and Carmania and the whole nearby region.'[21]

So Agatharchides' 'Asia', whose produce was distributed by the Sabaeans, was in fact all points east of Arabia as far as what is now Sind in Pakistan; the trade might date back to Alexander's foundation in 325 BC of Patala, a port near the Pakistani city of Hyderabad on the Indus delta; the ships that engaged in this trade were from such places;

and their operators seem to have already established their own trading settlements on Socotra. Assuming that there or thereabouts they exchanged goods with the Ptolemaic seafarers from whose reports Agatharchides obtained his information, the Isthmian Age of the Arabian peninsula as a landward stepping-stone had already ended. Thanks to Indian and perhaps Persian enterprise, a substantial chunk of the maritime spice route was already in place.

Of India beyond Sind, Agatharchides makes no mention; nor in writing of the local winds does he imply that they had a particular pattern which might be advantageous to such sailings. The inference must be that vessels passing between Sind and Socotra followed the coastline. Yet if this was indeed his understanding, it may already have been out of date. Arguably the greatest of all discoveries in the history of the spice route seems to have been made during the century in which Agatharchides wrote. The whole of western and southern India, plus the potential for further contacts beyond the Bay of Bengal, was about to be thrown open to direct trade from Egypt and the Red Sea. Thanks possibly to those enigmatic cinnamon traders, but more probably to a fortuitous or incredibly courageous experiment, navigators were about to throw off the tyranny of landmarks, provision their ships for shoreless nights and, embracing the open sea, entrust themselves to the blustery gods of the monsoon.

4

Hippalos and the Passage Across

Everything that is made in Limurike [Tamil Nadu] is brought to
these [Coromandel] ports, and nearly all the money that flows
annually from Egypt together with the many different products
of Limurike which are supplied through the Coast-Land.

Anon., *The Periplus of the Erythraean Sea*[1]

THE INDIVIDUAL PIONEERS of something as ancient as the spice
route are almost entirely unknown. There are no personalities
and practically no events. In attempting even the most basic kind of
reconstruction, research stands helpless without a spark of imaginative
licence. To navigators without names, dates or nationalities must be
assigned ships of plausible design undertaking seasonally possible
voyages laden with whatever cargoes a handful of texts and the gleanings of archaeology may suggest.

The Bible, supported by Herodotus, indicates that some of those
who once sailed down the Red Sea were Phoenicians; and from other
sources it seems that the commanders who later directed the operations of the Ptolemaic marine were often Greek. Their ships are
generally supposed to have resembled the open vessels depicted in the
Dayr al-Bahri reliefs; similar ships close-reefed in choppy seas are
found painted on an Etruscan vase of about 500 BC from Vulci (and
now in the Louvre). Propulsion could come from rowing, but for the
most part they relied on a large square sail rigged from a long yard-
arm comprised of two spars lashed together that was hoisted up a short
stout mast; for steering, in the days before the rudder, two side sweeps
resembling oars were used; and the only place for cargo was amidships.
The Sindi and Persian vessels that, according to Agatharchides, were

traversing the northern coasts of the Arabian Sea by 150 BC may have been of different design. Their hulls were probably of timbers sewn together with coir rather than nailed, and instead of the square sail rigged at right angles to the mast (so 'square-rigged'), they may already have carried the more triangular 'fore-and-aft' sail that would become known as lateen (or Latin) following its later adoption in the Mediterranean.

All else in respect of the identity of the early pioneers and their ships is conjecture. The Ptolemaic sailors who scoured the Red Sea's shores for elephants could have been Europeans (Greeks), Africans (Egyptians and Ethiopians) or Asians (Phoenicians and Arabs). Indian vessels, as well as coasting the Arabian Sea, may already have been sailing straight across it to the African littoral; so may the more mysterious ships, or 'rafts', laden with cinnamon from either Indonesia or Sri Lanka. Along the African coast various local craft, from dug-out canoes to larger vessels with sewn planking and outriggers, were certainly busy.

On all these voyages it is likely that spices were often carried. But away from the Mediterranean with its craving for exotic fragrances and its inflated prices, the trade attracted less attention. The silence of the omniscient Pliny compiling his *Natural History* at a retreat on the Italian lakes, or the limitations of the Alexandria library where laboured all those geographers, is no proof that beyond their intellectual horizons other peoples were not actively engaged in ambitious voyaging. Like the navigators themselves, their achievements are simply unrecorded.

There are, though, two exceptions to this anonymity. Both Strabo and Pliny notice a mysterious Eudoxus of Cyzicus who around 110 BC sailed repeatedly to India but then disappeared during an ambitious attempt to circumnavigate Africa. And in a Greek text written by someone with a practical knowledge of the Indian Ocean, there occurs a most deliberate mention of the only other named navigator in the entire history of Graeco-Roman endeavour in the Indian Ocean. This man was called Hippalos; and in so exceptionally identifying him, the author of the text in question betrayed a profound regard. For, says this text: 'Hippalos was the first navigator who, by observing the position of the marts and the character of the sea, discovered a route across the ocean. Since then...when the monsoon of the Indian ocean appears to be south-west, it is called Hippalos from the name of the man who discovered the passage across.'[2]

Clearly this Hippalos deserves pride of place among the great names of exploration. Like Columbus, he may not have been the first to 'discover the passage across', merely the first to perform it on behalf of a people that considered the achievement significant. Like da Gama, he may have employed Arabs or Indians who knew about the monsoon, or he may simply have tracked one of their vessels. Quite plausibly, his linking of two continents may have been preceded by a succession of adventurous voyages involving ever longer forays away from the coast. But that Hippalos deduced the potential of the south-west monsoon, used it to make the first recorded blue-water voyage in the Indian Ocean, and so inaugurated a sensational expansion of the spice trade, seems indisputable. Had there been any doubt about the matter, his celebrity would scarcely have been sufficient for his name to be conferred on the monsoon itself.

Sadly this most promising of breakthroughs is beset by a host of historiographical problems. The text in which Hippalos' feat is recorded gives no date either for the man or his discovery. The text itself is also undated, and its author is unknown. We do have a title: *Periplus Maris Erythraei* in its Latin translation or *The Periplus of the Erythraean Sea* in English. It scarcely trips off the tongue. A *periplus* was a circumnavigation, or in this case a compendium of information relevant to a circumnavigation; several other peripluses are known, including ones covering the Black Sea and the Mediterranean. The Erythraean Sea was the name by which the ancients knew the Arabian Sea (including its Gulf and Red Sea inlets). Here, therefore, is a work recounting information relevant to a voyage round the western half of the Indian Ocean.

To deduce a date for the *Periplus*, scholars have focused on the text's few references to reigning kings and recent events. On the basis of such internal evidence it must have been written not earlier than about 50 AD and not later than about 130 AD. Obviously Hippalos preceded the text by at least as long as was required for his achievement to be widely recognised, his name to be accepted as that of the monsoon itself, and a regular trade to be established. This could well have been a century or more. Pliny, when writing his *Natural History* in about 77 AD, used the term 'Hippalos' for the wind but made no mention of the man, the inference being that the former usage was sufficiently well established to require no explanation. Strabo on the other hand, writing about eighty years earlier (so around the time of Christ's birth), mentions neither the man nor his wind.

Some have supposed that Hippalos must therefore have made his discovery before Pliny but after Strabo. Yet Strabo took it for granted that a trade between Egypt and the west (or Malabar) coast of India already existed. 'As many as one hundred and twenty vessels' were making the annual voyage to India, he says; his only regret was that 'very few of the merchants who now sail from Egypt by the Nile and the Arabian Gulf to India have proceeded on as far as the [mouth of] Ganges'.[3] Assuming that Strabo's 'Arabian Gulf' was the Red Sea, and that from there, as implied by his failure to mention any intervening locations, these merchants sailed straight for India, it looks as if Hippalos must in fact have pre-dated not only both Christ and Strabo but, with a time-lapse for the development of the trade, even Cleopatra (died 30 BC). He therefore put to sea in Ptolemaic times. Furthermore, several authorities regard his discovery not as the culmination of a series of ever more adventurous voyages but as their precursor. These voyages could have extended over several decades and have included those of the enigmatic Eudoxus of Cyzicus. In other words Hippalos may have made his momentous discovery more than a century before Christ.

The first century BC also witnessed the awakening of Roman interest in Egypt. Julius Caesar first landed there in 48 BC, Mark Antony returned there in pursuit of Cleopatra in 41 BC, and when both were defeated by Octavian (the future emperor Augustus) in 31 BC, the country was annexed to Rome. That the Romans arrived just as Hippalos' discovery began to pay off and Egypt to host the most adventurous and lucrative trade known to the ancient world smacks of more than coincidence. Whether it was the numbing allure of some exquisite Indian nard hanging about Cleopatra's person or just the spice-brimming warehouses on Alexandria's waterfront, Egypt had become irresistible.

How rapidly the trade developed under the Roman dispensation is evident from the *Periplus*. Its anonymous author being nothing if not brisk – his text runs to just sixty-six paragraphs thinly spread over thirty-seven pages in the English translation – he wastes little time on the Red Sea. Myos Hormos and Berenice were the two main Egyptian ports; beyond them on the African side came 'the land of the Barbaroi'. It was inhabited by fish-eaters and, inland towards Meroë (near Khartoum), by plant-eaters and wild animal-eaters. 'Ptolemais of the Huntings', once an elephant port, yielded tortoise-shell and a little ivory but had 'no harbour and can be reached only in small boats'. Adulis (near Massawa) had upstaged it as 'a customary mart' and was connected to the Ethiopian kingdom of Axum. Here was now the best place to buy ivory and rhinoceros horn and to dispose of Egyptian manufactures – cloth, glassware, iron and iron-mongery – or, when returning from the East, Indian manufactures of a similar description.

Next came the straits of Bab el-Mandab and then, along the north coast of the Horn of Africa, a succession of small ports almost exclusively engaged in the spice trade. They began at Avalites (in Djibouti), extended to a place that was actually called 'the Spice Emporium', and continued on round Cape Guardafui ('the Cape of Spices' as in Ptolemy's imminent *Geography*). The spices in question included Somali gum-resins like myrrh, quantities of unspecified 'aromatics' that were not gum-resins, and cinnamon and cassia in such abundance that the author of the *Periplus* advised that 'larger ships are needed'.

Continuing on down the African coast to Rhapta (possibly Dar es Salaam), the *Periplus* makes no further mention of cinnamon or cassia, an omission which rather undermines the case for their having been either grown in east Africa or transported there from Indonesia. It would seem, then, that the unspecified 'aromatics', as well as the cin-namon/cassia, available along the Somali coast must have been carried there by Indian, Sri Lankan or Arabian vessels. In all probability this string of minor ports on the Horn of Africa represented a residue of the pre-Hippalos and pre-Roman trade of the Indian Ocean.

Such casual speculation is not to be found in the *Periplus* itself. While Herodotus has his anecdotes, Agatharchides his homilies, Strabo his textual critiques and Pliny his harrumphing outbursts, the author of the *Periplus* remains thoroughly impersonal. Any idea of engaging the reader eludes him. Bald facts and curt directions are his currency, and he dispenses them in the flat and formulaic style of a literary layman. In fact the *Periplus* reads just like the seagoing log it almost certainly was.

Possibly as a ship's master but more probably as a chief merchant, its author had clearly visited many of the places he records; and therein lies the enormous value of the work. It is the only first-hand account of the spice route to survive from classical times, and its narrative, though threadbare, can be taken as descriptive of an actual voyage. How far down the coast of Africa this voyage extended is debatable, but on the other side of the Arabian Sea it certainly embraced most of west Asia's more important ports, including those of western India. Spectral and often painfully inarticulate, the author of the *Periplus* is well worth observing at close quarters. One may step aboard his ship and, without undue licence, at last sail east for spices.

As when heading down the African coast, the Asian voyage recorded in the *Periplus* begins in the Red Sea. The month is July, the wind a steady northerly. Ships heading only to south Arabia wait on at Berenice until September, but the fleet of India-bound vessels needs to cast off sooner and make all sail. Only by a speedy progress down the Red Sea will it reach the Indian Ocean in time to catch the Hippalos.

In high summer the dry northerlies of the Red Sea are breathing fire from the scorched uplands of Nabataea. There reigns King Malichas in stone-cut halls atop a subterranean water supply that makes his 'rose-red' city of Petra proof against siege and a magnet to desert traders. Incense caravans on the overland route from Sabaea pass through Petra, and from its rocky ramparts another road snakes down to Leuke Come on the gulf of Aqaba. Into this garrison-port Arab ships, 'though not large ones', occasionally struggle with more south Arabian gum-resins; they pay a twenty-five per cent *ad valorem* tax for the privilege. Sea-transport is still cheaper than camels; but since this is July, the wind is contrary and north-bound ships are not to be seen by those heading for India on a *periplus*.

As to the year, let it be, say, 80 AD, a mean date between the earliest allowable for the *Periplus* by scholars and the 106 AD annexation of the Nabataean kingdom by the emperor Trajan. Trajan will also resume work on the Ptolemies' Nile–Suez canal, a labour which the author of the *Periplus* would surely have noticed had it been undertaken in his lifetime. In 80 AD the emperor in Rome is Titus, briefly the tenth in succession to Octavian (Augustus). His empire is still counting the cost of the eruption of Vesuvius in the previous August. Besides Pompeii and Herculaneum, its victims included the inquisitive Pliny, then in command of the Roman fleet in the area; going ashore for a closer look Pliny had been suffocated by the fumes, so succumbing to an olfactory assault beyond even his gloomiest reckoning.

The seafarer who would undertake the *periplus* needs to brace himself for different dangers. To port, the Arabian coastline is uninviting. 'Scoundrelly people who speak two languages' lie in wait for unsuspecting vessels; any survivors of a piratical attack are invariably sold into slavery. Moreover the entire country is said to be 'without harbours, with bad anchorages and a foul shore, unapproachable by reason of rocks, and in every way formidable...For this reason...we hold to the middle course towards the [south] Arabian country and press on all the more as far as Burnt Island, after which are continuous regions of civilised people with nomadic herds of cattle and camels.'[4] These pastoralists herald the Yemeni port of Mouza (south of Mocha) in the throat of Bab el-Mandeb. Mouza is an 'established port' and 'the whole place is full of Arabs, ship-masters and sailors, and hums with business'. It imports from Egypt mainly cloth and clothing, plus wine, some manufactured perfumes, and *crocos*, or saffron, from Asia Minor, a spice with a will of its own in that it seems to be going in the wrong direction. Arab vessels trade from here both across the straits to the Somali coast and across the ocean to India.

A twelve days' march inland from Mouza would, says the *Periplus*, bring one to Saphar, the capital of the country and a city currently shared by the ancient Sabaeans and their upstart rivals of the Himyarite tribe. The Sabaean kingdom, though still famous for its incense-traders, has been in some disarray since 26 BC when the emperor Augustus entertained designs on its accumulated wealth. 'He hoped either to enjoy the Arabians as his rich friends or to subjugate them as his rich enemies', according to Strabo.[5] The former option had been preferred when the Roman army commanded by Aelius Gallus got lost in the Arabian desert, then had to abandon the siege of Marib for want of water. Now the relieved king of the Sabaean–Himyarites thankfully styles himself 'Friend of the Emperor' and bombards Rome with embassies and gifts.

A notable casualty of these hostilities had been the erstwhile 'city' of Aden, beside an excellent rock-girt harbour that hoves into view just beyond the straits. In the days before direct sailings between Egypt and India had become normal, Aden, like the ports on the opposite coast of Somalia, was where ships from India exchanged cargoes with the Arabians for onward shipment to Egypt. 'But now,' says the *Periplus*, 'not very long before our time, Caesar [Caesar Augustus] destroyed it.'[6]

Beyond Aden 'a long line of continuous beaches stretching for 2,000 stades' (roughly 350 miles/600km) reaches to Cane (west of Mukalla). Only 'fish-eaters' are found on the beaches, but Cane is a sizeable place and the main port of the frankincense-producing Hadramawt. Its king 'Eleazos' lives inland at 'Saubatha' (Shabwa). All frankincense cultivation is controlled by him, the crop being brought in 'as to a warehouse' by camel-trains, boats and local rafts made of inflated hides. Storax – for smoking out those flying snakes in the incense groves – figures in Cane's list of imports as given in the *Periplus*; in its list of exports the laxative aloes and red cinnabar, both from Hadramawt's subject island of Socotra, defer only to frankincense. In fact, such is the worldwide demand for frankincense that Cane has 'reciprocal relations [with] all the marts on the opposite side [that is, in India], of Barygaza and Skythia and Omana, and the neighbouring regions of Persis'.[7]

The author of the *Periplus* is proving himself a fund of information. After watering either in the straits at Ocelis or beyond them at Aden, the fleet presses on again. Ships bound for India cannot afford the time to trade their way from port to port. The chief merchant (assuming that is what our Periplusian is) is just airing his experience of these places for the benefit of others. Frankincense, for instance, is not ready in August when the India fleet comes sailing by. The harvest is not due until September, which is why ships trading specifically to south Arabia make a later departure from Egypt.

Now clear of the Gulf of Aden, the sails of the India-bound fleet are billowing with the stormy gusts of the Hippalos. In an average year the south-west monsoon breaks in June and blows tempestuously through July; but it becomes more manageable as it tapers off in August and September. This is the time for 'the passage across'. A final landfall is made east of Cane at 'the greatest headland...called Suagros' (Ras Fartak, about half-way along Arabia's southern coast-line). Thence the fleet stands out into the still stormy void of the Indian Ocean.

Reflecting this, the *Periplus* says little about the remainder of the Arabian coast, and still less of the Gulf. The Gulf has good pearl fisheries. Ships from India and elsewhere sail up it to the ports of Apologou (near Basra) and Pasinou Charax (on the Euphrates), from where Palmyrene caravaneers handle westward consignments. But the Gulf is not a route with which our chief merchant is very familiar. Nor is he well informed about the desert shores of Persia and Makran (Baluchistan) east of the Gulf. The places that he next knows well are all 'on the opposite side'. 'Skythia', or Scythia, is the name extended to the lands of the Indus by virtue of their recently being under Scythian, or Saka, rule. Then come the great marts of India itself, Barygaza, Kalliena, Muziris and Nelcynda.

The course as set from the headland of Suagros depends on which of these marts is the ships' destination. If heading for the Keralan pepper ports of Muziris and Nelcynda, the ship bears away to the east-south-east, 'turning its bows against the wind' nearly as far as the sail will allow. The square-rigged Roman ships may not sail as well as their Indian and Arab counterparts, yet they venture into the heaviest seas. To ensure a return voyage within the year, they may even be risking 'the passage across' earlier than their rivals.

For, if Roman-built, these ships can afford to trifle with the tempest. They have the strength of siege-engines. Most shipbuilders, both before and since, begin by laying down a strong framework comprising the boat's keel, stem and stern-posts, and its rib-like frames; then they clad this skeleton with planking to form the hull. But the Romans began with the cladding. Jointing the planks end to end and side to side, they made a rock-solid hull for which a frame and ribs were later cut and fitted. As one scholar puts it, with a veritable fretwork of mortise and tenon joints, all secured by dowelling, the hull of a Roman vessel was less the product of carpentry than of cabinet-making.[8] Immensely strong, they could also be built bigger, perhaps with a length of 180 feet (60m) and a displacement of up to 500 tons. That the Periplusian is himself accustomed to a comparatively spacious vessel may be inferred from his always disparaging references to craft of lesser size.

For the benefit of his text – though rarely in practice because it would involve missing the return monsoon – the voyage is to include all the ports of India in sequence. The ship therefore bears south-east 'for not more than three days' at which point, 'clear of land', it runs before the wind east-north-east towards the low-lying coast of Skythia. This leg may be 'risky, but with the monsoon it is the most direct and shortest'.

Skythia is the land whence 'comes the river Sinthos [Indus], the greatest of the rivers which flow into the Erythraean Sea'. While still out of sight of land, the sea is discoloured by the river's silt. Sailors note the appearance in the water of thousands of 'snakes', a phenomenon which, allowing for the difficulties of translation, could refer to anything from jellyfish to alligators. In the first century AD the delta of the Indus, ever a changing wilderness of sandbanks and mangroves, has seven 'mouths'. Only the middle one is navigable, and beside it stands the mart of Barbarikon (possibly near Karachi), a place supplying cargoes of costus and spikenard brought down from the western Himalayas as well as bdellium and lapis lazuli from Bactria in Afghanistan. Silver-plate and coinage figure prominently among the acceptable imports, implying that stock Roman exports, like glassware and amphorae of wine, are insufficient to offset the purchase price of the spices. Inland the country is now ruled by the Parthians, a quarrelsome people 'who are continually expelling each other'.[9]

After the river Sinthos there is another gulf [running] northwards and not yet explored. It is called Eirinon. One might say that in reality [there are two bays], one small and the other large. The sea in both is shoaly with continuous shifting whirlpools far from land, so that often, while the shore is still out of sight, ships run aground; and if they are swept further inland they are wrecked.[10]

As a description of the great Rann of Kutch ('Eirinon' is from the Sanskrit *irina*, meaning 'a salty swamp'), this could scarcely be bettered. It is matched, after rounding the coast of 'Saurastrene' (Saurashtra), only by the Periplusian's display of knowledge concerning the tidal hazards encountered in the gulf of Cambay. These are such that to reach the great port of Barygaza (Bharuch, Broach), all foreign ships must wait for pilot vessels. The Periplusian is so obsessed with the dangers of this coastline that one supposes his vessel may once have come to grief here. While he expatiates, 'royal fishermen' in fully crewed longboats emerge from the mouth of the Narmada river. They come alongside and a tow-line is secured while they wait for the rising tide; then cautiously they ease the ship through a maze of sandbanks to attain the 'appointed berth' in the port's basin just as the tide is reaching its height. This timing is critical. The ebb 'exposes land where a little before ships were sailing', and the flow is accompanied by a tidal bore that sounds like 'the shouting of an army heard from afar' and tears ships from their moorings 'with a hissing roar'.

Barygaza is ample reward. The chief merchant describes its delights with all the relish, and in nearly the same words, as will his English counterparts when as factors of the East India Company they first touch Indian soil at the neighbouring port of Surat in the early 1600s. Corn, rice and cotton grow lushly in the Gujerati countryside, and 'there are in it too great herds of cattle'; sesame oil as well as ghi is produced in abundance. Some of Alexander the Great's forces had returned down the Indus, and the Periplusian, who is probably Greek himself, wishfully credits them with preceding him to Gujerat. The great Hindu temples with their elaborately stepped tanks, or wells, he supposes to be of Greek construction.

More convincingly he notices other relics as Macedonian. 'There are still current until now in Barygaza ancient coins stamped with Greek letters – the inscriptions being those of Apollodotos and Menander who reigned after Alexander'. Largely on the basis of just such coins, originally minted in Greek Bactria and collectable throughout north-west India long after the *Periplus*, nineteenth-century scholars have since reconstructed the early dynastic history of north-west India and assigned dates and kingdoms to Apollodotus, Menander and a host of other Greek-sounding kings. Unwittingly the author of the *Periplus* himself contributes data of value to students of ancient India's history by noticing a contemporary rivalry, if not an outright war. It concerns supremacy over this valuable stretch of the Gujerati coastline and pitches the Scythian/Saka 'satrap' in Saurashtra against one of the mighty Shatavahana kings of the Deccan.

To Barygaza comes cotton-cloth from Minnagara (Mandasor in Saurashtra) plus, courtesy of the trade-minded Shatavahanas, great wagon-trains of onyx and muslins from 'two very important marts' in Dakshinabades (the Deccan), namely Paithana (Paithan) and Tagara (Ter). More Himalayan spices are brought down from as far as Poklais (Charsadda, near Peshawar) by way of Ozene (Ujjain), 'which was previously a seat of government'. In fact it was the capital of western India under the emperor Chandragupta and his Mauryan successors.

On current affairs in Gujerat and Maharashtra the Periplusian waxes most knowledgeable. The range of his observations and their accuracy leave no doubt as to his being a familiar figure in the bazaars of Barygaza. Here most of the merchants deal in spices and, as later, they include both financiers, who are as often Jains as Hindus, and commercial hauliers who may be Buddhists. Spices and other trade goods are the life-blood of the region, and Barygaza's exports have a decidedly spicy flavour. Spikenard, costus and bdellium head the list, followed by ivory, a local myrrh, some Chinese silk and the first mention of pepper, albeit of the long variety.

The city's imports make a more extensive list, but if one excludes the 'gold and silver money which can be changed with much profit for the local currency', they are not more valuable. Wine comes first, 'chiefly Italian and also some Laodicean and Arabian', followed by copper, tin, lead, coral, 'crude glass', some cloth and a few pigments. It is notable that these are mainly heavy cargoes, an important consideration in the ballasting of the ship, and that they are nearly all in the nature of raw materials; India's manufactured goods can hold their own against those of Rome and Egypt. The only prestige items are not trade-goods but such things as 'expensive silver plate, musicians, pretty girls...and first quality wines', all intended as gifts for the local sovereigns.

South from Barygaza, the ports come thick and fast. Soupara (Sopara, near Bassein) has yielded evidence of one of the emperor

Ashoka's famous inscriptions, so authenticating the port's prominence in ancient times as implied in the *Periplus*. Another, Kalliena (Kalyan, in greater Mumbai/Bombay), had once been 'a legal mart' but, because of the rivalry between the Sakas and Shatavahanas, is closed to foreign traders of the first century AD; all who ignore this interdiction are stopped and 'sent under guard to Barygaza'.

Further south, the Konkan stretch of coast hosts seven named ports. From one of them, perhaps 'Erannaboas' (Malwan), Roman artefacts found their way to Kolhapur, a Shatavahana city 40 miles (60 km) inland. Resisting the ravages of two millennia, mirrors and assorted handles of bronze cast in Capua during the first century AD have been found here, along with with a fine bronze statuette in Hellenistic style but probably of Roman manufacture. Appropriately enough, it is of the sea-god Poseidon with a hand raised for his missing trident.[11]

At the time of the *Periplus* the steep Konkan coastline is already infested by pirates. Operating from its rocky inlets, they contest the sea-lanes in Graeco-Roman times just as they will in the years of Arab, Portuguese, Dutch and British dominance. The Periplusian wastes few words on them. Ahead, long beaches fringed with waving coconut palms command his attention. A first sharp whiff of peppercorns carries out to sea; soft lagoons and meandering waterways beckon from beyond the surf. Voyage's end has a look of paradise, and the merchant mind rejoices, scenting lively business.

> Then come Naoura [Cannanore] and Tundis [Tanor], the first marts of Limurike [that is, 'the Tamil country']; and after them Mouziris [Cranganore] and Nelcynda [Kottayam], which are now busy places. Tundis is in the kingdom of Keprobotos [Kerala-putra] and is a well-known village beside the sea. Muziris, belonging to the same kingdom, is a flourishing place with ships from Ariake [Gujerat] coming to it and also Greeks…Nelcynda belongs to another kingdom, that of Pandion [Pandya], and it too stands on a river.[12]

All these places can be confidently identified, though some of them only after help from Claudius Ptolemy's *Geography*. Ptolemy's 'Damirike' or 'Tamil-Land', for instance, corresponds to the *Periplus'* 'Limurike'. (The Greek letter delta is evidently an acceptable rendering of the 't' of 'Tamil'; and delta's capital form 'Δ' is often understandably mistranscribed as 'Λ', the Greek capital 'L' – and vice versa.)

This being Kerala, the main export is pepper; and the main way of paying for it is with the 'large volumes of coinage' which top the list of imports. The pepper is 'grown in quantity' and comes from a 'place near these marts called Kottanaric'. Two millennia later nothing much has changed. The same region in the backwaters south of Cochin, having surrendered the name 'Kottanaric' to the town of Kottayam, is still today a hive of pepper-dealers busy about the harvest of the neighbouring forests. Then, as now, there was both black pepper and white, the black being simply the unshelled form of the white. And then as now the vines from which the berries hang in clusters may be either wild, climbing freely on any host tree, or cultivated and twisting elegantly up some pre-positioned post. Picked, dried and, for ships without holds, bagged in palm-woven basketry, the peppercorns here await the world's shipping.

In the days of the *Periplus* the other specialities of the pepper-ports included pearls from the straits between India and Sri Lanka, tortoise-shell from Sri Lanka and 'Chryse' (Malaya or Sumatra), and ivory, diamonds and sapphires from inland south India. Two other spices are mentioned, 'Gangetic spikenard' and 'malabathron from the interior'. The spikenard presumably originated in the hills north of the Ganges; but 'the interior' from which came the malabathron was that of the south. The word 'malabathron' has been traced to the Tamil *tamala-pattra*, meaning 'dark leaf'. It always refers to the leaf of the Indian cinnamon plant, not the bark (which is usually 'cassia'). And one species of this cinnamon definitely grew in south India, where it was later known as *tejpat*.

Then, and more so since, malabathron was as prized as it was rare. Though mostly used in perfumes, Pliny took no exception to it because 'when added to lightly mulled wine its scent surpasses all others'.[13] In price, too, it 'approached the marvellous', reaching 400 denarii the pound. A still rarer version of the same plant features later in the *Periplus* as of quite exceptionally remote provenance.

But it was Kerala and its pepper that represented India's main attraction for a first-century Graeco-Roman merchant; and at Nelcynda/Kottayam the author of the *Periplus* may be taken to have completed his load. Tamil poems recited at the *Sangam* symposia of the Pandya court in the first century AD tell of the great ships and the boisterous conduct of the *yavanas*, a name derived from the word 'Ionian' and applied to all strangers from the west. Their 'wealth never wanes', says one verse in apparent reference to the cash payments made for pepper.

Poorer in coin but rich in pepper, the Periplusian set sail for home. The north-east winds, a longer-lasting and gentler version of the south-west monsoon, usually set in about October. Assuming the outward voyage had been direct from south Arabia to south India, the ship would have entered the Keralan backwaters in late September. With two months for conducting business, departure would have been by early December. This would see the Periplusian back in the Red Sea by the end of February and unloading his cargo at Berenice or Myos Hormos for the desert trek to the Nile by late April. That the Periplusian and his cargo made it without mishap we may safely assume from his subsequent, most revealing text.

As if reluctant to finish his work, or possibly as an afterthought, the author of the *Periplus* added for good measure all that he had been able to glean about the seas and lands beyond Kerala. These last few paragraphs are as enlightening as any in the entire work. Here occurs the only reference to Hippalos, whose discovery ended the age when the voyage from the Red Sea was 'made in small ships by sailing round the bays'. Here, too, he tells of 'Komar' (Cape Comorin/Kumari), to which the religiously minded flocked in pilgrimage to the goddess – and still do; of Palaisimoundou (Sri Lanka) which 'reaches nearly to the coast of Azania (east Africa)' – but never did; and of various ports on the Coromandel coast from which there sailed round Cape Comorin to Kerala large vessels 'made of single logs lashed together' – apparently catamarans or rafts.

> [But] those ships that cross over to Chryse and the Ganges and are called 'Kolandiophonta' are the largest of all. Everything that is made in Limurike [the Tamil south] is brought to these [Coromandel] ports, and nearly all the money that flows annually from Egypt together with the many different products of Limurike which are supplied through the Coast-land.[14]

If the author of the *Periplus* thought the size of these Coromandel ships notable, we may be sure that they were. Though shipping from

Egypt played no part in the trade with Bengal and south-east Asia, it seems that across the Bay of Bengal the sea-lanes were busy with bigger ships than were to be met with in the Arabian Sea. The most plausible explanation offered for the term 'Kolandiophonta' is that it represents '*k'un lun po*', 'the ships of the Kun Lun people'. Kun Lun being what the Chinese called south-east Asia, these must have been Malay or Indonesian craft, and 'almost certainly', says one authority, 'two-masted vessels with pointed ends and probably equipped with a stout outrigger'.[15]

In support of this Far Eastern activity we are told that all the produce of Limurike/Damirike and nearly all the wealth annually exported from Egypt found its way to the Coromandel ports, and that it did so 'through the Coastland' rather than round it. The meaning here is not entirely clear but it would seem that then, as later, the principal product of south India, namely cotton textiles, was being exported to the East, not the West; and that to finance the corresponding imports from the East, most of the cash received from the pepper trade with Egypt had also to be reinvested in this Far Eastern trade. Moreover such transfers of cash and produce between the Malabar and Coromandel ports were conducted overland rather than by sea.

All this information, though possibly mystifying to the author of the *Periplus*, has been handsomely authenticated by recent enquiry. The excavations at Virampatnam/Arikamedu (south of Madras near Pondicherry, the 'Podouke' of the *Periplus*), by both French archaeologists and the Indian Archaeological Survey under Mortimer Wheeler's direction, revealed the waterside facilities – large warehouse, reservoir, wells and storage-pits – to be expected of a thriving port. Less expected, according to Wheeler, was the discovery of Mediterranean artefacts in what was otherwise a wholly indigenous settlement. 'To it suddenly, from unthought of lands 5,000 miles (8,000 km) away, came strange wines, table-wares far beyond the local skill, lamps of a strange sort, glass, cut gems.' Shards of arretine ware and of amphorae specially treated for the storage of wine have led to the suggestion that the place might even have included 'a small foreign quarter'. Moreover the dates correspond nicely with those supposed for the *Periplus* in that 'the main development of the port...may be ascribed approximately to the middle of the first century AD, although its international usage may have begun half a century earlier'.[16]

No Roman coins were found at Arikamedu, but elsewhere in south India both individual finds and large hoards comprising hundreds, if not thousands, of gold aurei and silver denarii have been unearthed. Most date from the first century AD and depict Roman emperors prior to Trajan. They show little sign of wear but have usually been defaced by a mark of cancellation, suggesting that they may have been specially minted for the India trade. And the distribution of finds across the peninsula is strongly supportive of the existence of an east–west trade corridor through the Coimbatore region between Muziris (Cranganore) on the Malabar coast and ports like Podouke (Pondicherry) on the Coromandel coast.

It is tempting to suppose that the author of the *Periplus* may himself have once travelled this route to the 'foreign quarter' of a Coromandel port. If not, he must have been acquainted with fellow countrymen who had done so; for the detail supplied about, for example, the east coast's shipping is in marked contrast to the sketchiness that characterises his remarks about places further east. After mention of several tribes, probably in Orissa, he notes that the coast turns east just before it reaches the Ganges. This is 'the greatest of India's rivers', and from a port at its mouth that maybe the Tamluk (Tamralipti) of Mauryan times comes more spikenard and another variety of malabathron.

Then comes 'Chryse', meaning 'golden'. It is an island, 'the last place of the habitable world', and possibly signified Sumatra. Ptolemy will correct this, making the island a peninsula, or 'chersonese'. Hence the 'Golden Chersonese', a term vaguely referring to the whole of mainland south-east Asia that would resonate down the ages as the ultimate in romantic destinations, the goal of fortune-seekers and the epitome of all that was tropical and exotic, including spices.

Beyond this country, says the *Periplus*, 'the sea comes to an end somewhere'. But to the north there yet lies the land of 'This', or 'Thina' (for which Ptolemy would prefer 'Sina' or 'Sinai'). It is where the silk comes from that is brought overland to both Gujerat and the Tamil land, and to the author of the *Periplus* it is otherwise shrouded in mystery.

This Thina is not easy to reach. People seldom come from it and not many go there…[But] every year there comes to the boundary of Thina a certain tribe, stunted in body and with very broad faces and completely flat noses, and with white skins and of a wild nature, called Sesatai. They come with their women and children carrying great packs, plaited baskets, full of vine-like leaves.[17]

The leaves were of three qualities according to size; and all were mala-bathron (cinnamon/cassia leaves). Despite the lack of a shared language trading took place cheerfully enough, this being the occasion for a three-day festival. The Sesatai laid out their leaves and withdrew. The buyers then took their pick, rolling the leaves into little balls and threading them together on a bamboo. Hopefully, they also paid for them, perhaps with Indian long pepper. 'They [the balls] are then brought to India by those who prepare them.'

Where the author of the *Periplus* obtained this information is not revealed. 'Thina' was obviously China and the Sesatai have been vaguely supposed to be a Mongoloid people of the eastern Himalayas. The mute exchange, or 'trade fair', could have been at Gangtok in Sikkim, as suggested by one authority;[18] or it could have been just about anywhere between Lhasa and Hanoi. The interest of the passage is that it corroborates Chinese testimony to the existence of a trans-Himalayan trade route between the Yangtse and the Ganges at a time when direct maritime links between China and India had barely been established. That, and the gratifying revelation that the habitable world was already coterminous with the spice route. Spices were acknowledged as coming from the ends of the earth. They pegged out the known world, defining horizons and daring men to seek beyond them. By way of a conclusion the author of the *Periplus* could scarcely have written a more appropriate or challenging passage.

5

Land of the Luminous Carbuncle

SERENDIPITY … 1754. [f, *Serendip* (-*b*), former name of Ceylon + -ity, formed by Horace Walpole upon the title of the fairy tale *The Three Princes of Sarendip*, the heroes of which 'were always making discoveries, by accident and sagacity, of things they were not in quest of'.] The faculty of making happy and unexpected discoveries by accident.

Shorter Oxford English Dictionary

IN ROMAN TIMES, as later, the investment required for any trading voyage to the East was of crippling proportions; so was the risk involved. Both were more than any single merchant or business-house could handle and were therefore divided among several investing indi-viduals or groups. Each contracted to supply the capital required for a part of the investment, whether in goods or currency, and, all going well, each took a pre-arranged share of the return cargo or of the profits obtained from it.

A surviving papyrus describes the consignment received by one such Alexandria-based group of investors. The merchandise had come from Mouziris in Kerala and consisted of over 4,700 pounds (2,100 kg) of ivory, between 700 and 1,700 pounds (300–800 kg) of nard (prob-ably spikenard), and nearly 800 pounds (350 kg) of textiles (probably fine cottons). No pepper is mentioned; and since it is most unlikely that a vessel returning from Kerala would not have been awash with the stuff if only as ballast, the pepper presumably belonged to other investors. The consignment to which the papyrus refers was evidently more choice. The spikenard and particularly the several tons of Indian ivory suggest a merchant-house with important clients. Emperor Caligula had a stable built out of ivory; Seneca, a near-contemporary of Pliny's, was said to have fifteen hundred tusks serving as table legs; and Nero, Seneca's fickle patron, is credited with launching a major programme of African exploration partly to augment the dwindling ivory supplies coming from the much depleted herds of Ethiopia.

The one consignment of Indian imports on which we have some information may therefore be unrepresentative. Its total value of 131 talents certainly constituted an impressive sum, in fact one 'that could have purchased almost 2,400 acres of Egypt's best farmland'.[1] Yet if Roman vessels could carry 500 tons of cargo, there would have been more than a hundred other consignments, albeit of lesser value, on each of the perhaps two hundred ships annually making 'the passage across' – and this did not include the trade, by both sea and land, in mainly frankincense with south Arabia and myrrh with north-east Africa, nor the overland trade from the Gulf and via the Silk Road.

The spice trade in the early years of the Roman Empire probably exceeded anything seen in the West until the fifteenth century. It struck contemporaries as a remarkable development, transformed public ceremonial as well as domestic tastes, reinforced Roman conceits about commanding the resources of the entire world, and was heavily censured on moral and economic grounds by both the abstemious Pliny and those, like Seneca, who nevertheless consumed its yield conspicuously. Yet it was conducted on this grand scale for only as long as an expanding empire could support it; and just how grand it actually was in terms of value or volume is not easy to assess.

Various price-lists for imported spices have been compiled, mostly on the basis of information given by Pliny.[2] Apart from market fluctuations, these show a wide variation in the price per pound between different spices and so could be misleading in respect of the value of the total trade in each. The exorbitant sums charged for a pound of, say, malabathron, stacte (an oil obtained from myrrh) or the very best cinnamon bark reflect the limited availability of these rare products. Conversely, the comparatively affordable prices quoted for pepper or frankincense reflect ample supplies, bulk shipments, organised distribution and heavy demand. Thus the value of imports of black pepper, despite a price tag of only 4 denarii per pound, must have greatly exceeded that of, say, malabathron at up to 300 denarii per pound.

Pliny, always a reliable if disgruntled source, also provides the best clue as to the overall worth of the trade. Easing into the saddle of his favourite hobby-horse, he denounces the damage being wrought on the Roman economy by the irresponsible import of oriental luxuries for no higher purpose than the gratification of exhibitionists. At the funeral of Nero's consort Poppaea it was reliably reported that more aromatics were burnt than Arabia could produce in a whole year. While the gods received incense 'a grain at a time', it was being 'piled in heaps to honour dead bodies'. No wonder Arabia was so 'Felix', Pliny says, mimicking Agatharchides; it, and places beyond, was where all these smelly substances were coming from.

> And by the lowest reckoning India, Seres [that is China as the source of silk] and the Arabian peninsula take from our empire 100 million sesterces a year – such is the sum that our luxuries and our women cost us; for what fraction, pray, of these imports now goes either to the gods or the powers of the underworld?[3]

A hundred million sesterces, equivalent to 22,000 pounds (10,000 kg) of gold, does not sound outrageous as the gross value of the trade. The personal estate of Seneca, admittedly one of Rome's wealthiest citizens, was valued at three times as much; and the annual yield of gold from the new mines in Spain was put at 20,000 pounds (9,000 kg). But if, as seems probable, Pliny's figure referred only to the Red Sea trade and represented not its whole value (including exported manufactures and materials) but simply the value of the treasure and coinage required to keep it in balance, then the situation was more serious. An annual trade deficit of a hundred million sesterces was a significant drain on the imperial exchequer and was sustainable only as long as the empire's legions continued to bring in the treasure and tribute of neighbouring territories. Once these declined and new mineral discoveries ceased, Rome would be in trouble.

Meanwhile spices from the East, along with ivory, tortoiseshell, jewels and textiles, came gliding down the Nile from Coptos, eddied through the warehouses and workshops of Alexandria, and then spilled across the Mediterranean to ports like Puteoli for onward carriage to Rome. In 92 AD the emperor Domitian built new *horrea pipertaria* – literally 'pepper godowns' but used for the storage of all spices – near the city's Via Sacra. From shops in the *vicus unguentarius*, or 'perfume quarter', the carefully weighed spices were retailed to respectable Roman households for whom pepper had become as much a culinary essential as salt. Ready-ground in *molae pipertariae*, or 'pepper-mills', it was presented at table as a condiment either on *piperantes*, 'pepper-plates', or in the commoner *piperatoria*, 'pepper-pots'. Several examples of these, often in silver, have been found from Sicily and Pompeii to the Dordogne and Britain.

For the first time in history the doors of western Europe were open to the heavy scents of south Asia and the finest silks of China. Arabian joss-sticks burned in airy Tuscan villas as nard-pomaded citizens dressed diaphanously to dine adventurously. From kitchens savouring of a Gujerati eatery were borne boiled-and-spiced ostrich, curried crane, peppered parrot and roast flamingo with sesame seeds.[4] 'In one kind of food India is invoked, in the next Egypt, Crete, Cyrene and every land in turn.'[5] The ivory-legged tables with their tortoiseshell inlay groaned under Campanian wines impregnated with Indian ginger or Arabian resin, the much more exciting precursors of today's retsina. Spice-mulled punch was chased with iced fruit-juice laced with cinnamon. In its oppidan opulence Rome married the indulgence of the Orient with the sumptuousness of Sabaea.

To Apicius, a noted epicure, goes the credit for introducing his fellow countrymen to a whole new culinary repertoire based on spices. His *De Re Coquinaria* may have been begun about the time of Christ and would run to 478 recipes spread over several volumes. Innes Miller, with apparent relish, singles out the 'ragout *à la Baiae*' which called for 'minced oysters, mussels, sea-urchins, chopped toasted pine-kernels, rue, celery, pepper, coriander, cumin, sweet cooking-wine, fish vinegar, Jericho dates and olive oil'.[6] Apicius was especially good on sauces. For roast venison he recommended a simple glaze; take 'pepper, spikenard, malabathron, celery seed, dried onion, fresh rue, honey, vinegar, fish sauce: add Syrian dates, raisins and oil'.[7] Lampreys, on the other hand, called for a sauce whose ingredients were less exotic but more challenging:

Venafran oil of the first pressing, Spanish fish sauce, five-year old Italian wine to be added during the cooking (if adding after, wine from Chios will serve at least as well as any other), white pepper, and vinegar from the vineyards of Methymna on Lesbos. My own little innovation is to add fresh rocket and bitter elecampane [the root of a Mediterranean herb].[8]

As well as the spices mentioned, Apicius used ginger, cinnamon, an oil obtained from malabathron leaves, assafoetida and turmeric. Other spices from the East not mentioned but certainly available included costus, cardamom and amomum. Notable by their absence, though, are most of the south-east Asian spices including that distinguished trinity of cloves, nutmeg and mace from the Spice Islands. A 'macir' mentioned in the *Periplus* and elsewhere sounds a bit like 'mace' but is described as the bark of a tree-root; it cannot have been the delicate membrane of the nutmeg fruit. 'Comacum', on the other hand, was an oily extrusion from what was definitely a nut; it could have been nutmeg itself, except that the word 'comacum' is etymologically such poles apart from both nutmeg's Sanskrit name and its later Latin name (*nux moscata*) that this shared nuttiness must be coincidental.

Cloves, apparently, were known; Pliny mentions them. Or rather he mentions 'a grain like that of pepper but bigger and more fragile that is said to grow on the Indian lotos tree and is called *caryophyllon*'. He gives no price for it and simply says it is imported 'for the sake of its scent'.[9] No other first-century source refers to cloves, which then disappear from the record for three hundred years. Yet the word is correct. 'Caryophyllon' or 'Garyophyllon' would pass through the French *clou de girofle* to the English 'clove-gillyflower'. The *clou* refered to its *clou*-like, or nail-like, shape. This being its most distinctive visual trait, it is curious that Pliny calls it 'bigger' than a peppercorn, rather than 'longer', and that he says nothing of its notable medicinal or culinary properties. One must assume that he had heard tell of cloves but not actually encountered them. Perhaps some enterprising merchant had once picked up a few bags while sojourning in the 'foreign quarter' of one of those Coromandel ports to which the great *kolandiophota*, presumably Malay/Indonesian vessels, came laden with the archipelago's exotic produce. Like nutmeg and mace from the Banda Islands, camphor from Sumatra and Borneo, and sandalwood from Timor, the cloves of the Moluccas were already reaching both China and India but were perhaps too highly valued in these countries to be available for re-export. Not until the dying days of the Roman Empire would most of them become familiar in the West.

Indonesia's spices being practically unknown, there was no incentive to investigate their provenance. The Romans thought they had mastered the spice route in reaching India; thereafter the commercial and geographical horizons of the empire expanded only fitfully. As well as reports brought back by mariners and merchants like the author of the *Periplus*, diplomatic missions from south Arabia and India are known to have reached the Mediterranean. Emperor Augustus supposedly received deputations both from the Pandya kingdom in the extreme south of India and from 'Porus', evidently a Panjabi dynast in the far north-west. Porus sent gifts including a man with no arms, a large turtle, and a saddhu from Barygaza who later burned himself to death in Athens. There was also a partridge 'bigger than a vulture'; it might have been some strain of the domesticated derivative of the Indian jungle-fowl that was slowly conquering the world as the chicken; if so, to the hotly debated question of which came first, the chicken or the *tikka masala*, the correct answer would seem to be the *masala*.

According to the letter produced by his emissaries, King Porus was 'anxious to be a friend to Caesar and was ready, not only to allow him passage through his country wherever he wished to go, but also to co-operate with him in anything that was honourable'. All of which, declares Mortimer Wheeler, sounds 'like the effusive adumbration of a trade agreement'.[10] It also sounds like a reworking of some much quoted details from Alexander the Great's Indian incursion. He too had encountered a King 'Poros' who, after being defeated, was reinstated as a friendly feudatory in return for providing free passage across his territory. And from India Alexander had brought back his own religious renunciant. Called Calamos, this man was possibly a Jain, and he too made a great impression when, becoming ill, he walked to his own funeral pyre and climbed into the flames. Reverential encounters and deferential overtures were evidently what a would-be world-ruler might expect from India. In the case of Augustus they should not perhaps be taken too literally.

Yet the contacts continued. Four ambassadors from Sri Lanka, a place 'banished by nature beyond the confines of the world', waited on the emperor Claudius in Pliny's day. As with the queen of Sheba's curiosity about Solomon, the king of Sri Lanka had supposedly been moved to investigate rumours, perhaps retailed by a castaway, of Rome's power and justice. Early in the second century another Indian deputation was received by Trajan before his campaign to extend the Roman frontier through Mesopotamia; in old age Trajan is famously said to have frowned on the dancing waters of the Gulf and declared that, were he younger, his fondest wish would be to take passage to India. Over the next two centuries the emperors Antoninus Pius, Elagabulus, Aurelian and Constantine were also favoured with Indian and Bactrian missions.

Rome does not seem to have reciprocated other than commercially. A mission from Ta-t'sin ('Syria' or more vaguely 'the West') is noticed in the annals of the Chinese Han dynasty as having reached what is now north Vietnam in 166 AD. But it is unlikely that it got there under its own sail, or that its claim to represent the emperor Marcus Aurelius had any substance. Nor presumably did it ever return, for there is no mention of it in Roman sources.

There may too have been a small exodus of migrant-workers from Rome's eastern territories, as suggested by the tradition of the 'doubting' apostle Thomas. Either recruited or purchased by a Levantine 'gang-master', Thomas was supposedly whisked off to the Panjab to work on the palace of King Gondophares (Gudnaphar in Indian history). Later he is said to have sailed as a missionary to Kerala, whence he trod that coin-strewn trail across the peninsula to the Coromandel ports. Some of the Syrian Christians of Kerala (so called because they acknowledge the authority of the patriarchate of Antioch) trace their ancestors' conversion to this apostolic visit; and their association with the Malabar spice trade, which continues to this day, may be equally ancient in that Christian merchants of the later Roman Empire may have preferred to deal with co-religionists. On the Coromandel coast St Thomas is particularly associated with an area that is now part of Chennai (Madras) but which must have been adjacent to the one-time port of Sopatma mentioned in the *Periplus*.

The geographical knowledge that accrued from these contacts, though slight, no doubt augmented the material available to Marinos

Above: *Myristica fragrans*, the nutmeg tree, epitomised the mysterious provenance of spices, being native only to the remote Banda Islands of Indonesia. By a nineteenth-century Chinese artist

Right: A cinnamon merchant, from a fifteenth-century Italian manuscript of Dioscorides' *Tractatus de Herbis*. Fourteen hundred years after its composition, the work of this Greek physician was still Europe's primary guide to the medicinal use of Asian spices

Mary Magdalene as the patron saint of navigators and apothecaries, a role deriving from her use of the Himalayan spikenard to anoint Jesus' feet. From the *Book of Hours of Marguerite d'Orléans*

ameses III offers incense to Ptah. In the ancient world spices were used as much for
urification and perfumery as for cooking and medicine. From a wall painting in the tomb
Rameses' son at Thebes, *c*.1180 BC

tti making perfumes and ointments adorn the House of the Vettii at Pompeii, AD 62–79.
nically, the volcanic ash that preserved the frescos killed Pliny the Elder, the great
minator against the perfumed extravagances of Roman society

A boat on the Nile as depicted in a wall painting from the tomb of Sennefer at Luxor, 1426–1400 BC. The vessel's delicate construction suggests that the lands from which ancien Egypt obtained incense and spices may not have been particularly remote

The boat race portrayed on this black-figure cup of c.520–510 BC indicates the limitations ancient-Greek shipping. Cargo space, even for spices, was at a premium

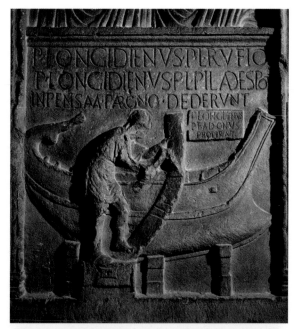

Above: Coin finds attest the Roman world's trade with the East. This gold aureus of the emperor Gaius (Caligula) was minted in Rome in AD 40 and was found in southern India in the nineteenth century. Though in mint condition, many such coins appear to have been defaced, suggesting that they had been produced exclusively for export

Above right: Funerary stela of Publio Longidieno, a boat-builder of Ravenna, first century AD. The sturdy interlocking hull of Roman ships, into which a frame and ribs were afterwards slotted, gave them vital strength for ocean sailing

Right: The 'Empress *piperatorium*', a pepper pot of gilded silver from Roman Britain, fifth century AD. It was one of several luxury pepper pots of the Hoxne hoard discovered in 1992

Above: Marco Polo's departure from Venice, from an illuminated version of his *Travels* produced in England in the fifteenth century. Polo's account of the spice producing regions of Asia was medieval Europe's main source on the then Muslim-controlled spice route

Right: An Arab trading ship, from al-Harari's *Maqamat*, AH 634 (AD 1237). The coir binding, which Marco Polo found such an off-putting feature of Indo-Arab vessels, is clearly visible

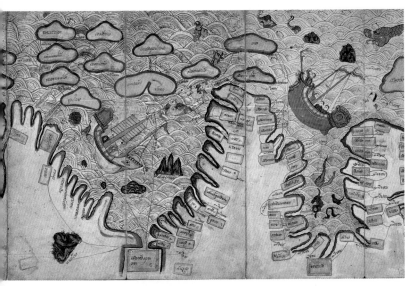

Chinese junk and a European vessel in Asian waters, from the Berlin Traiphum, a Thai cosmographical text of 1776. With south at the top, the three peninsulas are, from left to right, Indo-China, Malaya, and India

A navigational star-chart drawn by Cheng-ho for the Indian Ocean. In the early fifteenth century imperial China's maritime superiority was demonstrated in a succession of voyages via the spice route as far as Africa. From a wood-block print in a military treatise, *Wubei zhi*, by Mao Yuanyi, *c.*1621

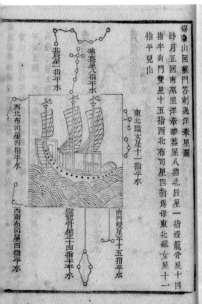

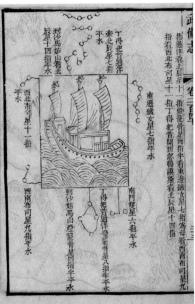

The Yongle Emperor
(r. 1402–24), Cheng-ho's
great patron and the last of
the Ming rulers to encourag
Chinese ventures abroad

Cheng-ho's giraffe,
brought to China from
eastern Africa and
there painted on silk by
Shen Du (1357–1434),
poet and artist to the
Ming court

of Tyre, a geographer whose works are lost but on whom Claudius Ptolemy drew heavily for his own compendious *Geography*. The most renowned of all the Graeco-Egyptian scholars who availed themselves of Alexandria's library and patronage, Ptolemy wrote in the mid-second century AD. Hadrian was by then emperor, a stern reformer remembered for his Northumbrian wall and other frontier demarcations. Consolidation rather than conquest was now the imperial priority as the first barbarian incursors moved into the Balkans and revolts rocked Judaea and Egypt.

More seriously for Roman participation in the spice trade, the Red Sea was becoming a hostile environment. The Himyarites, another Arabian people, were replacing the Sabaeans as the paramount power in southern Arabia, while the Ethiopians of Axum were asserting control of the sea's African shore. Both participated in the maritime trade between Egypt and India and may have largely ousted Graeco-Roman shipping. Of Trajan's Nile–Suez canal actually being used for transit between the Mediterranean and the Red Sea little is heard. Nor do the Egyptian Red Sea ports of Clysma (Suez), Myos Hormos and Berenice seem to have acquired the pillared permanence of their metropolitian equivalents inland at Petra, Jerash (north of Amman) and Palmyra.

The coin-finds in the south of India tell the same story of a trade already in decline so far as direct Graeco-Roman participation was concerned. While coins from the reigns of Augustus and Tiberius are plentiful, 'after Nero they dwindle markedly'.[11] This could be because Nero had debased the coinage and so discredited it as a medium of exchange. Or it could be that the 'passage-across' trade between the pepper ports of the Malabar coast and the Red Sea was being sapped by a revival of trade between Gujerat and the Gulf.

Trajan's advance into Mesopotamia had alerted Roman importers to this shorter route to India. On the proceeds of the transit trade between the Gulf and the Mediterranean, Palmyra was already profiting sensationally and building gloriously. A stele dated to 137 AD and known as the 'Palmyrene Tariff' lists the charges levied on some twenty-eight different kinds of trade goods handled by Palmyra's wealthy merchants. Assuming that the order in which these trade goods were recorded is significant, 'dry goods' including spices were second only to slaves, with perfumes and oils not far behind. Located on what was often the eastern frontier of the Roman Empire and acting as both carriers and financiers, Palmyrenes of the second to third century AD may have exercised a control over trade with the East as comprehensive as that later exercised throughout the Mediterranean by the Venetians. As the city's colonades marched proudly into the desert, so briefly did its political power. Septimius Odainat routed the Persians in 260 AD to claim the title of 'King of Kings'. His queen Zenobia, as regent, went still further, overrunning both Roman Arabia and Egypt.

Meanwhile Italy itself was entering an age of economic decline. Syria and the Levant were becoming the empire's most productive provinces. The imperial axis was edging east. Patterns of trade and fashions in ideas followed. Among emperors aspiring to semi-divine status and accustomed to a thurified and spice-laden life-style, Egyptian and Middle Eastern cults found both favour and converts. The less privileged classes looked east, too; in messianic cults like Christianity they found solace and strength.

Although Ptolemy's *Geography*, like the *Almagest*, his great work on astronomy, would invite the wrath of early Christendom's fundamentalists, it evaded the oblivion to which the Dark Ages consigned so much of classical learning. An era was dawning in which it was Christians who denied the empirically obvious, while Muslims gratefully appropriated and elaborated it. Ptolemy's *Geography* would enter the canon of Arab scholarship and thus be preserved to enlighten a Renaissance posterity and enjoy authoritative status well into early modern times. Its coastal topography of Africa and Asia would not be thoroughly revised until the Portuguese headed east; and some of Ptolemy's inland features – the 'mountains of the moon' in equatorial Africa and the 'stone tower' along the Silk Road – would still intrigue explorers in Victorian times. The *Geography*'s history spans the centuries much as its geography spans the continents.

Ptolemy himself would not have welcomed all this pedestrian attention. A purist in geographical matters with no sense of travel's romance, he was interested in the form and representation of the known world within its planetary context. Observations useful to a second-century traveller or merchant, let alone the colourful asides treasured by a twenty-first-century reader, are entirely absent. The *Geography* is revealed as essentially an index of almost unrecognisable place-names, each with supposed co-ordinates of latitude and longitude corresponding to its position on Ptolemy's barely recognisable maps.

The co-ordinates seldom have the certainty of an astronomical fix; usually they have just been roughly deduced from available itineraries. And Ptolemy disastrously underestimates the world's circumference. Four centuries earlier Eratosthenes had produced a figure for the girth of the earth that was almost precisely correct. Ptolemy's calculations shrank it by a sixth, so foreshortening each of the degrees into which he divided it. In terms of longitude, this error was compounded the further east his map extended from its base meridian off the Atlantic seaboard. Even supposing his sources had been more plentiful and reliable, his notions of the Far East would have been hopelessly compromised. As to what lay west of his base meridian, it was Ptolemy's shrinking of the world's circumference that would make a westward voyage to the Indies seem feasible and that convinced Columbus that the Americas, when he reached them, must be Asia.

Moreover Ptolemy's maps persisted with the idea that the Indian Ocean was as nearly land-locked as the Mediterranean. It was enclosed, though, not as in Strabo by an excessively pendulous India (Ptolemy denied India any peninsular protuberance at all), nor as in the *Periplus* by an elongated Sri Lanka (though Ptolemy's Sri Lanka was indeed inflated). Instead, he introduced an extremely droopy China whose ocean frontage, instead of turning north from roughly Hong Kong, spilled determinedly south. The resulting coastline appears to take in that of western Borneo and leaves the Celestial Empire fronting the Indian Ocean rather than the China Sea. Far from staring into the rising sun, Ptolemy's 'Sinai', the *Periplus*' 'Thinai' and Pliny's 'Seres' faced fondly towards the sunset.

On the other hand, Ptolemy's hundreds of named places and peoples, some gleaned apparently from written documents, others from hearsay, suggest a major advance on the *Periplus*, especially in respect of south-east Asia. In fact the advance is so great that some scholars have argued in favour of the text and maps of the *Geography* in their surviving form being not the work of Ptolemy at all. Rather were they 'probably compiled by an otherwise unknown Byzantine author of the tenth or eleventh century' who had access to Ptolemy's original.[12] However this may be – and the jury is still out – it says something for the enduring significance of the work. It also speaks volumes for the snail's pace at which Christendom's knowledge of the outside world advanced during the first millennium AD. If anything, Europe's discovery of the spice route was about to go into reverse.

Returning to the names in the *Geography* – and regardless of its authorship – east of the Ganges the Arakan coast of Burma makes its debut as the 'Silver' country, to be followed logically enough by the 'Golden' Chersonese of the Malay Peninsula. Here there are both named rivers and places, including 'Takola Emporion' which looks to have been in the neighbourhood of Phuket in southern Thailand. A corresponding 'emporion' near the mouth of the Godavari river on India's Coromandel coast is identified as 'the place of embarkation for those who sail to the Golden Chersonese'.[13] *Emporion*, or emporium, appears to have been a specialised term denoting a legally established place of trade. This routing across the Bay of Bengal between India and what is now southern Thailand was also established, and the mention of several Malay rivers strongly suggests an 'isthmian' crossing of the peninsula.

Much further south, in fact three degrees below Ptolemy's misplaced equator and near the extremity of the Chersonese, is located 'Sabara Emporion'. Archaeologists have sought it in the vicinity of Singapore or Melaka; and the establishment of an emporium thereabouts could indicate that the Malacca Strait was also in use as an east–west trade corridor. But if Ptolemy obtained this information from a mariner who had actually been there, he does not care to say so.

Of the Indonesian archipelago beyond, he has only the vaguest idea. None of his several islands is readily identifiable, let alone awarded any spices. His 'Iabadios', though the name suggests Java, boasts only much barley and the gold deposits usually associated with Sumatra; yet its dimensions are more appropriate to an atoll in the Nicobars. Applying various 'correction factors' to Ptolemy's longitude and latitude co-ordinates has failed to elucidate the matter. 'It would not be difficult to show that Ptolemy's islands have been located almost at random, or as from a pepper-caster,' quips one authority.[14] The most that can be said for them is that the sifting of these grains has sustained many academic hot dinners.

The one exception is the 'Island of Taprobane', or Sri Lanka. Here, better served by his sources than any predecessor, Ptolemy (or that anonymous Byzantine plagiarist) becomes positively chatty. The people are called 'Salai' and hence, rather improbably, the 'Palaisimondou' of the *Periplus*. 'Their heads are quite encircled with long luxuriant locks like those of women', and their country produces 'rice, honey, ginger, beryl, hyacinth and has mines of every sort'. It also breeds elephants and tigers; and its north cape lies 'opposite Cape Cory' (Comorin, Kumari). Ptolemy then lists some forty Sri Lankan coastal features and ports (all with co-ordinates), fifteen tribes and half a dozen inland towns including 'Anourogrammon, the royal residence' – which must be the sprawling site of Anuradhapura. Many other names have been satisfactorily identified. And, though far too large, Ptolemy's configuration is reasonably accurate. The tigers, then as now, were a figment of the imagination but, then as now, elephants were plentiful.[15]

Largely ignored by Pliny and the *Periplus*, Sri Lanka turns out to be Ptolemy's most notable addition to the West's knowledge of the East. His willingness to indulge in something approaching a description is taken to mean that ships from the Red Sea had just started calling there and that information on the island was therefore newsworthy. The few Roman coins found in Sri Lanka appear to support its belated discovery, with no emperors earlier than Vespasian being represented. Yet it is hard to imagine the great astronomer/geographer deviating from his co-ordinates simply to assuage public curiosity; and there may be an alternative explanation. By the time that that nameless Byzantine scribe turned his attention to the *Geography*, Sri Lanka's delights had been exposed by another Hellenistic writer, in fact by a bona fide traveller of loose literary habits but rigid cosmological beliefs that were poles apart from those of Ptolemy.

Cosmas Indicopleustes, if that was indeed his name, lived and wrote in the first half of the sixth century. This was nearly four hundred catastrophic years after Ptolemy. The Roman Empire under Justinian was in the evening of its days, perilously poised between decline and fall as it enjoyed a few last decades of lucidity in the midst of protracted death throes. Emperor Constantine had earlier adopted Christianity and removed the capital to Byzantium (renamed Constantinople) in 330. Looking less than eternal, the city of Rome had then been threatened by Alaric in 408; it was redeemed only after paying a ransom that included four thousand pieces of Chinese silk and 3,000 pounds (1,400 kg) of pepper. Two years later Alaric's Visigoths had sacked the city anyway. But clearly pepper was already scarce enough to be acceptable as treasure and expensive enough for a city's ransom. As such, it cannot have been considered the everyday condiment of three hundred years earlier. Its exclusion from Justinian's manifest of dutiable *species* cannot then be explained on the grounds of its being an everyday necessity.

India still interested Latin authors, but as a land of monsters and make-believe that was even more likely to be confused with Ethiopia. In the well-chosen words of one author, 'truly prodigious' was the ignorance now shown about India.[16] The trade in spices continued, though probably not in Roman hands nor in Romano-Greek ships under Graeco-Egyptian command, nor necessarily via the Red Sea. Limited quantities of a few new spices came on the market. In the late second century the physician Galen (Claudius Galenus) had mentioned camphor in one of his prescriptions, to which in the sixth century Aetius, another medical man, adds two more Far Eastern spices, galanga or galingale (a ginger-like root) and cloves. Both doctors worked for a while at Alexandria, but Aetius was from Mesopotamia and it was there that he encountered the galanga and the cloves. Far Eastern spices were evidently reaching the Roman world via the Gulf route from India and possibly from Sri Lanka.

Sri Lanka is a possibility on the basis of some unexpectedly meaty information provided by Aetius' contemporary, Cosmas Indicopleustes.

> [The island] is a great mart for the people in those parts...Being, as it is, in a central position, it is much frequented by ships from all parts of India, and from Persia and Ethiopia, and it likewise sends out many of its own. And from the furthest east, I mean Tzinista [China] and other trading places, it receives silk, aloes-wood, cloves, sandalwood and

other products, and these again are passed on to marts on this side, such as those of Male [Malabar] where the pepper grows, and to Calliana [Kalyan, in Mumbai] which exports copper and sesame logs and cloth for making dresses, for it too is a great place of business. And to Sindu [Sind] also, where musk and castor is procured and androstachys [spike-nard], and to Persia and the Homerite [Himyarite, i.e. South Arabian] country, and to Adule [Adulis, on the Red Sea's Ethiopian coast].

In the space of a paragraph Cosmas reveals more new spices and more about their routing than does Ptolemy in a tome. That Cosmas had actually been to Sri Lanka may be taken as established. Other references make it clear that he had sailed from the Red Sea and that, as a merchant-mariner following in the wake of the *Periplus*, he had earned both his sea-legs and his name, or nickname, of Indicopleustes – 'the India-sailor'. He had subsequently returned to Egypt and his native Alexandria. There, being a Christian of the Nestorian persuasion, he had joined a monastery and written his great work.

Whether 'Cosmas', like 'Indicopleustes', was also a nickname is uncertain. In translation his work is entitled *The Christian Topography of Cosmas*. It could rather easily have once been *The Christian Topography of the Cosmos*. And it might just as well be *The Christian Cosmography of Topos*; for of its twelve books, all but one (that on Sri Lanka) is concerned with asserting and endlessly reiterating a biblical, not to say bizarre, exposition of the workings of the universe. This has little to do with geographical topography and everything to do with debunking the cosmological heresies propounded by 'pagans' like Ptolemy. Cosmas, in other words, was a 'Flat Earther', his cosmos being a neat two-storey dwelling. Though for six hundred years every Greek and Roman scholar of repute had subscribed to the idea of the earth being spherical, Cosmas insisted that the planet was a plane.

To be more precise, it was a rectangle, twice as wide (east–west) as it was deep (north–south) and positioned like the table in the base of a tabernacle. The curved roof space of the tabernacle represented the heavens and the drape stretched between the heavens and the earth was the firmament. This was, of course, exactly as related in holy scripture. Moses had prepared the tabernacle in the wilderness and, according to Hebrews ix, 23–4, he had furnished it with votary objects to provide 'patterns' of how the universe was composed.

The tabernacle was therefore the only true microcosm. The sun circulated above the earth, disappearing behind high mountains to the north at night. The earth there ended in extreme cold just as to the south it ended in extreme heat. The idea of an antipodes, a whole southern 'hemisphere', was ridiculous; the rain there would have to 'fall *up*'. As for the movement of the heavenly bodies, it was the work of angels endlessly shoving them round; and as for eclipses, all those 'pagan' planetary conjunctions, ascensions, declinations and transitions were just an attempt to blind the faithful with professional jargon. The matter was not even worth consideration 'since by this our withers are unwrung'.[17]

Why, in the midst of such pious endeavour, Cosmas should break off to introduce a chapter (Book XI), and sketches, devoted to 'A Description of Indian Animals and of the Island of Taprobane' is not immediately obvious. After the Indian animals, among which feature the unicorn and, though 'found only in Ethiopia', the cameleopard or giraffe, there come two plants: the *argellia*, or coconut, and the *piperi*, or pepper. In his accompanying drawing the pepper appears to hang from a heraldic device of very un-tree-like symmetry. But the text is clear; 'like the tendrils of the vine' the pepper plant 'twines itself around some lofty tree'. Then Cosmas deals with the dolphin, the seal and the turtle; then comes Taprobane.

Taprobane is what the Greeks call it. But for this island of many names, says Cosmas, the Indians have yet another, 'Sielediba', from which would be derived both the medieval 'Serendib' or 'Serendip' and the later 'Zeylan' or 'Ceylon'. It lies out in the ocean 'about five days and nights sailing from the continent', and is indeed a serendipitous discovery. For 'one may say it is in the centre of the Indies' and, importing and exporting to all the seats of commerce, 'is thus itself a great seat of commerce'.

Once 'banished by nature [and by Pliny] beyond the confines of the world', Sri Lanka is now revealed as the hub of the East. Although Cosmas says nothing of its producing any spices, he harps on this centrality and on the island's importance as an entrepôt. Ships from India, Persia and Ethiopia frequent its ports, though none apparently from Egypt or the Roman world. Sri Lankan ships also participate in the trade. The movement of goods is predominantly from east to west, Sri

Lanka 'receiving' silk, aloes-wood, cloves, sandalwood and 'other products', then 'passing them on' to several marts 'on this side' (that is the west), like the five Malabar ports now handling the pepper trade and those of Gujerat (for cottons) and Sind (for musk and spikenard).

To the north of the island, two Coromandel ports, one of them Kaveripatnam at the mouth of the Kaveri river in Tamil Nadu, send to Sri Lanka tortoiseshell and something called 'alabandenum', but not the cloves, sandalwood, aloes-wood and silk. Presumably, then, these exotica were now reaching the island direct from south-east Asia or, in the case of the silk, perhaps direct from China. Cosmas knows only that 'the clove country' is 'further away' than Tamil Nadu and that 'Tzinista that produces the silk' is further still. Nor does he say who brings these products. But since this is the sixth century, conjecture may – and will – focus on the emerging pelagic empire of Sumatra's Srivijaya. As Europe's investors withdrew from the Indian Ocean and its trade in an end-of-empire disarray, Asia's producers were taking up the challenge of opening new sea-ways and exploring the spice route.

Not until the very end of his Sri Lankan digression does Cosmas reveal its purpose. In introducing the subject, he had noticed that the island was famous for 'the hyacinth stone' and that, of its two kingdoms, one possessed the main port, probably Trincomalee, and the other 'the hyacinth country'. Hyacinths were precious gems, possibly rubies or amethysts, of peerless quality and great size. The largest was mounted atop a temple on a hill and was 'as big as a great pine-cone, fiery red, and when seen flashing from a distance, especially if the sun's rays are playing around it, a matchless sight'.[18] Cosmas was enraptured and in no doubt at all that this beacon was the wondrous carbuncle supposedly mentioned in Genesis ii as peculiar to the land of Evilat, which he took to be south Asia. 'Clearly therefore does divine scripture, as being really divine, relate these things, even as the whole of our treatise goes to show.'[19]

The carbuncle, in other words, was the clincher. He had seen it with his own eyes; its fiery lustre was dazzling confirmation of both scriptural infallibility and Sri Lankan centrality. Thereafter the great carbuncle would insinuate itself into almost every description of the island. A century later the Chinese pilgrim Hsuan Tsang noticed it;

so would Marco Polo; Edward Gibbon would call it 'the luminous carbuncle'; and it is there, as 'hyacinth', in Ptolemy's *Geography*, interpolated surely by that mysterious Byzantine scribe. It may even be 'the carbuncle of unusual lustre' that would be purchased for the emperor of China early in the fourteenth century by the most intrepid of all 'India-sailors', Admiral Cheng-ho.

6

Insects on Splinters

There was once found in the Mediterranean, on the coast of Crete, some teak planks bored with holes and tied together with coconut fibre. They came from shipwrecks that had been the plaything of the waves. Now this sort of construction is used only on the coasts of the Abyssinian Sea [Indian Ocean]...It follows from this that the seas connect with one another, and that from the coast of China...the waters, encircling the regions occupied by the Turks, flow towards the Maghrib by one of the passages from the [Atlantic] Ocean. Otherwise God alone knows how it could happen.

Al-Masudi, *Fields of Gold* (translated from the French of Gabriel Ferrand)[1]

THOUGH WRITTEN SOURCES for the spice trade in the second half of the first millennium are tantalisingly inadequate, it would be a mistake to infer any kind of hiatus in activity. Rather was the trade realigned. As the West's major consumer of spices, the Roman Empire was succeeded by the Byzantine; as its immediate suppliers, Romano-Greeks and Ethiopians gave way to Persians and Arabs; and as the main corridor of supply the Gulf for a while largely replaced the Red Sea. Knowledge of the route beyond may thereby have receded from the European consciousness, yet among the actual participants it advanced dramatically.

Between 500 and 1000 AD merchants sailing from the Gulf to India or Sri Lanka first extended their journeys to south-east Asia and China; Chinese merchants probably reciprocated; and each briefly appears to have done so in their own ships – without, in other words, the transshipment of men and merchandise at intermediate ports. The first direct spice shipments between the Far East and the ports of Arabia and the Gulf must therefore belong to this period; and because these adventures were new, while the spice trade was not, it was maritime achievement and the opening of new markets that attracted attention. The surviving documentation reflects this, so that far more is known of the routing followed and the places visited than of the spices carried, and very little at all of the volume or value of the trade.

As to the vessels used and the navigational techniques practised, much can be inferred but next to nothing affirmed. The ships were evidently getting bigger; they could accommodate passengers other than merchants. A stream of Buddhist monks, from Shih Fa-Hsien (Fa-Hian) in the early fifth century to I-Ching in the late eighth, shuttled between their native China and the Buddha's native India, there to search for relics, texts, enlightening anecdotes and deeper understanding. Buddhism had first reached China overland, but in the fourth to ninth centuries many a Chinese pilgrim's progress to the Indian 'holy land' was by sea. Though just as dangerous, the sea route was less arduous than toiling through the Himalayas or trudging half-way along the Silk Road, and it afforded the consolation of study sessions, sometimes lasting years, in the then flourishing Buddhist monasteries of Sumatra. Spices found no place in the text-based curricula taught here, but their aromas, acquired during the close proximity of a sea voyage, must long have clung to the single monastic robe of the poverty-sworn pilgrim scholar.

By the ninth century, Arabic sources corroborate this traffic in men as well as merchandise, although not always drawing a clear distinction between the two. The bulk shipment of slaves from east Africa was a case in point; likewise the sex trade in under-age girls and exotic performance artists of both sexes. Such a consignment from a king of Sri Lanka to the household of the Ummayad caliph in Damascus prompted the first Arab advance into India of c.708. The Sri Lankan vessel had been waylaid by pirates off the coast of Sind and its passengers and cargo appropriated. Hearing of this, al-Hajjaj ibn Yusuf, the caliph's deputy in Iraq, determined on revenge. Landing-parties, then cumbersome siege engines, were sent to Debal (al-Daybol, near Karachi) by sea; and from this bridgehead the Arab conquest of Sind proceeded apace.

Two hundred years later the Persian sea-dog Captain Buzurg ibn Shahriyar of Ramhurmuz, a less fictional figure than Sindbad though not always a more factual raconteur, tells of the fate of a fleet of three 'extremely large and well-known' ships that carried between them, as well as a cargo of 'inestimable wealth', a grand total of twelve hundred men – 'merchants, ship-masters, sailors and others'. It sounds more like an entrepôt on the move than a one-off trading venture; perhaps there is a clue here as to how Indian Ocean seaports might suddenly acquire an Arabised component. Saymur (probably south of Bombay) was spared this make-over when the fleet, nearing the end of an unusually speedy voyage from Siraf (on the Persian side of the Gulf), was caught in a torrential storm. The only hope of saving the ships was to jettison the cargo; but reluctant to do so within sight of his destination, the commander waited too long, in fact until 'it was impossible to throw out anything because the sacks and bales were so heavy with the rain that what had contained a weight of 500 *manns* now contained 1,500'. All three vessels were lost; so were the brave twelve hundred, save for a handful who got off in a lifeboat.[2]

This appalling loss of personnel and capital, says Captain Buzurg, 'contributed to the decline of both Siraf and Saymur'. It also affords some not very helpful information on contemporary shipping. Evidently cargoes still lacked the adequate protection from the weather that a deck might have afforded; there was, though, a lifeboat or tender if anyone was of a mind to abandon ship; and the largest Arab vessels could each accommodate four hundred men (including crew) and at least five hundred *manns* of merchandise. The weight of a *mann*, or *maund*, is stated as 'varying from little more than 2 pounds to upwards of 160',[3] a generous margin that ought to permit a generalised assessment of the lading. Yet a calculation based on the maximum figure gives too small a total for the tonnage of a vessel capable of carrying four hundred men, while one based on the minimum figure gives too great a weight for the individual 'bales and sacks' if they were supposed to be portable. Perhaps Captain Buzurg was referring to an intermediate measurement based on a section of hold space or some other unit of stowage.

Important technical advances, like the universal adoption of the lateen sail as the standard rig in the Arabian Sea, the use outside China of the magnetic compass, and the navigational confidence that came from a greater knowledge of the stars and the use of the astrolabe, all belong to this period. Although practically nothing is known of their introduction, the credit for such innovations is usually awarded to either the Persians, the Arabs or both. In an invaluable work on *Arab Seafaring*, George Hourani, following the pioneering work of Henri Pirenne, draws attention to the prevalence of Persian words in Arabic nautical terminology, most notably *bandar* for a port (and so *shahbandar* for a harbour-master), *khann* for a compass point, *rahmani* for sailing instructions and *nakhuda* for a shipmaster. Such borrowings indicate a heavy Arab debt to the Persians, whose Sassanid rulers (successors to the Parthians) had established a land and sea hegemony in the fourth to seventh centuries which had on occasion reached from the Gulf to the Red Sea and Alexandria.

The Arabs of northern Arabia, to whom the Prophet revealed the Divine Word in the early seventh century, had no maritime traditions. As cameleers adrift in the desert beneath a night sky of sensational clarity they may have developed a working knowledge of the stars; and many Hijazi families, like that of the Prophet himself, were actively engaged in the overland incense trade. But unlike their Sabaean and Himyarite cousins in Yemen, they were not traditionally seafarers. Raiding parties might cross a bay or an estuary to surprise an enemy, but when Arab forces overran the Levant and reached the Mediterranean, the idea of taking on the Byzantine navy was unthinkable. Consulted about a possible invasion of Cyprus in 645, General Amr Ibn al-As famously cautioned against all maritime excursions. Despite assurances that the voyage hardly counted as such since the barking of Cypriot dogs and even the cackling of Cypriot hens could allegedly be heard from the Syrian coast, Amr would have none of it. For, he said, 'the sea is a boundless expanse whereon great ships look like tiny specks; nought but the heavens above and waters beneath; when calm, the sailor's heart is broken; when tempestuous his senses reel. Trust it little, fear it much. Man at sea is an insect upon a splinter, now engulfed, now scared to death.'[4]

The raid on Cyprus was postponed, and when the Arabs did finally take on the Byzantine navy at the 655 'Battle of the Masts', the ships in which they sailed had been built by others, mostly Egyptian Copts and Syrian Greeks. Similarly manned, these craft presumably resembled the many-oared war-galleys favoured in the Mediterranean since Roman times. After the squirting of fire-balls and other missiles, battle entailed getting to grips with the enemy by ramming and then coming alongside. Arabs comprised only the fighting force that mobilised for these final encounters and whose dexterity with bow, grappling iron and scimitar usually decided the matter.

In the Gulf and the Indian Ocean Persians, who had lately served in the Sassanid marine but were now under Arab rule, provided the Arab forces with the nautical expertise supplied by Copts and Greeks in the Mediteranean. But this subordinate role slowly changed following the 750 removal of the caliphate from landlocked Damascus to the riverine site beside the eastward-leading Tigris that became the Abbasid capital of Baghdad. 'A waterfront on the world', was how Baghdad's builder, Caliph al-Mansur, described his creation. Islam, already triumphant on land from the Atlantic to the Indus, was going maritime. 'This is the Tigris; there is no obstacle between us and China; everything on the sea can come to us by [the river],' the caliph knowingly declared.[5]

From Baghdad the Abbasids would preside over a fluctuating domain in which Persians, Arabs and other Muslims participated jointly and in which sea-lanes as much as land routes functioned as arteries of communication, commerce, pilgrimage and proselytisation. But they did so without the benefit of state direction. There was no Arab empire of the Indian Ocean and no enforced monopoly in respect of any particular commodities or the ships that might carry them. Piracy occasionally called for concerted action, but maritime exclusivity and the state's role in enforcing it, though practised within the confines of the Mediterranean and eventually extended to exclude the Christian powers from the Red Sea, were not supposed desirable or practicable in oceanic realms that seemed as indeterminate as outer space.

Meanwhile the seafaring peoples of south Arabia, though contributing little to the early eruption of Islam, became some of its major beneficiaries. In Aden, Oman and the Hadramawt, merchants whose ancestors had profited so sensationally from the export of frankincense directed their business acumen to extending trading activities right round the Indian Ocean. As shippers and financiers, the Hadramis were supposedly represented in the ports of the Malabar coast within a generation of the Prophet's death, and would soon extend their networks to east Africa, the Malay coast and especially the Indonesian archipelago. It was from the proceeds of this commerce, in eastern spices as much as home-grown gum-resins, along with the pilgrim trade of the *haj*, that the cities of Yemen would acquire their spectacular skylines and their cosmopolitan connections.

In respect of ships, we are better informed about Chinese, Indian and Indonesian vessels than about those lateen-rigged pioneers of the Islamic world. I-Ching, the eighth-century Buddhist monk, describes the vessel on which he sailed from China to Sumatra as having yards 'a hundred cubits long suspended from above in pairs' and carrying 'five-tiered sails'. He identifies the ship as a vessel of the *Po-sse*, a word which is usually taken to mean non-Muslim or pre-Muslim Persians – although as will be seen this could be misleading. The rig with its paired yards is obviously not lateen and sounds more like that of a junk. Indeed the Chinese written character used for the ship itself is that employed elsewhere for 'junks of two hundred feet that could carry six to seven hundred persons'.[6] Then, as later, the Chinese built big. But assuming the sails that hung from the yards were double the height of their width, as in later illustrations of junks, the masts would have been at least 330 feet (100m) high. I-Ching's 'a hundred cubits' has to be a bad guess or a wild exaggeration; perhaps the contemplation of still loftier matters distorted his monkish perspective.

Mention of the sails being 'five-tiered' also raises a puzzle in that five tiers are hard to reconcile with any rig of the period. 'Tiered' could be a mistranslation for 'masted', multiple masts being a feature of later junks; indeed they were often so designated as 'three-masted', 'five-masted' etc. Or it could refer to the folds in which the Chinese, by way of furling sails, neatly concertinaed the bamboo-jointed sheets of matting that served them as canvas. Unshackled from its hyphen, the 'five' might then indicate the three main sails plus jib and spinnaker with which the triple-masted junks known as *fuchuan* were rigged.

A vessel of similar rig, with five narrow sails and four masts, was evidently familiar in India, for it features in a painting at Ajanta that cannot be dated later than the seventh century. About 200 miles (320 km) from the ports of Gujerat but beside one of the trade routes from the manufacturing centres inland, the caves of Ajanta in Maharashtra honeycomb a fold of vertical rock on the edge of the Deccan plateau. A dusty approach promises nothing special; the only reward for the steep climb and the price of the ticket looks to be a good view. Remote and externally rather plain, the caves guard their secret well; the most impressive gallery of pre-medieval frescos in the world retains a capacity to surprise.

Within the bat-reeking bedrock, antiquity flickers into life with the aid of a torch like a slide-show projected from the musty depths of the past. Dry texts and doubtful references crumble into irrelevance as airy scenes of sumptuous colour and chaotic animation reach from the darkness. In choppy seas the captain of the 'four-master' is seen taking the helm. He perches among pots that could represent either his cargo of spices or his ginger-green precaution against scurvy. With its tall rectangular sails the vessel looks quintessentially a junk, except that the tiller is attached to an oar-like sweep rather than to the transom-mounted rudder invariably favoured by the Chinese. A billowing spinnaker completes the rig; and on the prow is painted a watchful human eye, a device that is still today *de rigueur* in much of south and south-east Asia. If this stylish vessel was typical of India's ocean-going fleet in the seventh century, the plausibility of regular sailings from the Gujerat and Malabar coasts to those of east Africa and Indonesia/Malaya can scarcely be doubted.

Four thousand miles (over 6,000 km) away and a century or so later, in the decidedly lusher surroundings of central Java's green-baize *padi* terraces, other Hindu–Buddhist artists addressed the challenge of portraying a ship in the unforgiving medium of stone. Indian ideologies had long since spread to south-east Asia in a prolonged and obscure process of acculturation that had little in common with the Hellenistic shock tactics administered by Alexander the Great in landward Asia. The process may, however, have been analogous to the assimilative tendency which was about to carry Islam down the length of the Asian archipelago. Trade rather than conquest seems to have provided the external dynamic, imitation rather than enforcement the internal incentive. Local rulers and élites had adopted Indian ideologies – devotional cults, cosmologies, rituals, taboos, social distinctions, literary, artistic and narrative traditions – because they served the purpose of legitimising and sanctifying their own status and because they were associated with attractive traits, like wealth creation, superior manufactures and a more sophisticated life-style. The kudos that a whiff of cool Sumatran camphor lent to a Byzantine boudoir was replicated in Sumatra by a glint of gold thread in the hem of an Indian-woven sarong at the court of Srivijaya. Social ascendancy, innocently disguised as high fashion, good taste or prestigious expenditure, was the same the world over.

Srivijayan sea-power based on Palembang in south-east Sumatra played a crucial role in reinforcing these Indian ideas. In the eighth century Srivijaya's influence was felt on the Malay peninsula, in the Menam basin of what is now Thailand, round the coasts of Cambodia and southern Vietnam (where the young Khmer kingdom of later Angkor fame was subservient) and in the neighbouring islands of the Indonesian archipelago, especially Java. The relationship between Srivijaya and the Sailendra kingdom of central Java is far from clear. But even if deadly rivals, they shared the same rich Hindu–Buddhist heritage; and in the early ninth century it was the Sailendras who realised its noblest expression by raising the squat grey ziggurat that is the stepped stupa of Borobudur.

Like the Ajanta frescoes, the relief panels with which the lower tiers of the Borobudur stupa are covered depict incidents from Indian mythology translated into a local vernacular. The famous ship running before a storm as her crew wrestles with the sails while the passengers crouch at the gunwales is thus a scene from contemporary life. Though chisel and stone scarcely lend themselves to the intricacies of nautical design, the sculptor has taken much trouble to emphasise the elaborate construction of the vessel. An outrigger, apparently of lashed bamboos whose hollowed buoyancy would act as a many-chambered flotation tank, identifies the ship as unmistakably Indonesian; likewise the hull, which in its mass of braced, bound and bundled timbers is the antithesis of the carefully jointed cabinetry favoured by the Romans. Instead of slicing rigidly through the waves, the Indonesian craft looks designed to ride to their rhythm and bend to the swell. As in most Indian Ocean craft – Arab, Indian and African – no nails are used, all timbers being stitched and tensioned with cords made of coconut fibre. Thor Heyerdahl's Kon-Tiki springs to mind. This is a ship for all seas and, being readily beachable, easy to repair and not impossible to disassemble, also a craft for all shores, a nigh-amphibious creation ideally suited to the reef and island-studded world of the archipelago.

As at Ajanta, the small scale of the composition has inhibited the artist's ability to convey the size of the ship; but the two masts and the great huddle of passengers suggest a considerable capacity. It may not be fanciful to suppose that the *kolandiophonta* noticed in the *Periplus* looked like this, and that just such vessels were still plying the archipelago laden with cloves, nutmeg, mace and sandalwood when the rest of the world finally woke up to the importance of this eastern-most extremity of the spice route.

The first mention of the Spice Islands, or Moluccas, occurs within half a century of the Borobudur reliefs. It is found in *The Book of Routes and Kingdoms* which was compiled by Ibn Khurdadhbih, an Abbasid official of Persian birth, while he was serving in 844–8 as director of postal communications in Samarra, a town on the Tigris north of Baghdad. Other Arabic writers, both scholars and story-tellers, would recycle and embellish Ibn Khurdadhbih's material, often without acknowledgement. But a few, like the geographer and poly-math al-Masudi, himself a traveller to India in the tenth century, hailed *The Routes and Kingdoms* as 'a priceless volume' and 'an inex-haustible mine of information that may ever be explored with profit'. Ibn Khurdadhbih looks, then, to have been an accepted authority of the period; yet he too must have amassed his material from correspond-ence and contacts with others, for he was no sailor, rarely mentions navigational matters, and has an uncertain grasp of eastern geography. On the other hand he spares his audience the tall stories beloved of Captain Buzurg, displays a wide knowledge of what commodities are available and where, and is exceptionally well informed about the islands of Indonesia.

'India' for Ibn Khurdadhbih, as for other Perso-Arab scholars, cor-responds to 'the Indies' of European literature minus Sri Lanka and the west coast of India itself (these regions being familiar enough to be specifically designated as Serendib, Sind, Malabar etc). 'India'

therefore has edged eastward and comprises all the Indianised kingdoms of south-east Asia, from Burma round to Vietnam, as well as
those of India itself. Indonesia is included, but because the outline of
its islands is not understood – and perhaps because Srivijaya's pelagic
authority had an almost tidal habit of invasion and retraction – Java
and Sumatra are either conflated into one island kingdom or fragmented into dozens, each corresponding to a known port or section
of coast.

Geographical identities become clearer in terms of their products.
Hence the 'Djawaga' where grow gigantic camphor trees is not Java,
as suggested by the name, but Sumatra. A hundred people can stand
in the shade of one of these trees; and for an Iraqi postmaster, Ibn
Khurdadhbih is exceptionally well informed about the method of
extracting the camphor.

> To obtain the camphor an incision is made at the top of the tree, from
> which the liquid camphor issues in such great quantity as to fill several
> jars. After tapping it, another incision is made further down towards
> the middle of the tree; from this comes the camphor that crystallises
> into bits; it is the tree's resin but is also found in the wood itself. After
> this operation the tree becomes useless and dries up.[7]

Elsewhere he says that much camphor is exported from 'the isle of
Balus', a barely disguised reference to Barus which, though not an
island, is a port on the west coast of Sumatra and would long be a
camphor outlet. It is inhabited by cannibals, says Ibn Khurdadhbih, an
aspersion that would be taken up by other writers to such effect that
all the islands off the west coast of Sumatra became synonymous with
cannibalism. Beyond Balus lies the great island of 'Djaba' – which, in
this case, is Java – and within a short distance of 'Djaba' are found 'the
isles of Salahit and Harladj'. Java's king is a Buddhist and wears a crown
of gold. 'The products of this island are coconuts, bananas and sugar-
cane; those of Salahit sandalwood, Indian nard and cloves...and two
weeks sailing from these islands brings you to the spice-producing
islands.'[8]

Curiously this first reference to the existence of 'spice-producing
islands' considerably beyond Java is about the only bit of *The Book of
Routes and Kingdoms* that was not plagiarised and embroidered by

others. 'Salahit', which could have been the sandalwood-producing Timor but was probably just a Javan port to which such produce from further east was shipped, crops up repeatedly. For Arabic geographers it would become an *ultima thule*, like Sri Lanka to the Graeco-Romans. It figures in the *Thousand and One Nights* when Sindbad, in the course of his third voyage, supposedly sails from island to island until he eventually reaches 'that of Salahat where sandalwood is plentiful'.[9] Harladj also reappears, usually in connection with a precipice 'which is one of the wonders of the world'. But Ibn Khurdadhbih's 'spice-producing islands' of the great beyond to the east of Java are mentioned by no one else. It as if they had quietly slipped back over the edge of the knowable world to enjoy a few more centuries of Elysian oblivion.

Elsewhere in his book the Samarra postmaster gives a useful summary of all the known products available to an enterprising eastern merchant in the mid-ninth century:

> As concerning what the eastern sea provides for export, from China comes white silk, coloured silk, damask silk, musk, aloes-wood, saddles, sables, porcelain, *silbanj*, cinnamon and galanga... from India [that is the Indies] several kinds of aloes-wood, sandalwood, camphor and camphor oil, the nutmeg, the clove, the cardamom, the cubeb [a kind of pepper], vegetable textiles, fine cottons and elephants.[10]

Like camphor, most of the spices here listed are more precisely located in the course of his text. Aloes-wood, for instance – the sinking timber of the Mekong forests that was so valued both as incense and in medicine – crops up as an export on both sides of the south-east Asian peninsula – in Bengal, Assam and Burma as well as Malaya, Champa (southern Vietnam) and Tonking (north Vietnam, then under Chinese rule). The few omissions in Ibn Khurdadhbih's list are made good in texts of the next century. Mace, or *barbasa*, joins the list of Indonesian spices in the work of Ibn Fakih, an early tenth-century writer. Captain Buzurg adds 'the famous cinnamon of Sri Lanka', a crop not mentioned by Cosmas, the Christian topographer of the sixth century, though by the tenth century reckoned of the highest quality and apparently too familiar to merit further comment.

Additionally ginger and especially pepper are still being shipped in quantity from the Malabar coast, though for political and environmental reasons the designated ports have changed. Quilon, for instance, has replaced the Nelcynda (Kottayam) of the Romans. Further north the pirates of the Konkan coast, together with severe estuarine siltation in Gujerat and Sind, have wrought similar changes with ancient ports like Barygaza (Broach) falling into disuse. To their replacements, like Saymur, Tana and Cambay, there still come from northern India, Afghanistan and the Himalayas the spikenard, costus and bdellium of old. And from south Arabia and the Somali coast, frankincense, myrrh and lesser gum-resins are still being exported both north to the Mediterranean and east to India and China.

With the exception of the Arabian Sea trade, the information collated by Ibn Khurdadhbih and his successors represents a major advance on later Roman knowledge. Those misallocations, most notably of cinnamon and cassia culture to Arabia or Africa, receive no credence from Perso-Arab sources; the attractions of the east African ports are gold, slaves, ivory and timber, not spices. The parameters of what constitutes a spice are being narrowed down to high-value vegetable products with distinctive properties and an Oriental provenance. Cloves, nutmeg, mace and sandalwood alone remain elusive. All other spices are confidently sourced; and the listings that do so are comprehensive. No more Asian spices await discovery; and no further progress will be made in exploring the Moluccan extremity of the spice route until the fifteenth century.

Reading authors like Ibn Khurdadhbih and Captain Buzurg, it is easy to suppose that in the eighth to tenth centuries Arab ships sailed to the Far East annually and in considerable numbers. George Hourani notes the existence of 'a very large village of *Po-sse*' on the island of Hainan in 748. He also draws attention to the *History of the T'ang*, in which it appears that, ten years later, 'the *Ta-shih* [Arabs] and *Po-sse* together sacked and burned the city of Kwang-chou (Canton, Guangzhou) and then went back by sea'. A century later 'regular' sailings are reported, with 'a great exchange of merchants' taking place, between Iraq and both India and China. In fact when in 878 Canton was again sacked, this time by a Chinese peasant army in rebellion against the imperial government, the carnage is said by one Arab writer to have included an improbable '120,000 Muslims, Christians, Jews and Zoroastrian Persians'.[11] Some of these must have been Chinese converts, others must have reached Canton overland, and most were probably not engaged in maritime trade. Yet that there was a foreign mercantile community on Chinese soil in which Perso-Arabs were prominent and numerous seems beyond dispute.

Whether they got there in their own ships is more debatable. Marco Polo in the thirteenth century and Ibn Batuta in the fourteenth make no such claims. By then large fleets of Chinese junks were frequenting the ports of the Malay peninsula, Sumatra, Sri Lanka and the Malabar coast. Merchandise from China and the Far East was exchanged for that of Arabia and the West at these intermediate ports; there was therefore no need for Arab ships to enter the China Sea or for Chinese ships to cross the Arabian Sea. Similarly Arab merchants wishing to do business in China simply took a connecting passage in a Chinese or Indian ship.

According to al-Masudi the same transshipment was the norm in the mid-tenth century. 'But in earlier days it was otherwise,' he says. 'China ships used to come to the land of Oman and Siraf and the coast of Persia and al-Bahrayn and al-Ubullah and al-Basra, and conversely ships used to go from these places to China.'[12] Certainly 'China ships' are noticed at ports in the Gulf, and '*Po-sse* ships' at ports on the China coast; but apart from the still disputed reading of '*Po-sse*' as 'Persia' (at least one authority believes that this troubling word refers to some far-sailing Malay or Indonesian people), it seems that a 'China ship' was not necessarily a Chinese ship. Just as later Dutch and English vessels might be called 'Indiamen' simply because they served the India trade, so a 'China ship' could be any ship engaged for a China voyage or for the transport of Chinese produce, regardless of who owned or manned it. In similar fashion the Spanish would call the galleons that annually sailed from Mexico to Manila *naos de China*. If the same principle applied to '*Po-sse* ships', the vessel on which I-Ching had sailed to Sumatra in 671 could well have been a junk engaged in the '*Po-sse*' trade (whatever that was).

The nationality attributed to a ship was not always that of the crew, and perhaps not even that of the country in which the ship was built.

China, India and most other places in the East enjoyed a decided advantage in shipbuilding: they had timber. More especially they had teak, whose strength, durability, easily worked qualities and resistance to worm made it every shipbuilder's preferred material. But the desert ports of Arabia and the Gulf were without any local timber at all. Both al-Ubullah at the head of the Gulf (the Apologou of Roman times) and Siraf about half-way down on the Persian side had extensive ship-yards, yet could hardly have been worse placed in respect of forests. In such yards every plank and spar had already made its maiden voyage by the time it was fitted in place. Even the coir cord used for sewing the timbers together had to be imported, often from the Maldive Islands. The wood came from the west coast of India or, more rarely, east Africa. More than pepper, timber probably provided the essential ballast for west-bound cargoes between India and the Gulf.

In his miscellany of seafaring yarns from the tenth century Captain Buzurg's favourite is 'the one about the teak log'. A merchant in one of the Gujerati ports – either Sindan or Saymur; the Captain can't remember which – sends his agent to Oman with a large length of teak and a list of items to be bought with the proceeds of its sale. The log is so big that it has to be placed down the centre of the ship and wedged under the bridge 'in such a way that it could not be extracted and jettisoned in a gale'. The ship then sails away, and two months later the same log washes up back on the Indian shore from which it had been sent. The merchant draws the obvious conclusion. 'He had no doubt that the ship itself had met misfortune.' How else could the log have broken free? The merchant weeps, colleagues comfort him, and in the fullness of time he goes back to business.

Another two months elapse. Then comes a report that must have sounded like a sick joke: his ship is in sight. He runs to the harbour. It is indeed the very same ship; and from it there steps ashore his beaming agent with all the items requested. Has the man not lost any-thing? 'We have not lost even a toothpick,' he replies. The teak? Sold for thirty dinars, he says. Itemised accounts are produced and congratu-lations exchanged. The merchant is enjoying himself.

It takes the incontrovertible evidence of the log itself to extract the truth. The ship had reached Oman, admits the blushing agent, but a storm had there overtaken it, scattering its cargo over the beach. All had been recovered except the teak log, which must have been washed away. 'The waves had carried it out to sea and returned it to its owner,' concludes Captain Buzurg with a near-audible slap of the thigh. 'It is one of the most amusing stories of this kind that I have heard.'[13]

Unquestionably it was the selfsame log because the merchant had 'put his mark on it', probably by branding. This was standard practice, and unsawn teak so marked, especially long butts, was imported in quantity; Baghdad's palaces were supposedly built of it. But given Indian and Chinese expertise in shipbuilding, and given the substantial Perso-Arab presence in ports like Canton and Saymur (where ten thousand Arabs eventually settled, according to al-Masudi), the option of actually building or buying ships on a foreign shore must have been irresistible. One authority prefers the term 'Indo-Arab' on the grounds that Arab-owned ships operating the long-haul trade, even when not Indian-built, conformed to Indian design.[14] But that many were indeed built in India seems as certain as it is that Portuguese ships were later built there and eventually even English and Dutch 'Indiamen'.

In the face of so much conflicting evidence, the most that can be said is that, by the tenth century, a trade in spices, silk, porcelain, textiles and much else between the Far East and the Arab world was well established. Shippers and merchants of many nations were involved and most were represented in the main places of call. These ranged from Basra, Apologou, Siraf, Oman and Aden to the various ports of Sind, Gujerat and Malabar, and on the other side of the Bay of Bengal, to Palembang, Kalah (on the Malay peninsula), Sanf (on the Vietnam coast), Haiphong and Canton. Cargoes could be transshipped at any of these ports and this was the usual practice. But Arab-owned vessels, as well as making regular sailings to east Africa, probably also ventured to south-east Asia and occasionally to the China coast. Indian vessels certainly reached Arabia, Africa and China. And in the early tenth century, but more so from the eleventh century onwards, Chinese vessels began to put in occasional appearances in the Arabian Sea.

The last word on this contentious subject may be left to Captain Buzurg. In another of his best-loved yarns he introduces a ninth-century Ulysses called Captain Abhara. Abhara is discovered bobbing about, alone but for a water-skin, in a small boat in the South China

Sea. It is off the coast of Vietnam, and the greatest seaman of his day seems quite content to stay there, despite his conviction that a typhoon is imminent. The story, a long one by Buzurg's standards, concerns Abhara's exorbitant conditions for being rescued, all of which are eventually met. In return the saved becomes the saviour by instructing his rescuers how to ride out the storm. But more instructive in respect of Arab sailings to the Far East is the paragraph in which Buzurg introduces his hero.

> Captain Abhara was a native of Kirman [in Persia], where he was a shepherd in the desert. Then he became a fisherman and then a sailor on a ship that went to India. Next he was on a China ship. Then he became a captain and sailed the sea in all directions. He went to China seven times.
>
> Only adventurous men had made this voyage before. No one had done it without coming to grief. If a man reached China without dying on the way, it was already a miracle. Returning safe and sound was quite unheard of. I have never heard tell of anyone except him who made the voyage there and back without mishap...He had many stories about it. This was one of the best.[15]

7

The World Travellers

> There was eke wexing many a spice,
> As clowe gilofre and Licorice,
> Ginger and Grein de Paradis,
> Canell and setewale of pris,
> And many a spice delitable
> To eaten when men rise from table.
>
> *Romaunt of the Rose* (Chaucerian translation of
> Jean de Meun's *Roman de la Rose, c.* 1230)

HAVING SURVIVED THE perils of the Indian Ocean, spices destined for medieval Byzantium and Europe had to navigate another zone of uncertainty. This extended from eastern Anatolia to Egypt and comprised the Abbasid heartland of Mesopotamia/Iraq together with the Levant. In the mid-eleventh century Iraq was ravaged by the Seljuk Turks, in the mid-thirteenth by the Mongols, and in the late fourteenth by the Mongols again; meanwhile the lands of the Levant and the Nile delta were being interminably contested between a still advancing Islam and a now crusading Christianity. The Near East in the Middle Ages, like the Middle East in nearer ages, was often a war zone.

From the ports of the Gulf, spices approached this seismic region by way of the Tigris to Baghdad. From there several options offered. Consignments might continue up-river through Samarra (where Ibn Khurdadhbih amassed his information on the East) to Mosul and then slip across the religious divide somewhere in the mountains of Anatolia. There followed a rugged descent to the Christian port of Trebizond at the eastern end of the Black Sea, with the onward journey to Constantinople being made by ship courtesy of the merchant marines operated by the Italian city-states of Venice and Genoa.

Alternatively, from Baghdad consignments of spices might take the old caravan routes across the Syrian desert to one of the Mediterranean ports, usually Ayas (north of Antioch), Tyre, Acre or Alexandria. At what point they crossed from the Islamic world to the Christian here depended on the current status of the Levant. When it was in Muslim hands, the transition would not take place until the subsequent voyage across the Aegean, but when under the Christian rule of the Crusader kingdom of Jerusalem, the transition might be in the vicinity of Damascus or anywhere along the fringes of the southern-stretching desert; while hostilities actually raged, of course, it might not be traversable at all. Whichever applied, the onward voyage to Italy, France or the Byzantine territories was again entrusted to Venetian or Genoan shipping, with Venice, in particular, aspiring to control the maritime trade of the Mediterranean and become the spice emporium of Europe.

The Near East was not, though, the only zone of religious confrontation. The two great power-blocs of the early Middle Ages watched one another along a much longer confessional fault-line that extended for over 2,000 miles (3,000 km); and contrary to much simplistic phrasing, it was aligned more east–west than north–south. Roughly, it zig-zagged along the Black Sea coast, cut down to the Levant, and then ran the length of the Mediterranean. The tide of Islam submerged the north African littoral and lapped at Europe's extremities from Rhodes to Sicily and Spain; Christendom clung to the rest of Europe.

Because the main confessional divide ran horizontally, Muslims were not strictly of the east, nor Christians of the west. Before the Crusades, Arabs knew all Christians as 'Rumi', a term derived from 'Rum', that is Constantinople. 'The West', on the other hand, was *al-maghrib*, comprising the Muslim lands of north Africa and Spain. Eastern Christians, like western Muslims, were heavily engaged in both war and trade; and of the two great world-travellers of the age, it would be a Muslim who represented the Occident and a Christian who represented the Orient.

A jurist from Fez in Morocco, Ibn Batuta took pride in being a Maghribi and would occasionally write as disapprovingly of the pagan East as would any buskined Portuguese *fidalgo* from Morocco's near-neighbour on the Atlantic seaboard. Marco Polo, on the other hand, though Christian, belonged to the Near East. His family hailed from Venice on the eastward-leading Adriatic, and their business interests centred on Byzantine Constantinople. It was from there that his father and uncle began the Polo affair with Mongol China. Joining them in his teens, young Marco would complete his education in the caravan-serais of the Silk Road and see no more of his home until he returned in middle age. If Venetians then failed to recognise him, he probably had difficulty in recognising Venice.

The waters of the Mediteranean, and less convincingly the Black Sea, divided the tectonic plates of Islam and Christendom and, naval encounters notwithstanding, to some extent absorbed the friction between them. Direct contact occurred only at the Mediterranean's extremities. There, in the Iberian peninsula at one end as much as in Anatolia and the Levant at the other, tremors and upheavals were an abiding hazard. Sudden fissures could open across trade routes favoured by geography and long sanctioned by tradition, and the resultant impositions, detours and temporary stoppages were much resented. Naturally merchants and consumers in Christian Europe blamed such disruptions and exactions on merchants and suppliers in the Muslim world. By Europeans, even a pacific Islam was seen, not as an intermediary and facilitator in the world trade in spices, but as an extortionate monopolist operating a stranglehold on legitimate commerce.

Nevertheless east–west trade was poised for dramatic expansion. Nothing if not resourceful, by the eleventh century merchants were moving spices from both the Gulf and the Red Sea to the Mediterranean for onward shipment to Italy, Spain and northern Europe in quantities not seen since the heyday of the Roman Empire. Recent study of the fragmentary documentation found in the Cairo geniza (a repository attached to a synagogue) has revealed the prominent role played by Jews in the economic life of the Mediterranean, and well illustrates the pre-eminence of spices in the tenth and eleventh centuries. 'A caravan of five hundred camels carrying oriental spices from Qulzum [Suez] to Cairo' is mentioned.[1] Though regarded as exceptional, and evidently a one-off in that the caravan accompanied the return of the annual *haj*, it nevertheless belies the idea that, before the Crusades, the Red Sea route was in abeyance or the trade in a state of suspension.

European merchants flocked to Alexandria and Cairo for the spice sales. Venetians were prominent among them and their trans-Europe trade was already well established. In the tenth century Venetian consignments passing up the Po valley were liable for a payment to the Pavia treasury of a pound (500g) each of of 'pepper…cinnamon… galanga…and ginger'. Pepper, ever the most ubiquitous spice, first surfaces in the economic life of England soon after. According to the statutes of King Aethelred (d. 1016), 'Esterling' (probably Hanseatic) ships arriving in London at Christmas or Easter must produce 10 pounds (4.5 kg) of pepper in part payment of a tax, presumably for keeping unsociable hours. By 1180 London's 'pepperers' had constituted themselves as a guild that would emerge as one of the city's earliest livery companies.

Europe's growing spice consumption intrigued the most distant of observers. In noticing 'a city in the land of the Franks on a river called the Rayn [Rhine]' – it was probably Mainz – one wrote: 'It is astonishing that although this place is in the Far West, there are spices there which are to be found only in the Far East – pepper, ginger, cloves, spikenard, costus and galanga, all in enormous quantities.'[2]

The writer was Zakariya al-Kazwini, a Persian cosmographer, who also produced an engaging *Book of the World's Marvellous Creatures and Curiosities*. This attributed more marvels than was their fair share to the Indonesian islands, including tree-climbing fish, giant cannibals, elephant-eating sea-snakes, a bird-like 'thing' that was too bright to look at, and a queen on a throne wearing nothing but her crown 'attended by four thousand virgins, also completely naked'.[3] There, too, were all the spices that the Franks of the 'Rayn' so coveted. But the mystery of where the rarest of them actually orginated and the marvel of how they reached Mainz, al-Kazwini did not address.

Al-Kazwini wrote in the mid-thirteenth century when the eastern Crusades were petering out in a fruitless contest with the Egyptian Mamluks. The Christian kingdom of Jerusalem had been established for well over a century and had been at peace for much of it. Commercial relationships and even military alliances spanned the religious divide, while a web of cross-cultural contacts further confused the situation. 'We who had been Occidentals had become Orientals,' confessed the chronicler Fulcher of Chartres after the First Crusade, 'the man who had been a Roman or a Frank has here become a Galilean or a Palestinian; he who used to live in Rheims or Chartres now finds himself a citizen of Tyre or Antioch.' Lebanese fiefs, Syrian retainers and Armenian, even Saracen, brides had turned Crusader households into Levantine babels where what Fulcher calls 'the most varied idioms' were shared by all.[4]

At the opposite end of the Mediterranean the caliphate of Cordova was being finally squeezed from the Iberian peninsula. Unlike in the Levant, in Spain the Crusades would enjoy lasting success. The Christian advance, though at first sluggish, achieved a quickening and eventually sea-borne momentum that would carry it over the Straits of Gibraltar to Moorish Africa, then down the African coast, across the Atlantic to America and around the Cape to India. The blood-red cross on Crusader tunics would be found emblazoned on Portuguese mainsails and fluttering from Spanish mast-heads; princes of Portugal would shed spurs won against the Moors in north Africa to rig spars for carrying the fight to the enemy in the East. All the blessings and incentives on offer to knights who 'took the cross' applied equally to nautical conquistadors, however much their Christian zealotry might be seasoned with a passion for spices. The dawn of Europe's age of expansion broke in the Mediterranean of the Crusades; and out of Near Eastern frustration would sail Far Eastern explorers. The year 1492 would encapsulate this linkage. Even as Columbus sighted what would become the 'new Spain' of Hispaniola, the kingdom of Granada, the last Muslim stronghold in 'old Spain', would capitulate to the Christians.

As suggested by al-Kazwini's observation on the spices in demand in Mainz, crusading upheavals, far from depressing the trade, had boosted it. In Iberia as in the Near East long familiarity bred a certain regard between the two sides. A few Crusaders learnt Arabic, there was a modest exchange of cultural forms and technology, and the common exigencies of life in a hot climate encouraged some domestic conformity. In Byzantium and Jerusalem as in Spain and Portugal, east as often met west (or north met south) across the dinner-table as on the battlefield. Boorish knights acquired a taste for piquant victuals, the physicians of both sides swapped simples and remedies, and swashbuckling clerics absorbed the heady aromas of eastern worship. When a colleague of Usama ibn Munqidh, the twelfth-century Syrian author of the semi-autobiographical *Kitab al-It'iban*, dined in a Frankish home in Antioch he was reassured to learn that pork was strictly banned and that all the cooks were Muslim Egyptians. 'I only eat what they prepare,' his Christian host explained.[5]

Palates were seduced, and demand excited. Like those eastern warriors of old returning from the campaigns of Alexander and Pompey, homeward-bound Crusaders nursed memories not just of unspeakable brutality but of exotic indulgence. Sunburnt squires and battle-scarred seigneurs trailed back to their estates and their loved ones with souvenirs other than the standard reliquaries and devotional knick-knacks. A pouch of cloves and a pinch of cinnamon for the lady of the house can rarely have gone amiss; likewise a philtre in a phial for her who had been missed the most. War was a mighty catalyst; and in its aftermath, manly appetites continued to crave the fiery flavours of Oriental memory while the fey heroes of medieval romance hankered yet for the smoke of aloes-wood and the swoon of nard.

Demand demanded and supply supplied. The spice traffic through Venice and the other Italian states would become the envy of Christendom – so much so that resentment over the supposed manipulation of the terms of trade was directed as much at Venetians as Muslims. Whoever the culprit, the complaints were prompted by feast, not famine. Across an awakening and urbanising western Europe spices had by 1300 become one of the most extensively traded of all commodities. By barge and buss (a North Sea coaster), in cart and pack, from Catalonia to Caledonia, they spawned a nexus of trails linking cities and serving the seasonal fairs held in market towns.

In Italy the spice bonanza inspired innovations in business and accounting methods that have been cumulatively dubbed Europe's 'commercial revolution'. By the 1320s the trade enabled one of that revolution's foremost exponents, Francesco di Balducci Pegolotti, to compile his most exhaustive listing of spices. At the other end of the European spice trail, over-indulgence brought a free-spending Sir

Roger Purslewe before the Court of Common Pleas in 1380 for non-payment of a grocer's bill – exactly £6 for a year's supply of 'pepper, saffron, ginger, cloves…powder of cinnamon, myrrh and [oddly] canvas'.[6] And before the century was out, the boom furnished Geoffrey Chaucer with botanical novelties to fill the forest through which the fantasising Sir Thopas trots in his Canterbury Tale.

> Their spryngen herbes grete and smale,
> The lycorys and cetewale
> And many a clowe-gylofre;
> And notemugge to putte in ale,
> Whether it be moyste or stale,
> Or for to leye in cofre.[7]

With some of the rarest spices – 'cetewale' was zedoary, a kind of turmeric, and 'clowe-gilofre' cloves – here making their debut in English literature, and with that reference to nutmeg, the product of the still unknown Banda Islands, being dunked in the stale ale of England, spices had indeed taken their place in the kitchen 'cofres' (cupboards) of furthest Christendom.

But to Chaucer's generation the mystery of their provenance remained. Largely unacquainted with the geographical works of Islamic literature, Europeans seeking an explanation of where spices originated still looked – if they looked at all – to classical authors. Apart from being readily available, the classics lent authority to otherwise speculative enquiry. Concocting his *Voiage and Travaile* in the mid-fourteenth century, Sir John de Maundevile, the probably spurious 'Knight of St Albans', assembled itineraries and pious details obtained while in the Near East as a Crusader. He then added some stock anecdotes dating back to Herodotus, tossed in a few meaty facts that originated in Pliny, and spiced up the whole mixture with a generous dusting of puerile invention.

Beyond 'Ynde', according to Maundevile, lay a mass of islands, each of which he deemed worth a short paragraph on account of some hideous local deformity or other biological peculiarity. Here, we are told, the people have dogs' heads, there birds' heads, and elsewhere no heads (their eyes being on their shoulders, like headlamps). On one island the men have such pendulous upper lips that they snuggle up in them at night; in another, on account of the great heat, it is 'mennes Ballokkess' that dangle extravagantly. 'Hangen doun to here knees', they require a king-size jock-strap well lubricated with special ointment 'to holde hem up', 'or elle myghte thei not lyve'.[8]

Amid all this nonsense interesting exception is made only for 'a gret Yle and a gret Contree that men clepen [call] Java'. Java has seven kings and seven islands. It boasts a large population and is both 'myghty' and 'rytche'. For:

> There growen all manner of Spicerie, more plenteous liche [plenteously] than in ony other Contree: as of Gyngevere, Clowegylofres, Canelle [cinnamon], Zedewalle [zedoary], Notemuges and Maces.
>
> And wythethe [understand] wel, that the Notemuge berethe the Maces. For righte as the Note of the Haselle [for just as the nut of the hazel] hathe an Husk withouten that the Note is closed in, so it is of the Notemuge and the Maces.[9]

Where Maundevile obtained this nearly correct notion of the relationship between nutmeg and mace is not known. If it featured in his original text, it is indeed 'note-worthy'; no other writer of the period so nearly approaches the truth. Yet he obviously never saw a nutmeg tree; Java had none, even supposing he had been there, and he is unaware that the nut is not in fact a hazel-like 'note' but the kernel of the stone of a peach-like fruit. The reference thus does nothing for the veracity of his book, and one can only assume that it was interpolated by a later scribe. Maundevile would have approved of this. Given the 'freeltee of Mankynde', errors and omissions might have crept into his text; 'Lords, Knights and other worthi Men' were therefore positively encouraged to 'redresse it and amende it'; and for this, as the author invariably has it, 'God be thonked'.[10]

Because Maundevile's supposed travels (1322–56) coincide almost exactly with Ibn Batuta's (1325–54), it is unlikely that he was aware of what his Muslim rival was writing; but he could have been acquainted with a version of Marco Polo's travels (c. 1270–95). The content of Maundevile's Javan and south Indian sections, and his final chapters on 'the gret Chan' (the Mongol qan, khan) of Cathay/China, bear a resemblance to those of Polo's odyssey, although the actual phrasing is more often that of Oderic of Pordenone, a Franciscan friar from near Venice who may have reached India and China in the 1320s. Indeed Oderic's distinguished editor does not doubt that, given perseverance, nearly all of Maundevile's text could be traced to such 'stolen' sources, so leaving 'the knight. .. almost in the buff'.[11]

This sudden proliferation of western travelogues, both factual and fictional, in the late thirteenth and early fourteenth centuries represented another spin-off from the Crusades. Beleaguered in the Levant, Christendom had long been on the look-out for possible allies and had eventually identified two, either of whom might surprise the Muslim foe in the rear. One was the Christian kingdom of Prester John, an elusive priest-king vaguely associated with the Ethiopian or Nestorian Churches, whose 'Abyssinia' was sometimes supposed to lie in deepest Africa, sometimes in furthest Asia. The Portuguese would still be looking for it in the sixteenth century.

More promising in the thirteenth century were the Mongol hordes who were running riot right across the East. By 1250 they had conquered most of China and all of inner Asia from the Yangtse to the Volga. They threatened Poland, Russia and Vienna, harassed the first Muslim rulers in Delhi, and in 1258 toppled the Abbasids in Baghdad. Better still from a papal point of view, they had yet to subscribe to the Quran and must therefore be eminently susceptible to the Bible.

Letters were exchanged, and a succession of Christian missionaries and emissaries rode the Silk Road to try their luck with Genghis Khan's descendants. One sent by St Louis (Louis IX) of France returned with a sheet of asbestos; it was a gift from Mangu Qan, grandson of Genghis, and its fire-resistant properties duly caused a sensation. It may also have been intended as a message. Trying to ignite the East with the flame of Christianity was not acceptable. Unconvertible as well as incombustible, the Mongols had little use for Christian allies and none at all for pious ideals that included love for one's neighbours and 'a world united in peace and joy'.

Such rebuffs were hard to counter; for a world united in peace (if not joy) was more or less what the Mongols had already imposed on inland Asia. If missions like that from St Louis could reach China, it was thanks to this *pax Mongolica*, as history would cheerfully hail it. Where missions and missionaries trod, merchants quickly followed.

Thanks to Mongol rule, the Silk Road was enjoying its last golden age. It was so safe, according to a later Muslim writer, that a man might journey 'from the land of the sunrise to the land of the sunset with a golden platter on his head without suffering the least violence from anyone'.[12] Pegolotti even produced a 'rough guide' for the overland traveller to China; it was a good idea, he wrote, to grow a beard, also to take a female companion, expecially if she spoke 'Cumanian' (a Turkish dialect); coin should be changed into the paper money current in China at Hangchenfu; and by following Pegolotti's recommended stages it was about 270 days travelling from the Levant to Beijing. A merchant with a dragoman, two servants and 25,000 florins-worth of merchandise should allow 60–80 *sommi* (ingots) of silver for a one-way trip 'and not more', provided of course that 'he manage things well'.[13]

Cathay-bound, the Polos and Friar Odoric all took the inland silk route. So did Ibn Batuta on his meanderings towards India. Yet it was not invariably their first choice. The outward journey chronicled by Marco Polo seems to have originally envisaged sailing east via the spice route; likewise Ibn Batuta's first effort to reach India involved getting there by ship. Although both voyages were aborted, this was not because they were impractical, simply because the travellers got cold feet.

The Polos – Nicolo, brother Maffeo and Nicolo's son Marco – started from the then Christian port of Acre in the Levant and described a long arc through Anatolia to Trebizond, Tabriz, Mosul, Baghdad, Basra and Hormuz at the mouth of the Gulf. Grave doubts surround their entire outward journey, this decidedly bandy leg of it being no exception. But they do appear to have reached Hormuz, of which island Marco manages a credible description; and the only possible reason for trailing so far down the Gulf can have been to take ship across the Indian Ocean.

Hormuz had replaced Siraf (following the latter's partial destruction by an earthquake) as the main port of embarkation for merchandise and passengers heading from and to the Gulf. From there, two to three weeks' sailing took one to Cambay in Gujerat and, with the north-easterlies of winter, another two to three weeks could see one boarding a Chinese junk in Quilon for the onward voyage to China. It need take no longer, and was surely cheaper, than the 270 days required for threading the oases of central Asia with herds of heavily laden camels and donkeys.

But the Polos took one look at Hormuz, took another look around the harbour, and turned back. Instead they headed sketchily north for Kerman, Khorasan, the Oxus and the Gobi. It is possible that they had mistimed their arrival on the Indian Ocean and so overshot the outward sailing season; but Marco does not say so. Rather does he offer, as the nearest thing to an explanation for turning back at Hormuz, some highly critical observations on late thirteenth-century Indo-Arab shipping.

> Their ships are wretched affairs, and many of them get lost; for they have no iron fastenings, and are only stitched together with twine made from the husk of the Indian [coco]nut…it keeps well and is not corroded by sea-water, but it will not stand well in a storm. The ships are not treated with pitch but are rubbed with fish-oil. They have one mast, one sail and one rudder, and have no deck, but only a cover spread over the cargo when loaded. This cover consists of hides, and on top they put the horses which they carry to India for sale…Hence 'tis a perilous business to go a voyage in one of these ships, and many of them are lost, for in that sea of India the storms are terrible.[14]

Half a century later Ibn Batuta seems to have reached much the same conclusion. On completing the *haj* to Mecca in 1332, he made for the Red Sea port of Jiddah and sought passage on a ship to India. 'But it was not decreed for me; [for] I was unable to find a companion,' he explains. Also unable to make up his mind, he sailed instead for Egypt in the opposite direction. Or at least he would have done if the ship had been in better shape. 'But it did not please me and I disliked the idea of sailing in it.' This was a lucky decision, or rather 'an act of providence of God Most High'. For as in Captain Buzurg's yarns, the ship foundered, all of its seventy pilgrims were drowned, and the fate of the few merchants who got away in the ship's boat was little better. On receipt of the news, Ibn Batuta decided to curtail his sailing still further. He made the shortest possible crossing of the Red Sea and tramped off towards the Nile.[15] Earlier in his narrative, and perhaps more plausibly, he had confessed to never having made a long voyage and being nervous of ships of any description, especially, he says, if there were camels aboard.[16]

Happily this was a phobia that he would conquer. For though initially neither of the great medieval world-travellers fancied the spice route, both in time became well acquainted with it. From their accounts, pioneers as well as plagiarists would over the next couple of centuries imbibe a heady mix of inspiration and information. Polo's exploits in particular became required reading. Columbus no less than da Gama would scan every landfall for a match to the Venetian's descriptions.

These descriptions dealt mainly with the Far Eastern section of the spice route. In the course of his allegedly distinguished career in the employ of the Mongol emperor, Marco Polo sailed south to Java, west to India, and then back to China – and possibly did so more than once – before all three Polos sailed the entire route to Persia. Ibn Batuta, while enjoying the more erratic favours of India's premier ruler, would do much the same in reverse; he sailed east to Java, north to China and then back to India, before he too completed the Indian Ocean spice route by continuing west across the Arabian Sea to Zafar in Oman. Both of the Old World's best-known overlanders thus became converts to maritime travel; and what reconciled them to the perils of the ocean was the fact that the more ambitious sections of these voyages were invariably made in Chinese ships – and without camels.

On seeing his first ocean-going junks, either at Fuju (Fuzhou) or Zayton (Quanzhou), Marco Polo's misgivings about ocean-going ships evaporated.

> These ships, you must know, are of fir timber. They have but one deck, though each of them contains some 50 or 60 cabins, wherein the merchants abide greatly at their ease, every man having one to himself. The ship hath but one rudder, but it hath four masts; and sometimes they have two additonal masts, which they ship and unship at pleasure...
>
> Each of their great ships requires at least 200 mariners, some of them 300. They are indeed of great size, for one ship shall carry 5000 or 6000 baskets of pepper.[17]

Ibn Batuta was equally impressed. He had been despatched to China by Muhammad Tughluq, the enlightened psychopath who, as sultan of Delhi, was as gruesome an enigma to contemporaries as he remains to historians. In charge of a truly palatial present for the great khan – six pavilions, a hundred slaves, a hundred nautch-girls, gold and silver ewers beyond the dreams of Aladdin, and a souk of priceless textiles – Ibn Batuta congratulated himself on his good fortune as he sailed down India's west coast from Cambay. He saw his first junks in the Malabar ports. At Quilon they were loading pepper; they were of three sizes, the largest being now even bigger than in Polo's day. The decks sported veritable market gardens and above them flapped 'anything from twelve down to three sails'.

> A ship carries a complement of a thousand men, six hundred of whom are sailors and four hundred men-at-arms, including archers, men with shields and arbalists, that is men who throw naptha [fire]...In the vessel they build four decks, and it has cabins, suites and salons for the merchants; a set has several rooms and a latrine; it can be locked by its occupant and he can take along with him slave-girls and wives. Often a man will live in his suite unknown to others on board until they meet on reaching some town. .. Some of the Chinese own large numbers of ships on which their factors are sent to foreign countries. There is no people in the world wealthier than the Chinese.[18]

With a little more encouragement from the Imperial government, such juggernauts clearly had a future along the trade routes of the East. None were as yet seen north of Goa, although from Chinese sources it would appear that they were already voyaging east to the African coast. Unwittingly Ibn Batuta seems to have been the only observer to have anticipated that the Chinese could soon have control of the entire spice route within their grasp.

Like Polo, he was especially impressed by the method of construction used in these junks. The hulls were cavity-walled, heavily clad and divided into compartments by watertight bulkheads so that, if holed, the damage could be repaired without the ship being endangered. Instead of being sewn, the timbers were nailed with huge spikes, some being 'three cubits [about 6.5 yards/6m in length'. The oars were 'as big as masts' and were operated by ropes pulled by opposing teams of rowers. Best of all, there were ample tenders and lifeboats, some towed, others slung alongside. For landlubbers, non-swimmers and anyone with a fear of plying the sea, a Chinese junk was the next best thing to *terra firma*.

★

Polo introduces his southern voyage with an account of Japan. He does not claim to have been there but mentions, while on the subject, that in the 'Eastern Sea of Chin' there are other islands, in fact 7,459 other islands. Such a number, it is presumed, must have included those of the Philippines, Borneo, Sulawesi and probably the Moluccas. Here, then, may be the first reference in European literature, however geographically imprecise, to the existence of what became known as the Spice Islands. For according to men who had sailed among them, says Polo, 'not one of those islands but produces valuable and odorous woods like lignaloe [aloes-wood]. Aye and better too; they produce all a great variety of spices.' Although the islands are remote and hard to get to, Chinese vessels 'do voyage thither'; a round trip takes a full year; and the merchants concerned 'make vast profits'.[19] All of which is consistent with the clove-producing Moluccas, including the nutmeg-producing Bandas.

Of their spices only aloes-wood and pepper are actually named by Polo; and since neither is particuarly associated with any of the supposed 7,459 islands, he must have been guessing. But corroboration of the existence of this obscure trade, and some vindication of his insistence on its comprehending 'all manner of spicerie', is afforded by Chinese sources. Chau Ju-Kua, the inspector of foreign trade in Quanzhou (Fujian province), was writing his *Description of Barbarous Peoples* at about the time that Polo was travelling. He lists both nutmegs and cloves as foreign imports and says they come from Java. But elsewhere he hints that they are in fact grown not in Java itself but in islands dependent on it though distant from it. He knows, too, that nutmegs and mace are produced by the same tree, and is wrong only in supposing that the mace is the flower, not the aril of the nut.[20]

Like Chau Ju-Kua, both Polo and Ibn Batuta also associate the rarest of spices with Java, although they fail to notice that they are not actually grown there. Java, for Polo, is the spice island *par excellence*. It produces 'black pepper, nutmegs, spikenard, galingale, cubebs, cloves and all other kinds of spice'. Vast numbers of ships come to trade for these precious commodities, with the result that 'the treasure of this island is so great as to be past telling'. It is also the world's largest island; it has a great king; Kublai Khan had failed to get possession of it; and the people are all 'idolaters', that is Hindus and Buddhists. Most of which is true, though none of it carries the conviction of chance detail that would suggest Polo knew the place well – or perhaps at all. His routing from southern China appears to have hugged the coasts of Vietnam and Malaya to the Malacca Strait, so bypassing Java completely. Not for the first time, the Venetian stands accused of blurring the distinction between observation and hearsay. Like that between actual experience and wishful association, it was part of the travel writer's art.

Ibn Batuta, more chatty and gullible than Polo, is generally more credible. Arrived in Java from Sumatra, he too identifies the former as the world's major supplier of exotic spices and solemnly promises to relate of them only 'what we have ourselves seen, have examined with care and verified'. He then launches into a series of botanical howlers that would have disgraced even Maundevile. The camphor tree, a giant of the Sumatran and Bornean rain-forest, 'is a reed'; it yields its tube-like resin only after a man, or in the more enlightened fourteenth century, a young elephant, has been 'killed at its root'. The clove tree on the other hand, whose buds may often be picked without climbing, is 'of great age and huge'. Its wood is the part chiefly in demand, and 'what falls from the flowers' is 'what people in our country call the flower of the clove'. As for the fruit of the clove, it is none other than the nutmeg; and 'the flower which is formed within it [i.e. the nut of the clove tree] is mace'. 'I have seen all this and been witness to it,' he adds.

Gullibility may be endearing, error attested as fact is not. Something strange has come over Ibn Batuta's Far Eastern narrative. On the Malabar coast he had been disastrously parted from the largesse entrusted to his care and intended for the Chinese emperor; the whole palatial caboodle, including slaves, dancing girls and pavilions, had been lost when the junk on which it had just been loaded was wrecked. Wisely the Moroccan had decided against returning to Delhi to report the loss. For lesser misfortunes his patron, sometimes called the 'bloody sultan', habitually had men flayed and stuffed while their cooked entrails were force-fed to their loved ones.

Ibn Batuta had preferred a long self-imposed exile in the Maldive Islands. There he had risen to high judicial office and, discovering an undreamt-of sexual proficiency in Maldivian maidenhood, had married four wives, one of them being a princess. This idyll ended when he fell out with his royal in-laws. An excursion to Sri Lanka followed, and after an abortive attempt to inveigle the ruler of Tamil Nadu into overthrowing the Maldivian monarchy, Ibn Batuta had finally turned his back on the tip of India.

Seemingly at this point in his peregrinations he also stopped taking notes. Either that or, when back in Morocco, he tired of writing them up. The measured narration of his exploits ceases, and the logic of his movements becomes more obscure than ever. A side trip up the Bay of Bengal and through what is now Bangladesh yielded only an encounter with a Sufi shaikh in the hills of Assam. Then, probably at Chittagong, he had found a junk and, without further explanation, taken passage to Sumatra, Java and China. A mini-chapter does for each; engaging discursions are pared into inconsequence; and after quarter of a century on the move the traveller seems to be pining for home. Under these circumstances attention to the niceties of botanical science was evidently beyond him.

Marco Polo, heading in the opposite direction, had at least noticed what sounds like the Malacca Strait and mentions thereabouts a 'fine and noble city' named 'Malaiur'. It has 'all kinds of spicerie' and 'a great trade is carried on there'. But any temptation to identify this place with the Melaka of imminent fame as the Muslim, and then Portuguese, entrepôt of the eastern spice trade is to be firmly resisted. More probably, say Polo's editors, 'Malaiur' corresponded to the 'Melayu' of I-Ching's day, which was otherwise Jambi in Sumatra and had briefly succeeded Palembang as the locus of Srivijayan rule.

Srivijaya's long aqueous hegemony had finally come to an end. In the eleventh century its domain had been assailed by the sea-borne forces of the Chola kingdom of Tamil Nadu. A much-quoted inscription in the great temple of Tanjore (Thanjavur, in Tamil Nadu) records this rare example of Indian overseas aggression and lists the places affected. Most appear to be on the Malay peninsula with prominence being given to the 'heaped treasures' obtained at 'Kadaram', or Kedah, perhaps the contemporary equivalent of the Isthmian 'Takola Emporion' featured in Ptolemy. Other places identified in the inscription include the Nicobar Islands and Srivijaya itself, whose 'jewelled gates' were wrenched from their posts to swell the Chola hoard.

Arguably this campaign was also about wresting from Srivijaya its control of the Malaccan sea-way; 'the jewelled gates' could even be a poetic reference to the strait. South Indian maritime contacts with south-east Asia and China had subsequently flourished, while the great pelagic realm of Srivijaya slipped slowly back into a watery oblivion.

In its place several north Sumatran port-cities contested control of the strait and rose to prominence as both international entrepôts and outlets for Sumatra's produce. These correspond to the 'eight kingdoms' into which Marco Polo reported the great island of 'Java Minor', or Sumatra, to be divided. Unlike 'Java Major', he clearly writes of some of them with the benefit of first-hand observation. His notice of 'Basma', for instance, contains mention of unicorns and small monkey-people; both are immediately identifiable from his descriptions, the first as the now endangered Sumatran rhino and the other as the equally endangered orang-utan; indeed 'Basma' was probably a mis-transcription of Pasei, a port of consequence that was not too far from today's 'Orang-utan Rehabilitation Centre' north of Medan.

'Ferlec', another of Polo's Sumatran kingdoms, has been more confidently identified. By some ingenious Arabic etymology it is equated with a site east of Aceh, itself on the north-east tip of Sumatra and a kingdom destined to play an important part in the European contest for control of the spice trade. Here, as throughout the island, says Polo, the indigenous people worship 'the first thing they see on rising in the morning'. They eat whatever they fancy, including one another, and 'live for all the world like beasts'. But exceptionally, 'this kingdom [Ferlec], you must know, is so much frequented by Saracen merchants that they have converted the natives to the Law of Mahomet – I mean the townspeople only.'[21]

This first mention of a Muslim presence in the Indonesian archipelago, and of Islamic proselytisation there, is corroborated by Malay sources which place the conversion of Aceh's ruler in the mid-thirteenth century. Other rulers would soon follow suit. By the time Ibn Batuta arrived in 1346 Pasei's twin 'kingdom', or perhaps its main city, was also Muslim. This was 'Samudra', the place from which the whole island eventually got a name of its own. The discovery that the sultan of Samudra employed jurists of the Hanafi school, to which Ibn Batuta himself subscribed, almost restored the Moroccan's affability. Under the supervision of such scholars, Islamic teachings were translated into Malay (or *Bahasa Indonesia*), which language acquired the Arabic script and became a vehicle for the transmission of both Islamic and Malay culture throughout the archipelago.

From the Minangkabau region in central Sumatra, of which both Polo and Ibn Batuta were ignorant, Islam would spread across the Malacca Strait to the Malay Peninsula. There a fugitive prince, possibly from Srivijaya, founded the settlement of Melaka in about 1400 and, welcoming Minangkabau settlers, quickly adopted Islam. By 1409 Melaka was predominantly Muslim, commercially active, and already well known to the Chinese. In that year the imperial envoy Cheng-ho, in command of the mightiest fleet yet seen in the East, would 'set up a stone tablet [there] and raise [the place] to a city'.[22] The most formidable Islamic state in fifteenth-century south-east Asia would owe its early success as much to links with China as to those with the Muslim world, a not inappropriate alignment given the role that later Chinese settlement would play in the development of Melaka's neighbour and successor, Singapore.

From Sumatra, Polo's junk sailed on via the Nicobar Islands to southern India and Sri Lanka. His observations on the Coromandel and Malabar ports provide copious confirmation of the pivotal role played by India's peninsular kingdoms in the movement of spices both eastward and westward. Vessels from Aden and the Gulf came as far east as Kayal, a port on the Gulf of Mannar between Cape Comorin and Sri Lanka; and vessels from China and south-east Asia are noticed no further north-west than the Malabar ports. The two great arms of the spice route were thus here interlocked in a cluster of estuarine anchorages dotted along some 200 miles (300 km) of beach at the apex of the Indian peninsula.

Chinese shipments outnumbered those of the Arab world by ten to one, 'a very notable fact' according to Polo. Local spices, especially black pepper but including ginger, cassia and brazil-wood (or sappan, from which a red dye was obtained), dominated the trade. From the west the main imports were horses and treasure, from the east Chinese manufactures, especially silks and porcelain, and more treasure. There was also a re-export trade in Far Eastern spices to the west and, though Polo is silent on the matter, of Arabian gum-resins, especially frank-incense, to China.

Fifty years later Ibn Batuta found little change in the peninsular trade. The commodities were much the same and so were the trading nations. Commercial activity had spread further up the Malabar coast with 'Qaliqut' (Calicut) emerging as a major port. Here the Moroccan witnessed pepper being weighed by the bushel. The sight took his breath away. By any but a Malabari merchant, pepper-corns were usually counted out like pearls and were nearly of equal value.

The only dramatic transformation was that which had overtaken the host kingdoms of the Indian peninsula. A few now had sultans instead of rajahs; all had sizeable Muslim communities. Wherever he landed, from Gujerat to Malabar, Ibn Batuta found shaikhs, sharifs and Sufis sufficient to satisfy his most inquisitive of Islamic minds. Polo's stock phrase for almost every Indian kingdom had been: 'The people are Idolaters' – by which he meant Hindus. Only one reference to traders from the Arab world, presumably Muslims, is found in his account of southern India; and after Sumatra no further 'Saracens' are sighted until he has conducted his readers right round India to what is now Pakistan. Ibn Batuta moves through a totally different world. It is merchants who are not Muslims, like rulers who are not sultans, who now merit mention. Even with due allowance for his Muslim perspective, Ibn Batuta's peninsular India has obviously undergone a confessional sea-change.

The transformation had in fact begun within a year of Polo's return to Venice. In 1296 an invading force from the Delhi sultanate pushed south into Maharashtra and in 1299 another conquered Gujerat. Thereafter until 1311 the kingdoms of the Deccan and the extreme south were frequently raided, ransacked and placed under tributary obligations to Delhi or one of its satellite kingdoms. Local sultanates emerged, ranging from that of the powerful Bahmanid dynasty in the Deccan to lesser dispensations like that of the Honavar (Honor, Onor) sultans near Goa. Although mass conversions were rare and many Hindu dynasties either bought off the enemy or joined them, Muslim merchants could now expect favoured treatment whatever the faith of the ruler. Minarets were poking above the coconut palms all down the

Malabar coast; large Arab and African Muslim communities were establishing themselves in Gujerat; and the fame of the Delhi sultanate had quickly spread beyond India. As the supposed protégé of Sultan Muhammad Tughluq, Ibn Batuta found himself fêted even in Sumatra. With Islam on a firm footing right down the west coast of India, another long stride towards south-east Asia would confer a virtual monopoly of the entire spice route. Provided, of course, that were no other challengers for mastery of the high seas.

8

East to West

> In the yeare 1300 after the coming of Christ, the great Soldan of
> Cayro commanded that the spiceries and drugs and marchand-
> ises of India should be carried through the Red Sea, as it was
> used before; at which time they unladed on the Arabian side at
> the haven of Juda [Jiddah] and carried them unto the house at
> Mecca, and the carriers of it were the pilgrims. So that each
> prince used a custome to augment the honour and increase the
> profite of his countrey.
>
> Antonio Galvão, *The Discoveries of the World*, 1563[1]

IN 1911, DURING the excavation of a culvert 'near the turn to
Cripps Road' in the Sri Lankan city of Galle, employees of the
Public Works Department hit a rock. The realisation that it was in fact
a dressed and inscribed slab resulted in the provincial engineer, a Mr
H. F. Tomalin – Sri Lanka was then under British rule – being sum-
moned from his bungalow. Tomalin found the slab to be nearly five
feet (1.5 m) long by 2.5 feet wide, 5 inches (13 cm) thick, and inscribed
only on one side. The corners of what appeared to be the top of the
stone were neatly rounded; here were lightly incised two dragons
facing each other; and below them, within a floral border, ran the
legend.

The writing was unusually small and in places badly worn. It
covered the whole face of the slab, and though no one was immediately able to read it, it clearly comprised three sections of unequal size,
for as on the Rosetta stone that had led to the translation of Egypt's
hieroglyphs, each section was in a different script. This was a feature
of great interest to epigraphists as suggesting significant subject-matter

as well as every chance of obtaining an accurate reading because of its probable triplication. Still more intriguingly, the script used in the longest section was recognisably Chinese.

So far as is known, Galle has never had much of a Chinese community. The town, barely a city, lies on the south coast of Sri Lanka and straddles a promontory, once an island, of obvious defensive potential. Here the Portuguese would build a modest fort, the Dutch would replace it with the massive bastions and ramparts that guarded their colonial township, and the British would clear and drain its linking isthmus for the cricket ground that still serves as a Test venue. The promontory also cradles one of Sri Lanka's few sheltered anchorages. Commanding the main sea-lane between the two halves of the Indian Ocean – the Arabian Sea and the Bay of Bengal – the port of Galle had been a natural place of call on the spice route for ships anxious to avoid the shoals of the Palk Strait between the north of the island and the Indian peninsula.

With the help of various scholars the 'Trilingual Stone', as it became known, was soon satisfactorily translated. Today it stands largely forgotten in a room crammed with other inscribed stones from Sri Lanka's earliest history in the recesses of the National Museum in Colombo. Having yielded up its secret, the slab has little to recommend it yet surely deserves better than the lapidary equivalent of a waste-bin. For Galle's Trilingual Stone is unique. It is the only certain archaeological evidence outside China of what may rank as the most ambitious maritime venture ever conducted.

Besides the Chinese characters, the stone's other scripts are Tamil, which had been widely spoken in Sri Lanka since at least the Chola invasions of the tenth century, and Arabic as used in Farsi, or Persian. Cosmas Indicopleustes had noticed a Persian presence in Sri Lanka in the sixth century, and by Ibn Batuta's time the king understood the language well. Making a pilgrimage to Adam's Peak, the Moroccan traveller had found the trail hallowed by the shrines of miracle-working shaikhs from Isfahan and Luristan. The choice of the Persian language, rather than Arabic, simply reflected the island's closer links with the Gulf than with Arabia and the Red Sea.

Although this Persian section of the inscription has fared the worst, enough is legible to indicate conformity with the Tamil and Chinese legends. Each, in other words, contains substantially the same information, and all are thought to have been engraved in China prior to the stone's being transported to Sri Lanka. Thus each concludes with the same date – 'the second month of the seventh year of Yung-lo'. Yung-lo (Yong Le) being the Ming emperor whose reign began in 1402, this gives 1409 as the year of the inscription and so probably 1410 as the date of the stone's supposed erection. The opening sentiments are best represented in the Tamil version: 'Hail! The great king of Cina, the supreme overlord of kings, the full-orbed moon in splendour, having heard of the fame of the Lord, presents offerings, by the hand of the envoys Cinvo and Uvincuvin, to the sacred presence of the Lord Tenavarai-nayanar in the kingdom of Ilanga.'[2] 'Cina' here is obviously China, 'Ilanga' (Sri) Lanka, and 'Tenavarai-nayanar' is said to be a Tamil designation for a local deity identified with Lord Vishnu. The remaining text in all three inscriptions deals largely with the specification and quantities of the offerings themselves – gold, silver, silks, sandalwood, oil and oil lamps. But with a nice ecumenical touch, the recipient differs in each case; so instead of the Tamil Lord Tenavarai-nayanar, Lord Buddha features in the Chinese version, and someone connected with 'the Light of Islam', possibly the Prophet himself although the lettering is too worn to read, in the Persian.

The Chinese version is most revealing as confirming previous Chinese contact with the island and in identifying the donors. Without it, few would have guessed that envoy 'Uvincuvin' is in fact an attempt at rendering Wang Ching-hung in Tamil; or that envoy 'Cinvo' is actually Cheng-ho (Zheng He), in fact *the* Cheng-ho, Grand Three-Jewel Eunuch, commander-in-chief of six great naval expeditions, national hero, explorer of 'over thirty countries large and small', and for a period of about twenty years undisputed master of the 'Western Ocean'.[3] Comparisons with Alexander the Great or with Albuquerque, the founder of Portuguese dominion in the East, suggest themselves; and had either of these giants been personally identified in just one extraneous inscription, it would probably not now be languishing in a room full of unrelated Sinhalese stelae from another millennium.

The Trilingual Stone has a further ambiguity in that its sentiments would prove highly misleading. Even the unimpeachable evidence of an inscription cannot always be taken at its face value. But perhaps history's predilection for irony is better illustrated by the Cheng-ho expeditions themselves; for quite unwittingly the Far East and the Far West had set their sights on the exotic produce of the Indian Ocean at almost exactly the same moment. When in 1420 Cheng-ho's treasure ships returned from their fifth voyage and a reconnaissance of the east African coast, Moorish traders were already pushing down the west African coast, Prince Henry 'the Navigator' was launching Portugal's first feelers in the same direction, and in that year the islands of Madeira were claimed by Lisbon as a forward base. A titanic encounter between the armadas advancing from the Pacific and Atlantic seaboards seemed inevitable; and assuming it proved as one-sided as the strength of their respective fleets suggests, the Chinese would have triumphed. The future tide of East–West relations would have been reversed and the course of world history fundamentally reshaped.

So it would have seemed, and so it would have been, had either received notice of the other's approach. In reality poor communications, the snail's pace of the western advance, and the blinkers of national prejudice interposed between the two a barrier of ignorance as dark as Africa itself. The Chinese, finding no one in the Indian Ocean to challenge their military and technological excellence or to upset their conviction of sublime cultural superiority, quickly withdrew from a clearly unworthy enterprise. And the Portuguese, finding – when eventually they got there – no sign of a serious rival to their commercial ambitions, indeed a trading world lulled into expectation of lucrative pickings from exotic fleets, took full advantage. Thanks to Chinese complacency, western dilatoriness and a whim of fate, Orient would succumb to Occident instead of the other way round.

China's break with its traditional isolationism may be traced back to those ocean-going junks that so impressed Ibn Batuta, and to an initiative of Marco Polo's patron, the emperor Kublai Khan. Ibn Batuta had noted, perhaps with some exaggeration, that trading junks carried four hundred men-at-arms. These warriors were not deployed to influence the terms of trade but to fend off attacks by the pirates who infested both the China coast and the Malacca Strait. Liquidating

predators in the name of legitimate trade was a task worthy of any protecting power and could easily be extended to harassing commercial
rivals. Yet trade, and especially trade with foreigners, ranked too low
in Chinese estimation for any urgent action. The Celestial Empire was
largely self-sufficient. Barbarians were at best tolerated as subordinate
neighbours; and negotiating with them on the equal footing funda-
mental to a trading partnership was anathema to Confucian tradition.

Kublai Khan, being of Mongol descent, had not been bound by
such inhibitions. By land his forces had repeatedly invaded south-east
Asia, and with sea-borne attacks on Japan and Java he had set a precedent for naval operations in support of overseas conquest and trade.
But the Japanese and Javanese expeditions had ultimately failed and
the precedent was not rapidly followed. In 1368 the Mongol dynasty
was overthrown by Chinese insurgents under an inspirational leader.
This man became the first Ming emperor, and Yung-lo was his successor but one. Reviving the Ming pattern of aggressive resurgence,
Yung-lo conducted incursions into Mongolia and north Vietnam
while organising his 'Western ocean' adventure.

Yet granted both the momentum and the means, the motivation for
the Ming voyages remains obscure. Much of the official documentation was destroyed, leaving the imperial intent to be surmised from
the actual conduct of the expeditions and from a few memorials.
Judged thus, the Ming initiative was primarily meant to reaffirm the
prestige of the Chinese emperor in the eyes of his subjects and of the
wider world. Although not usually the most compelling rationale,
prestige mattered much in the Celestial Empire and governed all
aspects of imperial policy. It was advertised, in this case, by despatching armadas of awesome, indeed excessive, magnitude, by lecturing
local rulers on the virtues of the Chinese emperor, and by requiring
from them tribute and ambassadorial supplicants in return for decidedly generous gifts and pious donations. Additionally gems, spices,
aromatics, rare animals and any other exotica deemed valuable or
curious were ostentatiously purchased; piracy, insurrection and insub-
ordination were ruthlessly suppressed; and exhaustive data on the
geography, produce, customs and peculiarities of the Western Ocean
and its peoples were collected. Other suggested motives for China's
sudden interest in the outside world, like establishing an overseas

empire, making contact with the West, or hunting down a refugee claimant to the imperial throne, are plausible but receive no support in the scant surviving documentation.

Cheng-ho himself emphasises 'the transforming power' of Ming virtue. In a retrospective of his expeditions recorded in a temple at the Chinese port of Chang-lo, he cites the 'kindness' shown to even the remotest barbarians and airs an uplifting idealism not unlike that later associated with the *mission civilisatrice* proclaimed by France's cultural supremacists.

> In the unification of seas and continents the imperial Ming dynasty has surpassed the three dynasties and even excels the Han and T'ang. Countries beyond the horizon and from the ends of the earth have all become subjects, and distances and routes can be calculated to the uttermost parts of the west and the farthest bounds of the north, however distant.[4]

As for domestic opinion, the preparation for the expeditions probably made a deeper impression than their outcome. Three hundred and seventeen vessels sailed on the first voyage of 1405–7, of which sixty-two were giant 'treasure ships'. The latter ranged from 'three-masters' to 'nine-masters' and in length from 130 to 230 feet (40 to 70m). They were easily the largest and most stylish vessels afloat. Each had at least fifty cabins; the main mast might be 100 feet (30m) high. Their accompanying flotillas included many-oared warships and lumbering transports – for horses and other livestock as well as stores and fresh water. Nearly all were built at shipyards on the Yangtse near Nanking. Docks had to be dug, shipwrights and a host of other craftsmen assembled, suitable timbers located, felled and transported, and special orders for export goods fulfilled, especially porcelain which was both in high demand and useful as ballast. If the Ming navy eventually boasted over 250 'treasure ships', their construction, outfitting and provisioning must have made a colossal demand on both manpower and treasure. Resentment of the exercise probably eclipsed its prestigious impact from the start.

Distributed among the 317 ships of the first voyage were nearly twenty-eight thousand men. A similar number is recorded for the third voyage (1409–11), the fourth (1413–15) and the seventh

(1431–3). Perhaps half were troops, a quarter sailors, oarsmen and marine craftsmen (caulkers, carpenters, sail-makers), and the remainder officials, merchants, secretaries, interpreters and other specialists (accountants, gemologists, cartographers). In attendance, too, was a veritable hospital of doctors, though their ministrations did little to staunch the alarming rate of fatalities.

Like a well-planned space exploration programme, each voyage built on knowledge already acquired and endeavoured to advance it. Landward camps were occasionally established, most notably at Melaka; and fleets might be divided up so that remoter realms could be reached within the two years that was normal for each voyage. Typically the main fleet sailed from Chang-lo in Fujian in January heading for Champa on the coast of Vietnam and then Surabaya in east Java. This was a convenient port for reaching the capital and court of Majapahit, the most illustrious of the archipelago's kingdoms since Srivijaya's submergence. Majapahit's ruler was a Hindu, but foreigners were settled in his country, including several thousand Chinese families and an already influential class of Muslim merchants 'from every foreign kingdom in the West'. 'The land produces sappanwood, diamonds, white sandalwood, incense, nutmegs, long pepper, cantharides, steel, turtles' carapaces and tortoiseshell,' says Ma Huan, who served under Cheng-ho.[5] As usual he failed to distinguish between the availability of these goods and their provenance, but at least he did not pretend to have witnessed their production.

With a formulaic mention of Majapahit's frequent tribute missions to 'the Central Country' – that is China – Ma Huan's 'Overall Survey of the Ocean's Shores' moves on to Sumatra and the 'Old Haven' of Palembang. Here some Chinese fugitives from Guengdong had established themselves and now derived a handsome income from piracy. Cheng-ho put a stop to this on the return leg of his first voyage. The pirate fleet was routed and its leaders captured, shipped back to China and executed. Perhaps to counter further piracy in the approaches to the Malacca Strait, and to discourage Thai encroachment from the north, in 1410 Cheng-ho elevated Melaka to a city and its chief to a king by conferring on him regalia and rank from the emperor. He also 'set up a stone tablet'. This has never been found, but Ma Huan does notice the wooden bridge over the Melaka River with booths and pavilions 'trading in every article' that would so impress the first Portuguese visitors.

From Melaka, Cheng-ho's third voyage, like his first, continued on to north Sumatra. Aceh was now a wholly Muslim sultanate but had yet to overwhelm the neighbouring sultanate of Pasei, whose port of Samudra was 'the principal centre for the Western Ocean'. Foreign ships were here 'coming and going in large numbers'. Ma Huan extolled the range of their exotic merchandise and for the first time identified black pepper as a notable local export. Sumatra's pepper came from somewhere 'against the mountains' and was not gathered from wild vines but grown by people who 'establish gardens for its cultivation'. Selling at the equivalent of over a pound for a pound (according to Ma Huan's English editor in the 1960s), it was ten times the price of Malabar pepper.[6] This probably says less for its quality than for the extreme difficulty of converting medieval Asian currencies into the mid-twentieth century's inflation-prone sterling – and then doing the same with the units of measurement. More intriguingly, the development of black pepper as a Sumatran cash crop coincides with the rise of south-east Asia's first Islamic states. It looks as if the anonymous pioneers of what would rapidly become the island's major export had brought their botanical inspiration, along with their faith, from the pepper plots of Indian Malabar.

In 1415, during his fourth expedition, Cheng-ho cemented relations with Pasei by defeating and capturing a rival claimant to its sultanate. The rebel was executed and the grateful sultan thereafter 'constantly presented tribute to...the [imperial] court'. Cheng-ho commanded great respect among Sumatra's Islamic rulers because he was himself a Muslim. A eunuch from youth (castration being a smart career move for one of modest background), he was a Muslim from birth. He hailed from China's rugged south-east Asian borderland in Yunnan and, supposedly a giant of a man, would ever sympathise more with the bold-speaking, decently attired sultans of Islam than with the bare-chested betel-chewing rajahs of Hindu or Buddhist persuasion. Sri Lanka, therefore, to which all his expeditions invariably proceeded from Sumatra, was likely to prove a less serendipitous landfall.

The friendly relations implied by Galle's Trilingual Stone referred to his first visit to the island in 1406. It was then that he may have purchased for Yung-lo the great red carbuncle noted by Cosmas. Returning there with the Trilingual Stone on the outward leg of his third expedition in 1410, Cheng-ho found himself drawn into a typically Sri Lankan power struggle. It pitched not just Hindu Tamils against Buddhist Sinhalese but also a popular contender against the royal incumbent of one of several rival thrones. If Cheng-ho expected Sri Lankan approval of the Stone's gracious sentiments, he was quickly disabused. His landing party was sent packing and a site for the Stone refused.

It is possible that it never was erected. Cheng-ho sailed off to the Malabar coast, leaving retribution till his return voyage; if he departed without the Stone, it may have been instantly consigned to the ditch from which Mr Tomalin's culvert-diggers would extract it five hundred years later. Tradition is vague on the matter, and no less so on the details of Cheng-ho's revenge. On his return journey in 1411 something in the nature of a war, both bloody and fraught, developed. It was the most serious engagement that the fleet's forces ever undertook and, though claimed as a success, it was followed not by the execution of the miscreant but by an imperial pardon.[7]

From Sri Lanka all the Ming expeditions proceeded to the Malabar pepper-ports. Quilon was now in decline, its Hindu ruler presiding over 'a small country' with a limited yield. Nearby Cochin, with a fine harbour and a more mixed population of Muslims, Chettiars (wealthy Tamil merchants who specialised in gems and spices) and Klings (whom Ma Huan describes as brokers), had supplanted it as an up-and-coming pepper outlet. But not even Cochin could compete with Calicut. Calicut was indisputably 'the great country of the Western Ocean', as Ma Huan puts it, twice. Cheng-ho treated its Hindu ruler with caution, showering him with honours from the emperor, concurring in the elaborate procedures for fixing the prices of all traded commodities, and erecting another stone as 'a perpetual declaration for ten thousand ages'. Its fate is unknown.

Side excursions to Thailand, the Maldives and Bengal were made from Melaka or Sumatra, but it was from Calicut that the most adventurous forays were mounted. Ships of the fourth expedition crossed the Arabian Sea to Hormuz at the mouth of the Gulf. Some of those of the fifth expedition continued along the base of the Arabian peninsula to Mukalla and Aden and then down the African coast to

Mogadishu (Somalia) and Malindi (near Mombasa); even da Gama's great voyage would scarcely cover as many nautical miles. The sixth expedition repeated this feat; and from the seventh a seven-man deputation sailed in an Indian vessel to Jiddah to attend the annual trade-fair held at Mecca.

These achievements were extraordinary enough, particularly given the short time-frame within which each voyage was usually made. They also raise the possibility of still further-flung landfalls. The difficulty of identifying place-names rendered into Chinese characters, the challenge of interpreting the stylised maps supposedly based on the voyages, and the likelihood that in fleets of this size a few vessels may have become unwillingly detached, have generated some extravagant speculation. Just about credible, though unlikely, is a Chinese discovery of Australia.[8] Distinctly incredible, though not exceptional in a field rife with fanciful suppositions, is an around-the-world voyage embracing (besides Australia) New Zealand, Antarctica, the Pacific, Mexico, Cape Horn, New England, a circumnavigation of Greenland and an expedition to the North Pole. Only in calling such claims 'epoch-making' does the book advancing them understate its case.[9]

Licence thrives thanks to the loss of both the official records and the voyages' logs. Where what is known is so surprising and where what is unknown so extensive, almost anything can be surmised. But if the Ming overtures conducted by Cheng-ho and his commanders, all fellow eunuchs, retain an air of improbability, a fitting explanation may be found in their emasculated nature; for the naivety of the original undertaking was exceeded only by the utter inconsequence of its conclusion. Like Galle's Trilingual Stone, the whole exercise was simply abandoned, consigned to a historical irrelevance from which it would not be exhumed for several hundred years. Opposition had never been dormant. To offset an enterprise entailing crippling costs and fatalities, returns that comprised an abundance of inessential luxuries (spices, gems, tortoiseshell, pearls), a menagerie of ailing animals (giraffes, lions, zebras, ostriches) and a trickle of passage-paid supplicants seemed paltry. Only the imperial court was gratified by such things.

Before his death in 1424 Emperor Yung-lo himself had been obliged to prune operations; the next emperor terminated them; and

after a brief revival for the seventh voyage, the following emperor outlawed even their memory by sanctioning the destruction of the
records. By mid-century the building of ships with more than two
masts had become a criminal offence, grass was growing in the
Nanking dockyards, and those private Chinese traders who somehow
circumvented all such embargoes rarely sailed beyond Melaka and its
strait. Military setbacks, financial cut-backs and ideological backtrack-
ing had put paid to prestigious foreign initiatives. The great adventure
was over, its memory hopessly discredited. The Celestial Empire once
more withdrew within its thick Confucian carapace. Cheng-ho's
handsome retrospect would stir only poets and other lovers of the fabu-
lous:

> We have traversed more than 100,000 *li* of the immense ocean and have
> beheld on the main huge waves rising mountain-like to the sky; we
> have seen barbarian regions far away hidden in a blue transparency of
> light vapours, while by day and by night our lofty sails, unfurled like
> clouds, continued their star-like course, traversing the savage waves as
> if they were a public thoroughfare.[10]

Though not primarily commercial ventures, the Ming expeditions
were mounted on behalf of the sovereign and were conducted with
an eye to the protection and promotion of Chinese trade. When the
emperor withdrew his support, China's oceanic intercourse dwindled.
No attempt had been made to establish permanent settlements,
exclude commercial rivals, or claim other than a formal and innocu-
ous supremacy.

Other contemporary examples of the state becoming involved in
the direction of overseas trade were less benign. They emanated
from the opposite end of the spice route in the Mediterranean
where, throughout the Middle Ages, naval galleys were deployed to
protect merchant fleets, especially those of Genoa and Venice, as
they made their annual sailings to Egypt and the Levant for spices.
Diplomatic activity was likewise directed to protecting mercantile
interests and redressing grievances. But with the rationale for foreign
trade never in dispute in Europe, attempts to restrict the movement
of shipping proved less effective than the interdictions of Yung-lo's
successors.

When in 1291 the port of Acre, the Crusaders' last toehold in the Levant, had been prised from them by the Mamluks of Egypt, the papacy renewed calls for a Christian embargo on all trade with the Muslim world. The main target was the export of arms and materials such as timber, iron and bullion, as well as manpower, that might be used by the enemy for warlike purposes. But spices and silks could not be paid for without the export of such things and so this trade too was banned. Eventually all travel to the Muslim countries, except of a bellicose nature, was also forbidden.

As is the way with sanctions, these injunctions were not very effective. The Mediterranean world was both more politically fragmented and more commercially interdependent than that of the China Sea; moreover papal authority lacked the bite of the Chinese empire's draconian powers of enforcement. Christian governments, like those of the Italian and Iberian states, paid lip-service to the embargo but were reluctant either to curtail their subjects' enterprise, prejudice their customs' receipts, or abandon vital trade links to the grasp of less scrupulous competitors. All manner of ruses were developed. Goods were misleadingly consigned and destinations concealed. Places on the confessional divide, like the ports of the Black Sea, Crete and Cyprus, did good business as sanctions-busting havens. And quasi-neutral intermediaries like the Jews and the Armenians assisted substantially.

Even the papal resolve proved limp in practice. It was more profitable to levy fines and to sell exemptions, absolutions and licences than to insist on the excommunication of offenders. The papacy could not afford to alienate republics like Venice and Genoa because it depended on their fleets for any offensive operations against the Muslim powers. Indeed the Church itself, no less than the Italian courts, was a major consumer of eastern produce, silk for chasubles being as indispensable as incense for thuribles.

But this papal pressure, plus high Mamluk tariffs in the Levant, led to some temporary displacement of the spice route. Imports from India via the Gulf, instead of passing through Baghdad and on to the Levant, were in the fourteenth century funnelled north round the Mamluk obstruction by way of Persia and Azerbaijan to the Caucasus and the Black Sea. A similar displacement would follow in the fifteenth century when the Ottoman Turks overran the area and took Constantinople. Following this same northern route in reverse, merchants from the Italian city-states opened direct relations with Persia, where quality silk was now being produced, and from there some Venetian and Genoese merchants travelled on to India and China either by land or by sea.

In about 1420–44, a century after Ibn Batuta, one of these adventurers, Nicolo de Conti, duplicated Marco Polo's maritime routing in south and south-east Asia. De Conti, like Polo, was Venetian; and like Polo, he dictated an account of his travels that is far from satisfactory. But he seems to have had a particular interest in spices. He speaks knowledgeably of ginger, provides the first convincing description of Sri Lanka's cinnamon production, and whilst in Java – if he was – collected information for a short but intriguing notice of the still unknown Spice Islands. 'At fifteen days beyond these islands [i.e. Sumatra and Java], two others are found to the eastward; the one is called Sandai, in which nutmeg and maces grow; the other is named Bandan; this is the only island in which cloves grow, which are exported hence to the Java islands.'[11]

Despite some obvious confusion, de Conti had rightly distinguished two islands (later revealed as groups of islands), from one of which came nutmeg and mace and from the other cloves. Moreover he had heard the name of one of them almost correctly. Tucked away in de Conti's little known account, the Banda Islands make their first appearance in the world's travel literature.

Nothing more would be learnt about the Moluccas for over half a century. But in 1502 another Italian, a native of Bologna who had converted to Islam, would also attain India from Persia, then continue east through Burma and Sumatra and not turn back until he had actually sailed among the volcanic archipelagos of Banda and Molucca. This was Ludovico di Varthema, whose overland journey would be undertaken within months of da Gama's epic voyage. Nine years later a draft of di Varthema's account of the Moluccas would be in Affonso Albuquerque's possession when he rounded off his creation of Portugal's sea-borne empire by storming the port-city of Melaka and from there making a grab for the clove and nutmeg trade. Nemesis was nigh for the Spice Islands. After a millennium as mysterious entities on the edge of the knowable world, by 1400 barely a century of isolation remained to them.

Only small quantities of high-value spices, such as nutmeg and cloves, can have been carried from the Gulf via Persia and Azerbaijan over the extremely circuitous northern route round the Mamluk dominions to the Black Sea. But that this was a favoured routing in the fourteenth century may be judged from the observation of a Florentine diarist. When Tana, a remote port on the Crimea's Sea of Azov near Rostov-on-Don, fell to the Tartars in 1343, spice prices in Italy shot up by, according to the Florentine, fifty to one hundred per cent.[12] Such was the volatility of the spice trade in an age of almost constant alarms and excursions.

The same considerations about avoiding Iraq (Mesopotamia) and the Levant had led to a marked revival of the Red Sea trade in the early fourteenth century. Cairo and Alexandria, supplied as in classical times from Aydhab and al-Qusair by way of the Nile, had resumed their role as the Mediterranean's major spice markets. By way of Jiddah, Mecca and the overland caravan route to Damascus and Beirut, spices from the Red Sea also made good the deficiency from the Gulf in the ports of the Levant. Business with the Italian city-states resumed at ports like Acre, albeit under Muslim control and with or without some form of papal dispensation.

This revival of the Red Sea routing occasioned an organisational phenomenon new to the Near-Eastern spice trade. Between the Yemeni entrepôt of Aden and the Mediterranean outlets, the trade was controlled, if not monopolised, throughout the thirteenth to fifteenth centuries by an enigmatic entity know as the *karim*. The *karim* was evidently an innovation, for there is scarcely a mention of it in the tenth- to twelfth-century documentation unearthed in the Cairo geniza. But quite what it was is far from clear. Historians reject notions of the *karim's* being purely a banking-house, a shipping monopoly, a trading corporation or even a loose guild. *Karimi* were not invariably Muslims; they might come from anywhere, trade in anything, and be based as far afield as India or Morocco. Ibn Batuta likened Indian pearl dealers to *karimi*, the implication being simply that they specialised in a particular commodity.

The *karimi's* main trade was undoubtedly in spices, their main axis was the Red Sea, and their main distinction was the accumulation of immense wealth. Perhaps the most plausible explanation is that the *karim* was originally a protection system whereby, for greater security against pirates, desert raiders and arbitrary exactions, those engaged in the Red Sea trade adopted a system of regular convoys and caravans. The *karim*, in other words, offered the support that in China and the Mediterranean merchants might expect from the state. Risk management and the pooling of transportation ramified into banking, shipping, warehousing and marketing. By the late fourteenth century the *karimi* exercised a stranglehold on the spice trade throughout the Muslim dominions.

As with most cartels, the *karim* brought to the spice trade a stability that was little appreciated at the time and an intransigence that was greatly resented. It epitomised Islam's monopoly of supply and therefore invited the censure of merchants from the Christian Mediterranean, whatever their nationality. At the beginning of the fifteenth century Genoa had a slight edge over Venice in the Levant trade; and unlike the Venetians, who invariably directed all trade through Venice itself, the Genoese were often content to act as long-distance carriers, trading between foreign ports without necessarily funneling merchandise through Genoa itself. Such was the case with the cogs – sail-powered bulk-carriers of up to 500 tons – that around 1400 began sailing direct from Alexandria and the Levant to Sluys (near Bruges) in Flanders and to Southampton on the south coast of England. Far Eastern spices, Near Eastern textiles and Mediterranean produce comprised the outward cargoes, woollens, furs and ores (copper from Germany, tin from Cornwall) the return cargoes. But in their dealings with the *karimi* and Muslims in general, the Genoese were less accommodating and less patient than the Venetians. Decisively worsted by Venice in 1386, then beset by domestic crises, Genoa gradually lost ground to its Adriatic rival.

By the fifteenth century Venice was entering its golden age as indisputably the busiest emporium of the West. Those who detected Oriental motifs, Islamic domes and even Buddhist arches on the façades of its piazzas and palaces or on the skyline of St Mark's basilica were not mistaken. No less than Palmyra and Petra, the city owed everything to its pre-eminence in Oriental trade – a term that was virtually synonymous with spices – and was proud to proclaim it.

Its golden age had been a long time coming. Originally an offshore refuge from the lawlessness that swept Italy during the last years of the Roman Empire, the low-lying islands that came to comprise the city possessed few natural advantages. As with barren Hormuz or swamp-ridden Melaka, seafaring, whether piratical or commercial, offered the only outlet. By the tenth century Venice was emerging as a respon-sible city-state and a considerable mercantile power. Thanks to the Crusading demand for maritime transport and naval support, it stead-ily extended its reach throughout the Mediterranean and the Black Sea.

Especially rewarding was the trade with Alexandria, whence came not only spices and eastern produce but also the bulk shipments of grain that had once sustained the Roman Empire. Venetian galleys – smaller and faster than cogs – had first reached the Thames and the Schelde in the late fourteenth century. By then the business-houses of the republic also dominated the landward trade of western Europe, making the 'merchant of Venice' a stock figure in every city of repute. Hauled over the Alps by pack-trains, merchandise continued north more by river than road to Nuremberg, Augsburg, Paris, Lübeck and beyond.

With consummate skill, the Venetians had weathered all that history could throw at them in the way of trade obstructions. Across France the Hundred Years War had smouldered for rather more than a hundred years (1337–1453). The Black Death (1347–50) had brought life everywhere to a standstill and decimated urban popu-lations. A mini-crusade had resulted in the sack of Alexandria (1365) and Mamluk reprisals that inevitably targeted the merchant community. Privateers and pirates, many of them from Catalonia, constantly harassed Christian as well as Muslim shipping throughout the southern Mediterranean, bringing more hefty reprisals. And to cap it all, in 1426 Barsbay, the new Mamluk sultan, at last discovered a mercantile role for the state by extending his heavy-handed man-agement of the Egyptian economy to claim the pepper trade as a royal monopoly.

As ever, pepper constituted up to eighty per cent of the value of all spice shipments to the West and rather more than that of their bulk. By Barsbay's intervention the *karimi*'s long reign as the spice kings of the Red Sea was effectively terminated; and the entire trade through-out the Red Sea, Egypt and the Levant was left at the whim of an avaricious autocrat. Christian merchants could buy only from the 'soldan's' agent and only in such quantities and at such prices as he chose to fix. The crisis, though it lasted little more than a decade, forcefully illustrated the extreme vulnerability of a very lucrative trade. Once again Christendom cast about for some way of circum-venting the Mamluk obstruction. And with the Black Sea and Persia now scarcely more welcoming than the Near East, it was to Africa that eyes turned.

In 1454, sixteen years after the death of Sultan Barsbay, a young Venetian called Alvise da Ca' du Mosto (or 'Cadamosto') joined one of the three galleys which had that year been assigned to sail from Venice to Flanders with spices. Though enrolled as an officer in the fleet's small corps of archers, Cadamosto was interested in navigational matters; and with an impoverished father to support, he was also trav-elling 'in the hope of profit', as he puts it. The fleet headed south down the Adriatic, then west through the Straits of Gibraltar.

Soon after they entered the Atlantic, adverse winds forced the Venetian galleys to put ashore. They were near a high and windswept promontory on the Algarve coast of south-west Portugal. Cadamosto learned that the promontory was called Cape St Vincent and that on a nearby country estate there presided 'Lord Infante Don Heurich', a prince of the Portuguese ruling family. Hearing of the stranded Venetians, this prince sent a deputation to wait on them. It was led by a man who, besides being one of the prince's employees, was also the Venetian ambassador to Portugal; and it came bearing samples – 'sugar from the island of Madeira, dragon's blood [a resin used as a dye] and other products of his domains and islands'. In the ensuing conversa-tion young Cadamosto was more an eavesdropper than a participant:

> He [the Venetian] said that his Lord [the prince 'Heurich'] had peopled newly discovered islands hitherto uninhabited (in proof of which he cited the sugar, dragon's blood and other good and useful wares) but that this was nothing to the other and greater achievements of his Lord, who had for some time past caused seas to be navigated that had never before been sailed, and had discovered the lands of many strange races,

where marvels abounded. Those who had been in these parts had wrought great gain among these new peoples, turning one *soldo* into six or ten…and if any of our nation wished to go thither, the said Lord would receive them gladly and show them much favour for he believed that in these parts they would find spices and other valuable products, and knew that the Venetians were more skilled in these affairs than any other nation.[13]

This news impressed Cadamosto more than it did his colleagues. He visited the prince, who was as good as his word, then returned to the fleet. His mind was made up; 'for I was young, well fitted to sustain all hardships, desirous of seeing the world and things never before seen by our nation, and I hoped also to draw from it honour and profit.' He disposed of his share in the galleys' cargo, bought whatever was requisite for his new destination, and said his farewells. The Venetian fleet resumed its northerly course to Flanders; six months later Cadamosto was sailing in the opposite direction for Africa.

Prince Heurich, or Henrique (Henry), was the youngest son of the Portuguese King João I and the uncle of the reigning King Affonso V. In 1415, little more than a century since the ejection of the Moors from the Algarve had reclaimed all Portugal for Christendom, the young Prince Henry had taken part in the Portuguese capture of the Moroccan city of Ceuta. This being the first time that the Christians of Iberia had carried their crusade to the Moorish Maghrib, it was hailed as a major triumph. Portugal had successfully asserted her right to act against the Muslim enemy independently of her rivals in Castille and Aragon. A Christian bridgehead had been established on the north African littoral; appetites were stirred by the spoils of gold and slaves that had there awaited the victors; and Prince Henry in particular had enquired minutely into the sub-Saharan sources from which this bounty came.

Retiring to his Algarve retreat of Sagres in 1419, Prince Henry had devoted his resources, his considerable influence and the rest of his life to the maritime exploration of the west African coast. Information was collated from all available sources, certainly from Ptolemy and Marco Polo, and probably from de Conti and a remarkable 'Catalan Map' produced in the previous century by a Majorca-based Jew who knew something of Arabic accounts; knowledgeable visitors from

Italy, Spain and north Africa were also quizzed and invited to participate as advisers or mariners. Charts similar to the *portulans* used in the Mediterranean and based on compass bearings and the dead-reckoning of distance were extended after each new voyage. Astronomical, instrumental and navigational know-how of use to sailors far from land was shared. And the vessels known as caravels, which incorporated the slim pointed hull and lateen sails of Arab craft, were adopted. Capable of sailing closer to the wind than the conventional galleys and cogs, caravels were 'the best of all sailing ships' according to Cadamosto.

Yet Lisbon, let alone Lagos, the Algarve's port and shipyard, was no Nanking. Each of Cheng-ho's 'treasure ships' probably displaced about 2000 tons; Cadamosto's first caravel displaced about 100 tons. While the Ming fleets enjoyed the support of an Asian empire with a population of two hundred million, the Portuguese fleets had the backing of one of Europe's smallest and most impoverished kingdoms with a population of around one million. The Chinese also had the benefit of close acquaintance with the route to India and of centuries of Indo-Arab contact with east Africa. The Portuguese knew something of the Canary Islands – as had Ptolemy – and possibly of Madeira and the Azores; Genoese and Spanish vessels had visited all three island groups, and the Canaries had received some settlement. But of the ocean beyond, and of the African coast south of what is now Western Sahara, a mere 800 miles (1,300km) from Gibraltar, no information whatsoever was available to the Portuguese.

Optimists supposed Africa to be a shallow continent bounded by a branch of the Nile; large rivers reaching the Atlantic from the interior were therefore of especial interest to explorers like Cadamosto, who more in hope than expectation persisted in calling west Africa 'Lower Ethiopia'. Pessimists doubted whether Africa was circumnavigable at all, citing as evidence Ptolemy's idea that the Indian Ocean was land-locked. All supposed the heat to be so insupportable, the people so inhospitable, the ocean so vast, and its winds and currents so unforeseeable that the only chance of survival lay in extreme caution.

Progress would therefore have been slow even without the distractions that had at times almost halted it. By 1455, when Cadamosto 'set sail in God's name and with high hopes', the furthest point reached was Casamance, the greener half of Senegal between Gambia and Guinea-Bissau. That represented an advance of about 2,000 miles (3,000 km) in twenty-five years (the total length of Africa's western shoreline is over 10,000 miles [16,000 km]). It was encouraging only to the extent that, when following the coast, the midday sun was now dead ahead or even slightly to starboard. They had rounded the continent's great western bulge.

The distractions included interminable arguments with the Spanish kingdoms over Madeira and the Canaries, some Ethiopic excursions up the Senegal and Gambia rivers in case they should prove to be connected to the Nile, and the periodic need to redeploy men and ships for the defence of Ceuta against Muslim forces bent on its recapture. There was also the matter of gold and slaves. Both were major items of the trans-Saharan trade and, though currently in Muslim hands, diverting this trade into caravels could only be to the greater glory of Christendom.

Lacking the resources of the Ming emperor, Prince Henry's whole programme was supposed to be self-financing. According to Cadamosto, participants could sign up on the basis either of the prince providing the ship in return for half of all profits, or of the adventurer providing the ship and the prince just a licence in return for a quarter of the profits. The young Venetian, being of straitened means, chose the former. In both cases, the cargo – Cadamosto took Spanish horses, Flemish woollens and Moorish silk – was the responsibility of the adventurer.

Trade, and its protection against all-comers, was essential to the whole enterprise. But no less so was the promulgation of Christianity and the dispossession, suppression and enslavement of both Muslims and pagans. Several papal bulls framed in accordance with Portuguese wishes had been issued to this effect; one (*Romanus Pontifex*) was published just weeks before Cadamosto's 1455 departure. It acknowledged the Portuguese effort in African exploration and Muslim conquest, applauded enslavement as leading to the conversion of African pagans, and urged further attempts to circumnavigate Africa and make contact with peoples in the Indies 'who it is said, honour the name of Christ' (a reference to the abiding myth of Prester John). It also solemnly awarded to Prince Henry and the Portuguese crown an exclusive monopoly of the navigation, trade and fishing in all regions already visited plus all those that might lie ahead as far as the Indies. Licence to trade with Muslims was also given, but only when necessary and excluding warlike materials; various ecclesiastical privileges were conferred; and all other nations were solemnly admonished against infringing the Portuguese monopoly or in any way impeding its realisation.

This bull has been called 'the charter of Portuguese imperialism'.[14] In the eyes of Christendom it conferred on the Portuguese sacred privileges that overrode the rights of all other nations with an interest in Africa and Asia. Those of Venetian, Genoese and Spanish competitors were confounded; those of the Muslims outlawed; and those of all the indigenous peoples of two entire continents utterly ignored. Cadamosto and his colleagues sailed from Sagres with *carte blanche*.

9

Christians and Spices

No pyrates we, who fare on ports to prey,
   and purse-proud cities that in war be weak;
   thieves, who with fire and steel the peoples slay,
   their robber-greed on neighbour-goods to wreak;
   From haughty Europe to the realms of Day
   We sail, and Earth's remotest verge we seek
Of Inde, the great, the rich, for thus ordaineth
The mighty Monarch who our country reigneth.
Luis de Camoes, Os Lusiadas, ii, 80[1]

AFRICAN EXPLORATION MAY seem tangential to the story of the spice route. Not since the time of Strabo and Pliny had anyone supposed Africa to be a source of spices; nothing was said about spices in the papal bulls of the 1450s authorising the Portuguese monopoly; nor are they mentioned by Cadamosto other than as part of the incentive package offered by Prince Henry. At the time, rounding Africa, let alone reaching the spiceries, remained a doubtful proposition. Papal reference to 'the Indians' among whom the explorers were to seek out Prester John's Christians could as well have meant African Ethiopians as anyone in Asia. It would be another quarter of a century before the Indian Ocean loomed large enough in Portuguese plans to make the spice trade a realistic objective. And yet, as if by way of an appetiser, spices, indeed pepper – the most widely traded of all culinary condiments – lay just around the west African corner.

Cadamosto failed to find it. His voyages of 1455 and 1456 are notable for conveying a rare delight in the African scene and for being practically the only Portuguese expeditions, out of dozens in the period before da Gama, that yielded a coherent narrative. Perhaps Cadamosto, once safely back in his native Venice, felt released from the bond of confidentiality under which the Portuguese strove to deny useful news of their discoveries to rivals. Certainly he displayed an open-minded interest in Africa's natural history and its peoples that was neither Crusader-like nor conducive to the rapid advance of geographical knowledge. In two years he records only one attempted conversion (it failed), no new discoveries other than that of the Cape Verde Islands (which was disputed), and no landfalls beyond Guinea-Bissau.

Much of his time was spent up the Senegal and Gambia rivers. Near the first, he was entertained by a chief called 'Budomel', who was excellent company despite being a Muslim. The chief had a wife in every village and had pressed on Cadamosto, before he had even met him, 'a handsome young negress'. 'He gave her to me for the service of my chamber.' She was only twelve, but this being considered a marriageable age and Cadamosto, at twenty-three, no Methuselah, 'I accepted her and sent her to the ship'.[2]

Cadamosto's seven Spanish geldings, each of which had cost about 43 ducats, fetched a hundred slaves. That was slightly better than the going rate, which stood at a horse for fourteen humans of acceptable age and gender. Back on the open market in Lisbon, he could expect 10 to 20 ducats apiece (or 'aperson'). It has been estimated that in the last half of the fifteenth century, Portugal received 'something like 150,000' African slaves.[3] Most were purchased rather than simply snatched, as had been the way in the first half of the century. Trading was better than raiding; there was less risk of damage to the merchandise and it gratified the local chiefs like Budomel. Christian consciences, far from being troubled, rejoiced over the 150,000 souls thus saved. Since baptism awaited them all, João de Barros could report with pride that 'human beings were brought here [to Lisbon] more for salvation than slavery'.[4]

From the desert-fringed Senegal river on that country's northern border with Mauretania, Cadamosto sailed south in company with a Genoese who had also joined Prince Henry's service. They headed for the Gambia river in the hope of finding the gold for which the region was supposedly famous. 'I have never seen a more beautiful coast,' enthused the Venetian as they passed the promontory now traversed by the breezy boulevards of Dakar. It had been named Cape Verde; 'big green trees' decended to the shoreline; and just inside the Gambia river elephants were surprised at the water's edge. The herd ambled off when approached, but not before Cadamosto had seen enough to set the zoological record straight.

> I must explain that these animals have knees, which they bend when walking. I say this because I have heard others who have formerly been in these parts declare that the elephant is unable to lie down and that they sleep standing on their feet. This is a great lie... Their trunk is on the lower [upper?] jaw and they can lengthen and shorten it at will. With it they gather all their food, and drink water, putting it in their mouths, which are in their breasts... it is like a very long nose.[5]

The Gambia river, a mile or more wide at its mouth, quickly contracted. On the first voyage the natives greeted them with a shower of poisoned arrows. The explorers fared better in 1456, and with a following wind, sped past the estuarine acres of tangled mangrove to a point about sixty miles (100 km) upstream. There slaves and some gold – but not much – were obtained. It was also there that Cadamosto encountered, as well as 'cockatrices' (crocodiles), his first '*pesse cavallo*'. Inexplicably his English translator faithfully renders this as 'river-horse'; 'hippopotamus' is more usual. 'It is formed thus:' reported Cadamosto, 'its body the size of a cow's, with short limbs, has cleft feet, and its head is shaped like a horse's, with two large tusks as a boar has'.[6] Somehow the description, so admirable in its accuracy, only lent credence to the freaks and monsters beloved of Maundevile. Science could validate the absurd as well as discredit it; to all but latter-day know-alls, the difference between a medieval fabulist and a Renaissance empiricist was not clear-cut. Thanks to the new technology of printing, Maundevile's book was reaching a wider readership, Polo was well known but more for his exaggerations than his observations, and Ibn Batuta and de Conti were nobodies.

When the hippo emerges from the water, continues Cadamosto, 'it walks about like a quadruped'; moreover 'it is not to be found in any other parts to which we Christians have sailed (unless, perchance, the Nile)'. To one who thought that the Gambia might be the Nile, or a branch of it, this possible exception was well worth mentioning. The preposterous hippo looked, in short, to be an excellent omen; up the Gambia river might lie the hippo-rich headwaters of the real Nile, 'upper' Ethiopia, Prester John's Christians, Islam's undefended flank, and a short tramp to the Red Sea and the Indian Ocean.

But the river being unsuitable for caravels, Cadamosto and his Genoese friend preferred to return to the coast. They pushed south to a red cliff that they named Cape Rosso, now the border between Senegal's Casamance and Guinea-Bissau. Sailing by day, anchoring at night, and landing to little purpose since none of their interpreters could understand a word of the local tongue, they finally turned back at the mouth of Geba river. From where today stands the city of Bissau, 'we proceeded towards our parts of Christendom, whither we sailed, so that God in his mercy brought us, when it pleased Him, safely to port'.

Cadamosto never sailed south again, but he stayed on in Portugal for another six years. He was there when in 1460 Prince Henry died, and he was there when, either just before or soon after, reports of pepper were confirmed. The first had come from Diogo Gomes who, while trading on the Senegal river, was offered 'a quart measure of *malagueta*, in grain and in its pods as it grows, with which I was highly delighted'.[7] About 1462, in the course of exploring the Sierra Leone coast, Pero de Sintra probably became the first actually to reach the pepper-producing country.

The written sources reveal little, being as tight-lipped about pepper as they are about this whole phase of Portuguese discovery; but maps offer a clue. Unusually, west Africa's south-facing coastline came to be divided up in terms of its tradable commodities; they, after all, had a stronger claim on the attention of Portugal's explorers than the sort of considerations – local custom, history, geography – that usually determine the nomenclature of new lands. Hence, running west to east from roughly Guinea-Bissau, there was designated first a 'Grain Coast', then a 'Gold Coast', then an 'Ivory Coast'. A 'Slave Coast' followed, although the term might reasonably be applied – and was – to all of them.

Nowadays the Ivory Coast remains as the Cote d'Ivoire and the Gold Coast has become Ghana; but the 'Grain Coast', as applied to such impoverished and cereal-deficient countries as Sierra Leone and Liberia, sounds like a cruel misnomer. In fact it referred not to corn but to a grain that the Venetians and Genoese knew, from the occasional imports reaching them via the Sahara and north Africa, as 'grana paradisi' or 'Grain of Paradise'. Otherwise the Latin *amomum meliguetta* and the Spanish, and hence English, 'malaguetta' or 'melegueta', this was the plant whose capsules yielded the seed-grains 'with a tail' that found favour as a peppery condiment. The association with Paradise implied great rarity and value. Substantial profits were anticipated, and in 1470 malaguetta was declared a monopoly of the Portuguese crown along with precious stones and 'unicorns' (or rhinoceros horns). Some malaguetta went to Italy and some was sent to the spice markets of Flanders.

But there rather abruptly the excitement ended. India's black pepper was 'held in higher esteem', says de Barros.[8] During the third quarter of the fifteenth century black pepper happened also to be cheap and plentiful. Venetian trade with the Levant and Egypt had staged a dramatic recovery. The demise of Sultan Barsbay had ended his efforts at economic management, and as the panic occasioned by the Ottoman conquests, including that of Constantinople, subsided, trade with Alexandria revived. By the 1480s pepper was selling in Venice at under 70 ducats a *sporta*, down from 120 in the 1430s. Malaguetta could not compete with it in volume, price or piquancy. Demoted to simply 'Guinea Grain', *grana paradisi* slumped to the status of occasional ballast and by the end of the century, after da Gama's first haul of Malabar pepper, had become an irrelevance. In the sixteenth century it was left almost entirely to interlopers from Brittany.

To speed the advance of Africa's coastal exploration, in 1469 the Portuguese crown hit on the idea of a concession dependent on progress. Fernão Gomes contracted to discover 100 leagues of coastline a year and to pay a fixed annual rental for the exclusive privilege of doing so. The arrangement lasted six years and carried the Portuguese advance along the Gold and Ivory coasts to what are now Nigeria, Cameroon and Congo. Here the shoreline had turned south again, presumably to Lisbon's consternation. But the Congo river, another candidate for Nilotic communication, would be reckoned some compensation; so was the island tucked into the sweltering armpit of Africa which was named Fernando Po after one of Gomes' commanders.

A seven-year hiatus then intervened as the Portuguese again fought the Moors in north Africa and became embroiled in the dynastic affairs of Castile. The 1479 treaty of Alcaçovas-Toledo settled the latter dispute, as well as providing a basis for the great carve-up of the colonisable world that would be enshrined in the later Treaty of Tordesillas. Exploration resumed. In 1481–2 a fortified factory and forward base was established at El-mina on the Gold Coast. The *mina*, or mine, for which it was named would yield some gold-dust; and among the gold-digging explorers who gained valuable navigational experience on this voyage were Bartolemeu Dias and Christopher Columbus.

A supposed native of Genoa, Columbus, like Cadamosto, had been stranded in Portugal in the course of a voyage to the North Sea. London being his destination, it was England's loss that became Portugal's gain when he too had opted for the opportunities of advancement and profit on offer in Lisbon. He was well connected, scientifically knowledgeable and immensely determined. Back from the Gold Coast in 1483, he immediately started lobbying for Portuguese backing to undertake his own voyage towards the Indies. Its only novelty was that he proposed to get there by sailing west.

The idea was not new. Ptolemy's contraction of the world's girth, and his and Polo's exaggerated notion of the distance between Seres/Cathay (China) and Cipangu (Japan), brought the latter within what current maps suggested was a sailable distance. The Atlantic was supposed the same ocean as that which encircled Japan; and by heading west no further than the Portuguese were already sailing south, a ship must surely reach that fabled island. If it missed it, there was every chance of sighting another of Polo's 7,459 islands in the 'Eastern Sea of Chin'; thence it should be a formality to pass on to China, Java or India. Columbus was supremely confident about this, indeed perhaps suspiciously so; but Lisbon refused to be distracted from the African route and declined its backing.

Columbus tried again in 1488 and received an even firmer rejection. For by then another concerted series of African voyages had just culminated with that of Bartolemeu Dias. Dias was Portuguese and already a noted navigator. Given command of three ships in 1487, he had coasted what is now Namibia and then been swept far out to sea by a storm. Weathering the worst of it, the ships turned to rejoin the African coastline only to find it not there. Seemingly the continent had disappeared. They bore north, and when they finally sighted land, it was different from what they expected. The air was cooler, the people communicated in a language that was not just incomprehensible but unspeakable, and the shore, instead of running just east of south, ran distinctly north of east. Dias was in the vicinity of Mossel Bay, midway between what would become Cape Town and Port Elizabeth. The coast's northward trend was confirmed by continuing a short way beyond; somewhere in the heaving swell of the past week the fleet had passed imperceptibly from the Atlantic Ocean to the Indian.

After decades of straining to find Africa's ultimate cape, the Portuguese had rounded it without realising it. Dias turned for home, paused to make good this deficiency by discovering Table Bay, and reached Lisbon with the glad tidings in 1488. No celebrations are recorded, although the significance of the achievement was clearly appreciated. India's trade-rich ocean, its supposed Christians and its bonanza of spices were at last within navigable reach, in fact within striking range. The way was clear, the stage set; but the elaborate preparations needed for Portugal's grand entry would take another decade. Meanwhile the Congo (Zaire) river was excluded, much like the Senegal and the Gambia, as a possible short-cut; and in Castile Christopher Columbus finally won from Queen Isabella the backing denied him by João II of Portugal.

This long hiatus – and the previous ones – in Portugal's erratic history of discoveries, coupled with uncertainty over the number of voyages undertaken and the sketchy nature of the documentation, have excited as much speculation about unrecorded excursions as have Cheng-ho's voyages. Like the Chinese, the Portuguese often memorialised their landfalls *in situ*. They carved names and dates on convenient trees and latterly erected stones or pillars. De Barros mentions an uninhabited island just below the equator where a Portuguese inscription dated to 1438 was found in the bark of a tree;

the location that he gives suggests Ascension Island. Antonio Galvão repeats this story and adds that 'then also there were places, countreys and islands discovered which before were never known to us since the Flood'.[9] Cabral's discovery of Brazil in 1500 would itself be incidental to an eastward voyage. It is not therefore impossible that Portuguese navigators of the fifteenth century knew more than is recorded. They may well have chanced upon some part of the south American coast before Columbus sailed west in 1492. Columbus himself may have been aware of this and emboldened by it.

Why the Portuguese were quite so slow to capitalise on Dias' discovery of the Cape route is not clear. It had been long enough coming and had lately been anticipated. In 1487, the year in which Dias set sail, João II had despatched two scouts to travel east overland. They were to obtain advance information on trading conditions in India and to sound out the disposition of Prester John's Christians. One of these men soon died; but the other, Pero de Covilha, reached India from Hormuz and then returned to Cairo. From there he confirmed by letter the spices available at Calicut and the navigability of what he called 'the Guinea Sea' between India and Sofala, a place on the African coast in what is now Mozambique.

This should have been encouraging; Sofala is in fact under 500 miles (800 km) from where Dias had turned back. But it is not known whether Sofala's latitude had been established, nor whether de Covilha's letter and its good tidings ever reached Lisbon. Meanwhile de Covilha himself, thinking that it had, headed off into Ethiopia to complete his assignment. He there found a king, whom he hailed as Prester John, and many Christians. They welcomed him as the emissary of some long-lost sister-church, although later report had it that they then detained him. More plausibly they seduced him, for he married, settled down on a rolling Ethiopian estate, raised many children and for thirty years lived happily ever after.

Possibly King João delayed the next voyage in expectation of the letter that may not have arrived; possibly he waited in hope of the news concerning Prester John that may never have been sent. As he waited – if he waited – the king suffered from declining health. He died in 1495 after a long illness, which may have further retarded plans.

Other good reasons for the delay are to be found in the complications arising from Columbus' discoveries on behalf of Isabella of Castile. From his first voyage of 1492–3 Columbus returned confident that the lands he had found did indeed pertain to Japan. China and the spiceries must then by all accounts be within easy reach; and this being the case, the economic viability of the Cape route was suddenly thrown into question. If a few weeks of uncontested westward sailing could open up the East to Christian enterprise, Dias' long haul round Africa looked like a waste of time. Moreover the anticipated contest with the Muslim world for control of the spice traffic might be avoided. With both demand in the Mediterranean and supply in the Indies being siphoned off by Columbus' new transatlantic route, Islam's trade would find itself high and dry in the Indian Ocean. Such considerations, along with worries about the cost of the Portuguese programme, may have weighed heavily with the council that advised the new king, Manuel; for the council, it was reported, opposed the de Gama voyage, 'the majority holding that India should not be discovered'.[10]

The king thought it should, and with good reason. It so happened that, on his return, Columbus' storm-tossed ship had fetched up in Lisbon. This coincidence, accompanied by the bombshell of his news, had led the Portuguese to register an immediate claim to his discoveries. They did so on the basis of the Alcaçovas–Toledo treaty which reserved all territories 'below the Canaries and towards Guinea', whether discovered or still to be discovered, to the Portuguese crown. In return Castile had got the Canaries themselves. But the treaty had understandably failed to anticipate other westward discoveries; the Carib 'Indians' whom Columbus had brought back with him were clearly not 'Guinean' Africans; and so Castile, in the persons of Queen Isabella and her husband Ferdinand of Aragon, strongly contested any Portuguese interest in the matter. There followed much heated diplomacy before the Spanish appealed to Rome. The pope was the accepted referee in such matters. As guarantor of the earlier treaty, he was the obvious person to interpret it; and at the time he just happened to be Spanish. The Castilian claim to

Columbus' discoveries was accordingly upheld in a flurry of papal bulls.

But it remained to reconcile these with Portugal's claims, in defence of which Lisbon now threatened hostile action. This was averted by the Tordesillas Treaty of 1494. Under its terms both sides accepted a neat bisection of the world and all its sailable seas, tradeable commodities and baptisable peoples. It was much like the halving of an apple with a sharp knife. The cut ran vertically down the middle of the planet along a pole-to-pole meridian drawn 370 leagues west of the Cape Verde Islands; all territorial, commercial and proselytising opportunities to the east of this line were reserved exclusively to Portugal, all to the west of it to Castile (which kingdom, being now dynastically aggregated with Aragon and León, in effect meant Spain). Positioning the line in mid-Atlantic was supposed to create clear blue water between the two rivals' spheres. But it failed to do so when south America was found to straddle it, so leaving much of what became Brazil on the Portuguese side. Whether the Portuguese were aware of this at the time is not known. They certainly were by 1506 when another papal bull finally confirmed the Tordesillas carve-up.

The treaty having cleared the air, both parties resumed operations. Timber had to be cut and keels laid for the larger ships deemed necessary for the long voyage round the Cape; Lisbon was taking no chances. Columbus, on the other hand, had already set off again, his object being to ransack the Caribbean for the silks and spices that would prove it indisputably part of Asia.

When he returned with no silks and only unrecognisable spices, Spanish hopes slumped. But the Portuguese were encouraged; preparations accelerated. More determined than ever that India should not go undiscovered, on 8 July 1497 King Manuel was reportedly rowed out to da Gama's fleet in the mouth of the Tagus. A Mass had been said, and a vigil held, in the nearby chapel of Our Lady of Belem. From there the Christian argonauts processed to their ships amid candles and censers in a buzz of prayer. 'A great multitude came together...and led them down to the boats. Not the priests and monks alone, but all the rest of the concourse prayed aloud to God with tears that this perilous navigation might turn out well for them and that all, having well performed the undertaking, might return safely.'[11]

Anchors were weighed, sails filled, and as the four ships slipped away, the king is described as still gazing seaward, 'his boat lying on its oars until they disappeared'. Such scenes, often rehearsed during the fifteenth century and endlessly re-enacted during the sixteenth, lacked nothing in poignancy. That in 1497 the king was almost certainly not in attendance scarcely mattered. In retrospect the magnitude of the occasion excused the manipulation of its details. Participating in what was more an act of faith than an historical endeavour, the hopeful raised their voices in hymn while the Jeremiahs joined their hands in prayer. To Bishop Osorio, the far from starry-eyed historian of Manuel's reign, 'the weeping and lamentation was made by so many that it seemed as if funeral rites were being performed'.

A week later da Gama's fleet anchored in the Canaries; by the end of the month they were in the Cape Verde Islands; parted in the first by fog, they had been reunited in the second beneath a cloudless sky. 'We gave vent to our joy by many times firing off our bombards and sounding the trumpets.' This being the last landfall before the long reach into the south Atlantic, they took on meat, wood and water and made some 'much-needed repairs to our yards'.

They left on 3 August and did not sight land again until 4 November. At ninety-three days, this was easily the longest voyage in open water on record (between the Canaries and the Bahamas, Columbus had been out of sight of land for only thirty-six days), and in navigational terms it was the most notable achievement of the whole expedition. Instead of an interminable progress down the African coast, the fleet had made a wide westward loop around the Atlantic doldrums almost to Tristan da Cunha and had then picked up the westerly trade winds and currents of the southern ocean to home in on southern Africa. Whether by chance or design, they had pioneered an ocean route to the Cape that took maximum advantage of the available winds and was sufficiently devoid of obstacles for round-the-clock sailing. It would thereafter become standard for all outward voyages.

At its end, the low-lying shore of an ample but empty bay had embraced them. The ships 'drew near to each other,' says the record, 'and having put on our gala clothes, we saluted the Captain-major by firing our bombards, and dressed the ships with flags and standards.'[12]

Like *The Periplus of the Erythraean Sea*, the only first-hand account of da Gama's epic voyage lacks literary pretension and, despite the best efforts of scholarship, remains annoyingly anonymous. Near-contemporary writers of far greater lustre, including Luis de Camoes, the national bard, would make handsome amends. Their dazzling accounts introduce some notable drama and much detail. None of it is necessarily fabrication; but inconsistencies arise, and any consensus as to the details of what was the most adventurous voyage of exploration to date is notably lacking. According to an American scholar, doubts surround 'when the voyage was planned, why Vasco da Gama was chosen to lead it, when the ships were built, what the names of all the ships were, what types of ships there were, how many men were in the crews, how many died on the voyage', and much else besides.[13]

Da Gama is credited with outstanding navigational skills on the grounds that only a man of such attributes would have been chosen as the fleet's captain-general. In fact, he relied on the services of much more experienced navigators, including one who had sailed with Dias. The youngest of three bothers, da Gama was of modest birth and had previously been attached to the royal household; little else is known of him before his appointment. Of ships, there were four. Some accounts say three, presumably discounting the least impressive of the fleet which acted as a supply ship. One was a caravel, commanded by Nicolau Coelho; the other two were *naus*, which were bigger, square-rigged (though possibly with a lateen-rigged mizen-mast) and specially built for the voyage. These were commanded by Vasco da Gama himself and his brother Paulo. Their capacity, probably between 100 and 200 tons, afforded only limited space for cargo because of the generous provisioning and crewing (estimates of the total manpower vary between 118 and 260) thought necessary for a voyage of such uncertain duration. They were also heavily armed. The 'bombards' would have been mortars rather than catapults; they fired grape-shot and cannon-balls of both stone and iron. The fleet's anonymous chronicler records the 'amusement' they afforded on an island in Mossel Bay. Seals and walruses 'as big as bears' were blasted from their rocks; penguins on the march were bowled over like nine-pins; 'we killed as many as we chose'.[14]

The long awaited landfall on the coast of southern Africa had been made at St Helena Bay about 150 miles (250km) north of the Cape. They stayed there a week, long enough to make repairs, take on wood and water, and antagonise the natives. In a beach affray, the first blood went to Africa, Vasco da Gama himself being among the several wounded by flying spears; how many Africans were peppered with grape-shot is not recorded. They rounded the Cape at the third attempt on 22 November 1497. A friendlier reception awaited them at Mossel Bay where the supply ship, being now deemed redundant, was broken up, cattle were purchased, and only the wildlife was decimated.

Christmas came and went on the coast of what was duly dubbed Natal. Near the future Lorenzo Marques (Maputo) they again put ashore and declared the region the 'Land of Good People'. Then came the 'River of Good Omens', where the natives were bolder and some traders examined their stock of gifts with a refreshing indifference. One of them appeared to claim that he had seen ships as big as theirs before. Evidently they were approaching more civilised regions. They careened their vessels and spent a month ashore recovering from the effects of scurvy. Tacking against the Agulhas current that would lead many later navigators to prefer a passage to the east of Madagascar, they missed Sofala, the port mentioned by Pero de Covilha, and made their next landfall amongst some offshore islands. It was a measure of their progress towards more civilised regions that these needed no christening; they already had a name.

'Moncobiquy', or Mozambique, exceeded their wildest expectations. Sailing ships came forth to meet them; and the chief people were dressed not in penis sheaths or skins but in robes of fine linen and cotton. Rarely can Christians have been so delighted to encounter a disdainful sultan, to hear fluent Arabic spoken, and to find themselves surrounded by 'Moors'.

> They are merchants and have transactions with white Moors, four of whose vessels were at the time in port, laden with gold, silver, cloves, pepper, ginger, and silver rings...all of which are used by the people of this country. We understood them to say that all these things...

abounded where we were going to and that precious stones, pearls and spices were so plentiful that there was no need to purchase them as they could be collected in baskets...that there were many cities along the coast...and that Prester John resided not far from this place...This information, and many other things which we heard, rendered us so happy that we cried for joy and prayed God to grant us health so that we might live to behold what we so much desired.[15]

They were disconcerted only by the contempt shown for the assorted hats, basins and bits of coral with which they expected to appease Indian Ocean dignitaries and by the news that the coast ahead was beset with shoals. Da Gama's inadequate presents, an oversight born of Christian conceit, Portuguese penury and the unsophisticated traditions of west African trade, would prove an abiding and near-fatal handicap; but the navigational hazards could be offset by acquiring local pilots. Two men were promised, but only one materialised, and in pursuit of the other the bombards were again fired in earnest. A running battle then developed. Apparently their hosts had at last divined that, contrary to initial opinion, they were not fellow Muslims from some far western outpost of Islam but gate-crashing heretics from detested Christendom; amicable relations were not to be expected of such people, a surmise that da Gama obligingly confirmed by 'bombarding' both native craft and the town itself. 'During the three hours we were so employed, we saw two men killed,' says the anonymous chronicler. 'When we were weary of this work, we retired to our ships to dine.'

Da Gama was at last showing his mettle. The next landfall was named the 'Island of The Flogged-One' in honour of their Muslim pilot. This was not the man originally supplied; he, after being casually tortured in an effort to discover the source of Mozambique's gold, had been 'chastised forever when killed by the artillery'.[16] It was therefore one of his two replacements who, on the grounds that he had wilfully misrepresented the island as the mainland, was here 'well flogged'.

Mombasa, the next port of call, brought more pilot trouble. Obsessed by the idea of joining forces with Prester John, the Portuguese naively supposed that all non-Muslims must be, if not savages, Christians. It was a delusion that even close acquaintance with

India's religious diversity would fail to dispel; and it now led them to interpret their pilots' reports about Mombasa having a substantial infidel community – in fact it was one of Hindu merchants – as evidence that they were at last among co-religionists. With confidence, therefore, after exchanging hostages, they approached the harbour.

Near its mouth a minor collision involving the flagship brought them to a halt, at which point most of the Muslims hostages who were held aboard unexpectedly made their escape. Treachery, readily suspected, was painfully confirmed. 'By dropping boiling oil upon their skins', two Muslims who had failed to get away were induced to blurt out that it was Mombasa's intention to avenge the bombardment of Mozambique. A second dose of 'questioning' produced no further revelations, only a couple of suicides; one of the wretched informants threw himself overboard with his scorched hands still tightly tied, 'and the other did so during the morning watch'. Although a retaliatory raid was easily repelled, the city itself remained disappointingly out of range. They sailed away, pilot-less but unscathed, on Good Friday 1498. 'Our Lord had not allowed the tricks practised upon us by these dogs to succeed.'

Easter Day found them off the whitewashed and palm-fringed frontage of neighbouring Malindi. They celebrated the risen Christ by capturing a boatload of innocent day-trippers to serve as go-betweens and then be ransomed for a pilot. This precaution proved superfluous. Malindi was habitually at war with Mombasa; allies of any persuasion were therefore welcome. Informed of the Portuguese purpose, Malindi's king greeted them with a boat laden with six sheep and 'quantities of cloves, cumin, ginger, nutmeg and pepper'. To meet da Gama, the king even ventured forth from his pungent capital in person; lesser figures from both sides exchanged home visits; and the captives were gratefully repatriated. Malindi evinced none of the religious fanaticism of Mombasa and Mozambique. Its 'Christians', though Indian and almost certainly Hindu, won Portuguese hearts by showing great reverence for a picture of the Madonna and Child. Better still, when some of these good people discharged their guns in a ceremonial salute, they shouted what the Portuguese took to be 'Christ, Christ'. More plausibly, the words may have been 'Fire, Fire'.

After nine days of mutual felicitations, the wind being fair and the tide of expectation rising, the expedition embarked on its final leg across the Indian Ocean. Africa had not brought out the best in Vasco da Gama. His brutal, not to say demonic, conduct had embarrassed even his brother Paulo and had set an ominous precedent. Lacking the wealth and resources of its Indian Ocean rivals, Lisbon could compete for favours and trade only by a ready recourse to arms. But at least Malindi had been secured as an ally and future safe haven; and there a trustworthy pilot had at last been found.

This man is described as a 'Christian', so probably a Hindu, by the on-board chronicler. Other contemporary sources identify him as a Gujerati Muslim. None calls him an Arab, and the tradition that he was in fact Ahmad ibn Majid, the greatest of all Arab navigators as well as the prickly author of the compendious 'Book of Profitable Things Concerning the First Principles and Rules of Navigation', seems to be apocryphal. Ibn Majid was certainly a contemporary, but he would scarcely have been an obliging hireling, nor is it likely that such a celebrated man of science would have been found roaming an east African port in the hope of a ship. The misidentification was perpetrated by another Arab writer who evidently had a grudge against Ibn Majid. As well as blaming him for admitting the infidels to Islam's Indian Ocean preserve, this writer accused him of the no less heinous crime of succumbing to the Captain-general's liquor. In the words of Ibn Majid's English translator, it was all, surely, 'a deliberate piece of libel written out of spite' and wholly undeserving of the wide credence later given it.[17]

Yet whoever the pilot was, he must have drawn on the traditions of Arab navigation and astronomy as organised in Ibn Majid's great work and have treacherously made this knowledge available to the Portuguese. Thanks to his directions, da Gama's fleet 'steered straight for the open sea from Malindi', so avoiding the danger of shipwreck on the African coast and ensuring arrival on the Malabar coast before the worst of the monsoon closed its ports. The crossing took only three weeks; and their first sighting of India was of the Western Ghats only 20 miles (30km) north of Calicut. They anchored off Capocut, about 10 miles (15km) from Calicut, on 20 May. The total voyage from Lisbon had taken 316 days.

Unsure of his welcome, da Gama despatched ashore 'one of our convicts'. (Condemned felons and heretics being disposable, a supply of them was carried for just such risky assignments.) This man, who, though the first recorded European to set foot in India without passing through the Middle East, remains sadly anonymous, was directed to the house of two Tunisian merchants who happened to be resident in the place and who knew both Spanish and Italian. 'The first greeting that he received from them was in these words: "May the Devil take thee! And what brought you hither?" Then they asked what he sought so far away from home, and he told them that he came in search of Christians and spices.'[18]

This was a fair summary of Portuguese objectives; da Gama could scarcely have put it better, and during the ensuing weeks of comings and goings between the fleet and the city he amassed ample detail on both of these long-sought commodities. The Portuguese had no hesitation in offering prayers in what they took to be a church, actually a Hindu temple, and falling to their knees before a statue of Our Lady that was probably Mariamma, the smallpox goddess. 'Many other saints were painted on the walls, some with crowns,' says the chronicler. 'They were painted variously, with teeth protruding an inch from the mouth and four or five arms.'

As for the king of Calicut, or its Zamorin (an Arabicised version of his Hindu title of 'Samudri-raja'), he was also deemed 'Christian', albeit of a most unorthodox sect. But regrettably, it was concluded that His Highness was not a free agent, being in the hands of the city's Muslim merchants. These gentlemen 'could ill digest us', says the anonymous chronicler.

> They had told the king that we were thieves and that once we navigated to his country, no more ships from Mecca, Cambay and Hormuz nor any other part would visit him. They added that he would derive no profit from this trade [with Portugal] as we had nothing to give and would rather take away, and that thus his country would be ruined.[19]

The inadequacy of the Portuguese presents lay behind this all too acute prognosis. At first the formalities had gone well. To explain their rather pitiful fleet, the da Gama brothers had concocted a story about their ships being breakaways from a great Portuguese armada laden with all the rich gifts to be expected from what the Zamorin was given to understand was the most illustrious kingdom in Christendom. But when no further ships materialised, and when all the Captain-general could produce by way of a presentation was his wretched collection of red hats and copper basins, relations had cooled.

More was expected of pale-skinned strangers in tall ships; for there is good evidence to suggest that the munificence of Cheng-ho had not been forgotten. According to Girolamo Sernigi, a Florentine merchant based in Lisbon who interviewed the first returnees from the da Gama expedition, Calicut still cherished the memory of certain white but beardless 'Christians' who, some eighty years previously, had been wont to make biennial voyages to the Malabar coast. They came in '20 or 25 large vessels', each with four masts, and they brought 'very fine cloth and brass vessels' to exchange for spices. Whence they came was uncertain. 'If they were Germans,' conjectured Sernigi, 'it seems to me that we should have had some notice of them; possibly they may be Russians if they have a port there.'[20] Like Cheng-ho, da Gama too attached great importance to memorial pillars, the erection of one at Calicut being his last task before sailing home. That the Zamorin took him and his men for the harbingers of another exotic treasure fleet seems certain. All the greater, therefore, was his disappointment over the expedition's dismal presents and its lack of trading capital.

The Portuguese understood none of this. Blinded by religious prejudice, they exculpated all but Muslims and saw 'Moorish' machinations and treachery behind every reverse. It was the Muslims who disparaged their gifts, misrepresented their intentions, soured relations with the Zamorin, and plotted their detention. Calicut, or 'Alta India' (as opposed to 'Lower India', which was otherwise Prester John's 'Alta Ethiopia'), was indeed the place whence came all 'the spices which are consumed in the East and the West', says the chronicler. They included 'much ginger and pepper and cinnamon', although the best quality cinnamon was imported there from Sri Lanka. Cloves too 'are brought to this city from an island called Malequa', that is, Melaka. But at the time all this trade was controlled by 'Mecca vessels' and directed exclusively through the Red Sea and the realms of Islam. It could be diverted round the Cape only by contesting the Muslim monopoly head-on.

'Christians and spices' thus complemented one another; the interests of Christendom would be well served by commandeering the spice trade, and commandeering the spice trade would be best effected under the blood-red cross of crusading Christendom. In respect of the Portuguese eruption into the Indian Ocean, spices constituted both an economic incentive and an iconic imperative.

10

Peppered Ports and Curried Friar

Who does not know that [the dominions of your Portuguese
Majesty] stretch from the beginning of Africa to China, including the whole of Africa and Asia... and an infinity of islands, very
rich, great and populous within their boundaries?... Who can
doubt that your armadas are the largest in the world... so that no
one has power to navigate anywhere in your dominions without
your permission, and the Moors at the farthest ends of the earth
are as much intimidated as those in the centre?

Tome Pires, *The Suma Oriental*, 1512–15[1]

B Y THE TIME Vasco da Gama regained Portugal in the late summer
of 1499, his achievement was already known. Nicolau Coelho in
command of the fleet's caravel had reached Lisbon on 10 July, and a
vessel not attached to the fleet had since brought word of da Gama
himself, then storm-bound in the Azores. The news that they had
actually reached India caused a sensation; but the details, as they fil-
tered through to King Manuel, were not all encouraging.

In respect of finding powerful new allies, the expedition had largely
failed. Prester John remained a will-o'-the-wisp, and the supposedly
'Christian' credentials of India's majority population were soon being
doubted, though not by da Gama himself. Only with Malindi on
the east African coast and Cannanore on the Malabar coast had amicable relations been established. In both cases this was more thanks to
existing rivalries – between Malindi and Mombasa and between
Cannanore and Calicut – than to the captain-general's thumbscrew
diplomacy. Future Portuguese overtures could expect to be received
with trepidation but never enthusiasm. The absence of any political

cohesion, or even collusion, among the port-cities of the Indian Ocean was noteworthy. But while it made infiltration comparatively easy, it did not bode well for the exercise of a cheap and unchallenged monopoly.

The immediate commercial dividends were also disappointing. With the fleet lacking either adequate funds or ample hold-space, pepper, cinnamon, cloves and ginger had been obtained only in sample quantities. They would be sufficient to reward participants in the voyage and to whet the financial market's appetite for subsequent voyages, but not to defray the expenses already incurred. A large quantity of cinnamon-leaf loaded at Anjediva, an island off India's Konkan coast, might have done so but would prove not to be cinnamon at all. (Columbus was being similarly fooled by spicy look-alikes and smell-alikes in the Caribbean.) Worse still, the human cost of the voyage had escalated alarmingly during the homeward journey.

Da Gama had taken his departure from Calicut in September, which is before the favourable north-easterlies of the winter months set in. As well as being anxious to escape the clutches of the city's Muslim authorities, he had been bent on a quick return and early recognition of his feat. But the monsoon proved unresponsive. As in Kipling's 'epitaph drear' of 'A fool lies here who tried to hustle the East', haste confounded speed and exacted a heavy price. Frequently becalmed, the fleet had been forced north, taking nearly three months to reach the African coast instead of the three weeks of the outward voyage. The water became undrinkable, the food inedible, and scurvy claimed another thirty lives. This was as many as had been lost on the entire voyage to date. 'Only seven or eight men' per ship remained at their posts, says the chronicler, and by the time they made an African landfall near Mogadishu, 'even these were not as well as they should have been'; some were unable to eat because their bulging gums had grown over their teeth, others were unable to stand because their distended limbs had become as useless as garden marrows.[2]

Though the good king of Malindi provided some excellent oranges, it was too late for many of the invalids. Two days south of there, Vasco da Gama was obliged to beach and burn brother Paulo's great *nau*. 'It was impossible for us to navigate three vessels with the few hands that remained to us,' explains the on-board chronicler.

Paulo himself then went down with scurvy; so, seemingly, did the chronicler. His account, after stuttering round the Cape, manages a sentence on the crossing of the Gulf of Guinea, and then expires with an abrupt full stop somewhere in the latitude of Bissau.

Paulo da Gama, now aboard his brother's flagship, had lasted a few weeks longer. A storm having separated this vessel from Coelho's, it was driven into the Azores just in time for Paulo to breathe his last on *terra firma*, then be decently buried in it. The loss, added to that of at least half of those who had sailed from Lisbon two years earlier, might have been expected to cast a gloom over the captain-general's eventual homecoming. In fact Vasco da Gama curtailed his mourning to concentrate on garnering the rewards that he considered his due.

King Manuel, for his part, was already basking in the success of the voyage and busily organising the next. In a letter to Ferdinand and Isabella in July 1499, some royal gloating was understandable.

> As the principal motive of this enterprise has been...the service of God Our Lord and our own advantage, it pleased Him in His mercy to speed [the explorers] on their route...[Now] we learn that they did reach and discover India and other kingdoms bordering upon it... entered and navigated its sea, finding large cities...and great populations among whom is carried on all the trade in spices and precious stones...
>
> As we are aware that your Highnesses will hear of these things with much pleasure and satisfaction, we thought well to give this information...Moreover we hope that with the help of God the great trade which now enriches the Moors of those parts...shall in consequence of our regulations be diverted to the natives and ships of our own kingdom so that henceforth all Christendom in this part of the world shall be provided with these spices.[3]

A month later in a letter to Rome, Manuel was styling himself not just 'king of Portugal and the Algarves' but 'Lord of Guinea and of the Conquest, the Navigation and the Commerce of Ethiopia, Arabia, Persia and India'. This mouthful required no justification. 'Conquest', rather than simple exploration, was now acknowledged policy, and what he called 'apostolical grants' already awarded him full enjoyment of 'the sovereignty and dominion of all that we have discovered'. Given the recent voyage, however, His Lordship of such extensive territories and multifarious responsibilities thought that 'a fresh expression [from the pope] of satisfaction with reference to a matter of such novelty' might be appropriate.[4]

After years of dilatory endeavour Portugal's far-flung offensive at last slid into overdrive. There would be more new discoveries in the coming generation than in the previous three, more triumphs over the Moors in the next two decades of eastern buccaneering than in the past four centuries of Mediterranean Crusading. Unknown in the East before 1498, by 1520 the Portuguese crown would indeed be lording it over 'the navigation and commerce of Arabia, Persia and India', not to mention a string of spice-rich destinations beyond.

During their three months in the vicinity of Calicut, da Gama's men had counted 'about fifteen hundred Moorish vessels arriving in search of spices'. Some were big, up to 800 tons, some smaller; but all were supposed 'frail' because they were still held together by coir rather than nails; and more notably, according to Girolamo Sernigi's informants, 'none carry either arms or artillery'.[5] Evidently the trade itself was inexhaustible, yet its capacity for defence negligible. The Portuguese, with a reputation as ruthless fighters won in Morocco, lacked only funds. But if a hundredweight (50 kg) of pepper, which might be selling for anything from 60 to 90 ducats on the volatile Venice market, could be bought for the equivalent of just 3 ducats on the Calicut waterfront, investors would not be found wanting. The banking houses of Europe queued up to help; from the best German foundries came cannon and chandlery, from Florence and Genoa investors and seafarers, from France and Flanders spice buyers, and from Rome the moral sanction and the diplomatic support essential for scaring off any Christian competitors.

By March 1500, just six months after da Gama's return, the next fleet was weighing anchor in the Tagus. There were thirteen vessels with about twelve hundred men, and this time King Manuel was definitely in attendance. Command of the fleet had gone to Pedro Alvarez Cabral; under him served both Coelho from the previous expedition and Dias, the conqueror of the Cape. With the favourable winds of an earlier departure – March would become the usual month for beginning the round trip known as the *carreira da India* – they sped south in da Gama's wake. Edging slightly further west than had the

Captain-general, within six weeks they stumbled on their first discovery. A ship was sent to convey the good tidings back to Lisbon, and from there further contacts would be made direct.

They called this new find the 'Land of the True Cross', which was soon amended to the 'Land of the Holy Cross'. More popularly it was the 'Parrot-Country'. But here, as in west Africa, hard-nosed commerce finally prevailed: as the 'Brazil-country', and hence 'Brazil', it was conclusively named after what it could yield. Not Brazil nuts but Brazil-wood or sappan, the south Indian timber that produced a red dye, was abundant in this part of what is now Bahia (about 700 miles/1,100km north of Rio de Janeiro). It quickly became the region's most valued product, so providing one of the earliest examples of an American 'spice' usurping an Asian one. The people, of impressive physique behind the odd feather, were also of a suitably reddish hue. But the name change was not without controversy. The devout thought it a sacrilege with many, like João de Barros, declaring it the work of the Devil. For only Lucifer could have 'wrought... that the name of the Holy Cross should be lost, as if a wood for colouring cloth were of more moment than that wood [of the Cross] which imbues all the sacraments with the tincture of salvation, which is the Blood of Jesus Christ'.[6]

The Almighty, as if anticipating the outrage, wreaked an early revenge. A south Atlantic hurricane scattered Cabral's fleet, consigning four ships to the deep and jeopardising the whole voyage. Among the disappeared was Bartolomeu Dias; he was presumed drowned within no great distance of his greatest discovery. Diogo Dias, his brother, who commanded another ship, looked to have shared the same fate. In fact he had been blown so far off course that his next landfall was made on what proved to be Madagascar. Diogo Dias discovered not only that island but the often easier outer passage up its east coast. He then continued to pursue an erratic course. Reaching the African mainland near Mogadishu, he sailed round Cape Guardafui, the old 'Cape of Spices', to Berbera, from where he finally pin-pointed the location of Prester John's elusive Ethiopia. He did not enter the Red Sea, but from its coast a Portuguese expedition would reach the Ethiopian highlands in 1508. It never returned, and subsequent contacts proved equally fraught. By 1540 the Ethiopians, far from affording the Portuguese any assistance, would be pleading for their help against the incursions of Muslim Somalis.

Minus a third of its ships, Cabral's fleet had re-formed at Mozambique, touched at Kilwa and Malindi (but given Mombasa a wide berth) and anchored off Calicut in September 1500. There the Zamorin, under great pressure, and in the light of Cabral's more appropriate presentation, eventually agreed to the establishment of a Portuguese *feitoria* – a 'factory' or trading establishment. But relations with the city's Muslim merchant community remained tense, and when the Portuguese casually captured one or more of their ships, the aggrieved happily massacred some forty of the *feitoria*'s inmates and appropriated their property. As a reprisal for the reprisal, in what amounted to an escalation into war, Cabral fired several ships, making sure that their crews burnt with them, then for two days bombarded the city. This caused further fatalities and so enraged the Zamorin that he finally espoused the cause of his Muslim subjects. Of his supposedly 'Christian' beliefs, no more is heard.

The matter of the Calicut massacre would not end there. Cabral, however, had other priorities. He sailed south to Cochin whose rajah, apprised of Calicut's fate, welcomed the idea of Portuguese trade plus a *feitoria*, an alliance, and anything else that would mollify these aggressive strangers while strengthening his own position vis-à-vis his neighbours. In Cochin, and again at Cannanore, Cabral loaded spices in vast quantities. He also made contact with India's only real 'Christians' – those of the Syrian Church, some of whom traced their conversion back to St Thomas. A priest of this persuasion accompanied the fleet back to Portugal and there put paid to the myth of Hinduism's deities being distorted versions of Christianity's saints.

The voyage home was notable only for one of the ships visiting Sofala, the port whence gold from Zimbabwe reached the east African coast; gold and silver being still the preferred form of payment for spices, access to this port and its trade was earmarked for future attention. By late June 1501, Cabral's fleet was trickling back to Lisbon. Over half his ships were now missing, but the four or five that remained sat low in the water and filled the Atlantic air with exciting fragrances. Cabral's one hundred tons of pepper, plus lesser quantities of cinnamon and ginger, represented the first major consignment of spices to reach Europe without passing through Arab hands. A national thanksgiving was declared, processions stomped the cliffs and the beaches, and the celebrations lasted for weeks.

The side-effects were immediately felt in the eastern Mediterranean and nowhere more so than in Venice. In 1502 the fleet of Venetian galleys sent annually to Beirut, now one of the main Levantine ports, brought back 'only four bales of pepper'; 'those returning from Alexandria had also found very little.' The shortage, which was attributed to Cabral's haul and that about to be made by da Gama's second voyage, sent prices through the roof. Black pepper reached 100 ducats a hundredweight (50 kg) on the Rialto, a level unheard of since the bad old days of Sultan Barsbay.[7] Girolamo Priuli, a Venetian diarist and banker, predicted the ruin of the city and rated the new Portuguese challenge more serious than the republic's ongoing war with the Ottoman Turks. He estimated the profit made on Cabral's cargo at a hundredfold and anticipated that all those who formerly bought spices in Venice – 'Hungarians, Germans, Flemish and French, and those beyond the mountains' – would in future take their business, and their money, to Lisbon.[8]

That the Portuguese were in earnest was self-evident. Cabral's forceful methods, added to his sovereign's Christian zealotry, had committed them to a confrontational policy in the Indian Ocean that was uniquely provocative. Despite the misgivings of his councillors, King Manuel was determined to see it through. The idea of any state, let alone a minor Iberian kingdom, conducting warlike operations, enforcing its commercial supremacy and constructing a viable empire all of 10,000 sailing miles (16,000 km) from home challenged even European conceits. The logistics would be mind-boggling, the risks as immense as the presumption. In the absence of any known blueprint, trial and errror would seem to have played a major part. So would sheer good luck; and so too navigational expertise, superior gunnery, Crusader-like bravery, and a level of brutality not exceeded by that of the conquistadors in the Americas. But the rewards were worth it.

Another fleet, the third in the succession of India voyages, had already sailed from Lisbon ahead of Cabral's return. Comparatively small, its only notable discoveries were also small; the island of

Ascension was sighted on the outward journey and that of St Helena on the return. More ominously a fourth fleet, larger even than Cabral's, was under construction and being heavily armed. It was to fetch more spices, make further discoveries, set up new *feitoria*, leave a permanent fleet in the East to protect these establishments, and above all avenge the Calicut massacre.

Its vanguard of fifteen ships sailed in February 1502; a further five followed behind. Many of these vessels are described as *naus* but they were probably of greater capacity than those of da Gama's first voyage and anticipated the many-tiered carracks and galleons of later fame. Their artillery included both fixed cannon and the movable falconets and swivel guns. Fore and aft there reared fretwork castles from which missiles, boiling oil, flaming arrows and grape-shot could be poured into enemy craft.

Cabral was given the command but was replaced at the last minute by Vasco da Gama. Conflicting reasons are given for the change; none is very convincing but all tend to the conclusion that da Gama was preferred because, for the prosecution of a war, his natural belligerence and lack of scruple had much to recommend them. 'He was a very disdainful man,' says Gaspar Correa, 'and ready to anger, very rash, much feared and respected, very knowing, and experienced in all matters.'[9] Already raised to the rank of *dom*, as well as captain-general he now enjoyed the title of *almirante*, or admiral.

The outward voyage went according to plan. Only one ship was lost in rounding the Cape; at Sofala, African traders gravely deposited little mounds of gold beside each bundle of the tawdry textiles purchased by the Portuguese at Mozambique and laid out for the purpose; and to encourage this trade Mozambique itself was persuaded to accept a small *feitoria*. Kilwa, an island and a gracious port-city in the south of what is now Tanzania, was less obliging. Not until the ships' crews had ransacked the place, and not until its more distinguished inhabitants had been stripped naked and left to broil in an open boat, did the ruler agree to meet the Portuguese demand for a hefty tribute.

There then arose a further complication. 'In the city there were some very beautiful women,' says Correa, the most chatty of da Gama's memorialists. These Kilwa ladies allegedly resented being kept in purdah and so made it known that they wanted to become

Christians and to sail away with the Portuguese. Da Gama, though sympathetic, vetoed the plan. The conversions might not be sincere and the ladies might prove troublesome shipmates; at sea, declared the admiral, preserving discipline was more important than saving souls.

But in explaining all this, Gaspar Correa lets slip that the women were in fact already aboard. There were more than two hundred of them. All had been removed from hearth and home by the sex-starved sailors when they ransacked the town. Nearly every Kilwa female of pleasurable potential must have been abducted; and if they were now reluctant to return, it was because, defiled by heretics, they would surely be rejected, or worse, by their husbands and loved ones. Da Gama exacted assurances that there would be no retaliation on pain of the city being levelled on his return. He then sailed away taking 'about forty' for whom no minders had been found; most of these would eventually be carried to Lisbon. But since he never would return to Kilwa, the fate of those left behind goes unrecorded, indeed defies conjecture.[10]

At Malindi, the next port of call, the king extended his customary welcome to 'his great friend Dom Vasco da Gama'. Presents were exchanged, provisions were paid for, and the fleet's purchasing agents were the only ones allowed ashore. Everyone was on their best behaviour for what was still Lisbon's only certain ally on the east African littoral. They left on 18 August, and though a gale scattered the fleet in mid-ocean, all safely reached the Indian coast at Dabhol, south of the future Bombay/Mumbai.

There the caravels 'rigged their lateen sails and mounted their artillery', says Correa. For inshore work the more manoeuvrable caravels were ideal – and so they quickly demonstrated. Onor (Honavar), a small estuarine sultanate near Goa, looked inviting. Its river approach was navigable, its defences contemptible. After its shipping had been sunk, the town, 'which was large', was 'burnt with all that was in it'. This action had nothing to do with avenging Calicut or advancing Portuguese commerce. It was undertaken at the whim of the fleet's highly unreliable interpreter who had declared 'Honor' and its ruler to be 'thieves'. Later the same ruler would be acknowledged a doughty patriot and useful ally who would introduce the Portuguese to neighbouring Goa.

The next place was Batticala (Bhatkal, north of Mangalore). Its only offence seems to have been that of not raising a white flag quick enough. After the first attack, which had been met with a shower of stones, an old man came forth to remonstrate with the admiral on behalf of the 'king'. Da Gama thereupon 'sat down in his chair, trimmed with crimson velvet, with a carpet beneath it' and composed himself. He let the old fellow kiss his feet, says Correa, and he then deigned to outline, with infinite patience, the logic and methodology of a European-style *imperium*. 'I did not come with the design of doing injury,' he began, 'but when I found war, I ordered it to be made.' (The 'war' he found was presumably a reference to the stone-throwing.)

> For this is the fleet of the King of Portugal, my sovereign, who is lord of the sea, of all the world, and also of this coast; for which reason all the rivers and ports which have got shipping have to obey him and pay tribute for their people to go forth in their fleets; and this [they must do] only as a sign of obedience, in order that thereby their ports may be free, and that they may carry on in them their trade in security, neither trading in pepper, nor bringing in Turks [i.e. Muslims], nor going to the port of Calicut, because for any of these three things the ships found to have offended will be burned, with as many as may be captured in them.[11]

Batticala was given a choice: pay tribute every year or be reduced to cinders every year. It chose the former, and in return for fifteen hundred 'loads' of rice, says Correa, the admiral 'gave his *cartaz*'. This was a safe conduct, and although not necessarily annual, it would become the standard instrument by which the Portuguese would endeavour to regulate the trade of the Indian Ocean. Without a *cartaz* no ship was supposed to sail and no port to operate. Its issue usually depended on a payment in some form, and it would invariably be contingent on the recipient forswearing any dealings with Portugal's usually Muslim enemies and refraining from any unauthorised participation in the trade in pepper and other spices. Such, at least, was the rule, later numerous and glaring exceptions notwithstanding.

Da Gama then pressed on. Wafted inexorably southwards, he was now closing on Calicut. From the strongest of all the Malabar port-cities, spirited resistance could be expected; but in what was taken to be a sign of divine favour, Calicut played straight into his hands. A massive vessel owned by one of that city's most hostile merchants and captained by his brother was intercepted on the high seas by da Gama's caravels. Sailing under the protection of the Cairo sultan and perhaps part-owned by him, it was found to be awash with treasure for the purchase of spices, to have been consigned from Mecca's port of Jiddah, and to be crammed with hennaed pilgrims, both men and women, returning from the *haj*. In da Gama's bloodthirsty estimation, a maritime abomination better appointed for a spectacular demonstration of Christian righteousness could scarcely have been devised.

Escorted to the Portuguese flagship under a safe conduct, the ship's skipper was given to understand that the Portuguese required only 'things of small volume' by way of 'a present'. These were delivered. Da Gama's officers then went aboard and chose what else they fancied. Finally followed their ships' crews under orders 'to go and pillage it… until it was empty'. The operation took all day. They were to leave aboard only the passengers and crew, of whom Correa says there were eight hundred, de Barros 260. 'Then he [da Gama] ordered them [his men] to set fire to the ship.'

At this point those about to be burned objected 'because', supposes Correa, 'it was very expedient'; they offered to exchange their lives for enough spices free of charge to fill all the Portuguese holds. Da Gama's officers thought this a good deal; and they were also inclined to agree with the Moors' contention that, since surrender had been made without a fight, the captives were entitled to their liberty. Under any rules of knightly conduct – international law would be the modern equivalent – their claim to life should have been respected. Da Gama disagreed. The offer of spices was just a bribe, he said; honour was served not by coveting an enemy's property but by effecting his death. In an odd variation on Scripture he contended that 'he who spares his enemy dies at his hands'; and on the even stranger grounds that 'we have gained nothing in this country by arms, only by friendly methods', he declared that heaven would hold him to account if he did not extirpate those whose continued existence might endanger later Portuguese visitors.

'Alive you shall burn,' he announced to the Moorish skipper, who now found it expedient to offer resistance. Some hidden weapons were produced and the captives engaged in a desperate struggle. At one point they managed to board and nearly commandeer one of the Portuguese ships. It made little difference. The Muslim ship was sunk by the combined artillery of da Gama's armada, and the survivors 'were left swimming' until 'the boats plied about killing them with lances'. Out of the 260, only twenty children and a hump-backed pilot were spared according to de Barros; out of the eight hundred, none was spared according to Correa.[12]

There followed a less bellicose visit to Cannanore. Da Gama evidently suspected that he was being overcharged for ginger, the town's main export. Its septuagenarian ruler denied this but capitulated when threatened with the cancellation of his *cartaz* and a taste of Calicut's imminent fate. Allies, he was told, should not assume that Portuguese favour entitled them to charge what they wanted. On the contrary, as well as a monopoly on the purchase of spices, the Portuguese would endeavour to establish a fixed tariff for them.

And so, like the avenging angel, da Gama, burning-eyed and black-hearted as he appears in his early portraits, descended on Calicut. 'The admiral, on arriving at Calicut, was in a passion,' says Correa, for 'the port had been cleared, and in it there was nothing to which he could do harm because the Moors, knowing of his coming, had all fled and hidden their vessels and *sambuqs* [coastal craft] in the rivers.' Nor was his temper improved by the arrival of an emissary disguised as a friar and bearing a white flag tied to a pole. Correa calls this man a Brahmin, Bishop Osorio says he was an Arab, and de Barros mentions several envoys. The disguise, like the flag, was supposed to ensure a safe reception, but as to his actual mission there is no consensus.

Taking all three accounts together, it seems that the Zamorin via his intermediary first proposed that, since da Gama had already killed far more men and commandeered far more valuable property than had been lost in the *feitoria*, Lisbon and Calicut should call it quits and start anew. At this 'the admiral, already indignant, became even more enraged'. A second proposal, to the effect that the men actually responsible for firing the *feitoria* might be handed over, fared no better. Again, we are told, the admiral 'was greatly enraged'. By way of the final straw, it was then suggested that the men who were to be handed over would actually prefer to pay a hefty premium and stay alive. To this 'the admiral did not choose to respond as he was losing time'. Instead he ordered the whole fleet to take up position along the shore-line and 'all day, till night, he bombarded the city, by which he made a great destruction'.

Worse was to follow. While da Gama was arranging for part of the fleet to stay at Calicut and pursue the vendetta with the Zamorin, a convoy of two large vessels and twenty-two lesser ones hove into sight. According to Correa they had come from the Coromandel coast where they had been freighted with rice, ghi and cotton piece-goods. Whether these strangers, who included Hindus as well as Muslims, thought the fighting was over, or whether they were just unaware of it, is unclear. An easy prey for the caravels, they were rounded up and inspected. Six vessels sailing for Cannanore were released. The rest were relieved of as much of their cargoes as the Portuguese required. With greed satisfied, the fun could begin.

First there was crossbow practice. For the benefit of anyone watching from the shore, the human targets were tied by the feet from the spars and yard-arms of their ships, there to be riddled with arrows until they moved no more and the archers tired of the sport. The ships, their rigging now a forest of prickled corpses, were sent ashore for the edification of the onlookers.

> Then the admiral commanded [his men] to cut off the hands and noses and ears of all the [remaining] crews, and to put all that [i.e. the body parts] into one of the small vessels, into which he ordered them to put 'the friar', also without ears or nose or hands, the which he ordered to be strung round his neck with a palm leaf for the king, on which he told him to have a curry made of what his 'friar' brought him. When all these Indians had been thus mutilated, he ordered their feet to be tied together, as having no hands they could not untie them; and in order that they could not untie them with their teeth, he ordered his men to strike upon their teeth with staves, and they knocked them down their throats.[13]

The thus pruned but still squirming bodies were then piled in a boat; its sails were set for the shore, and the boat was set on fire.

Further atrocities, some even more revolting, abound in the Portuguese accounts. It was, as they say, a brutal age, especially where religion was concerned. Death prior to dissection might be considered a kindness; martyrdom minus evisceration scarcely counted. The Spanish, Dutch and English, no less than the Portuguese, delighted in casual mutilation, experimented with vivisection, and as part of the judicial process took torture for granted. It is supposed that since all Europeans lived in mortal fear of the multitudinous East, exemplary punishments inflicted on whoever was to hand served as a necessary deterrence. With the possible exception of Bishop Osorio, the panegyrists and annalists record these actions without embarrassment; in conveying the surgical ingenuity shown by the perpetrators, they clearly approved it, even relished it. Squeamishness was not a European trait.

But to the peoples of the East such behaviour may have been novel. Polo and Oderic of Pordenone say little about such things; it was the dimensions of Oriental society, its magnificence and wealth, that impressed them, not its savagery. Captain Buzurg's salty yarns contain nothing about piratical excesses; nor are the 'One Thousand and One Nights' filled with agonised cries from the dungeons. It could be that such things were too commonplace to merit comment. Straightforward massacres of astronomical proportions certainly accompanied the Mongol victories and some of the triumphs of Islam. Yet the shivers of horror that greeted the punishments meted out by Delhi's 'Bloody' Sultan Muhammad Tughluq, Ibn Batuta's patron, argue otherwise. Such excesses seem to have been regarded as exceptional, and in the context of innocent trade, as unprecedented.

The Zamorin of Calicut vowed revenge and began assembling every available craft for a retaliatory strike. Da Gama contemptuously turned away and took most of his fleet to Cochin. It was now November; the nor-easterlies were blowing; a cargo was urgent. The Cochin *feitoria*, as established by Cabral, reported excellent relations with the local rajah and stocks of pepper ready and waiting. Cochin would serve as Portugal's main eastern base for the next decade. More immediately, while the twelve *naus* bound for Lisbon were being loaded, encouraging news came from Cochin's neighbours. The 'queen' of Quilon also had pepper for sale and would welcome Portuguese patronage; and the largely Christian port of Cranganore hoped for favours and friendship. In fact Cochin, though the better harbour, largely relied on these places for its own pepper supply since they were nearer the pepper-producing hills and were linked to Cochin by Kerala's network of inland lagoons and waterways.

In agreeing terms with Quilon as well as Cochin, da Gama won a potential monopoly of southern Malabar's pepper output. This was much the most important producer-region, and its acceptance of Portuguese terms probably undermined Calicut's primacy as effectively as did the hostilities with the Zamorin. To punish Cochin, therefore, and bring it back into subordination, the Zamorin's hastily assembled fleet was directed south. It was assumed that da Gama's ships, if they had not already put out into the Arabian Sea, would be too heavily laden to manoeuvre for battle.

This calculation took no account of the caravels that were being left behind to patrol the coast, nor of the *naus*' artillery being little affected by heavy sailing. The Portuguese kept their distance, evaded boarders and plied their guns. In consequence, the Zamorin's makeshift armada was badly mauled, many vessels being sunk and others fired with all hands aboard. Osorio gives the death toll as three hundred, Correa makes it sound more like three thousand. By way of a parting shot, on the way up the coast Calicut itself was again bombarded, its third taste of Portuguese marksmanship in as many years. Da Gama then loaded ginger at Cannanore and sailed for home at the end of December. The later departure meant favourable winds. He reached Malindi 'within a few days' and was back in Lisbon on 1 September 1503. A service of thanksgiving was followed by an audience with the king and further promotions and favours. The ten, possibly twelve, vessels laden with spices, along with the loot from innumerable engagements and the tribute from several kings, made it much the most successful voyage to date.

Once again existing rivalries and what seemed like chronic disarray among the port-cities of the Indian Ocean had played into Portuguese hands. With the establishment of factories and a permanent fleet in Indian waters, King Manuel now enjoyed the lion's share of the pepper trade plus the privilege of directing western Europe's first colonial enterprise in Asia. Known as His Majesty's Estado da India, or State of India, this watery imperium received its first governor and viceroy in 1505. Annual fleets of around twenty vessels being now standard, the new governor Francisco d'Almeida arrived in command of no less than twenty-two ships.

They were needed as much for defence as for carriage. Despite its maritime superiority, the Portuguese presence had as yet made no impression whatsoever on south Asia's continental power structures. Land, and its yield in terms of produce and manpower, formed the basis of dominion in India. Delhi and the other great sultanates, most of them located hundreds of miles from the coast, fielded vast armies of infantry, cavalry and artillery but gave little thought to naval matters. The sea was strategically irrelevant and economically marginal. Overseas trade could be left to private initiative and its protection to local potentates; the export of spices, though remunerative, mattered less to the peninsular kingdoms than the import of cavalry horses, principally from the Gulf.

Ludovico di Varthema, the somewhat mysterious Bolognese traveller whose wanderings in India coincided with Almeida's viceroyalty, made no mention of the Portuguese – or the 'Franks' as they were known to his Muslim companions – until he reached Cannanore. There he found that the 'Frankish' *feitoria* was being upgraded to a fort, while at Calicut trade was still minimal because of the war in which 'the King of Portugal has killed, and every day kills, great numbers'. But the impact of these events seems not to have penetrated much beyond the shaggy foothills of the Western Ghats. Up on the Deccan plateau at Bijapur, the bedomed capital of the nearest major Muslim sultanate, and at Vijayanagar, the sensationally endowed metropolis of the nearest Hindu kingdom, Portuguese effrontery passed almost unnoticed. According to di Varthema it was not Frankish firepower but the 'Frankish epidemic', otherwise syphilis, that posed a threat to Indian society. If the Zamorin of Calicut seemed in a permanent ill humour, it was as much 'because he had the Frankish disease and had it in the throat' as because of the hideous punishments meted out by da Gama.[14]

For support and revenge the Zamorin turned, therefore, not to his overlord in Vijayanagar nor to rival Bijapur but to trading partners dotted along the Indo-Arab spice route around the Arabian Sea. The sultan of Gujerat was immediately sympathetic. His subjects included the most enterprising class of merchants and mariners in the entire

Indian Ocean; and his ports, especially Cambay and Diu, supplied most of northern India with bloodstock from Arabia and black pepper from Malabar. Portuguese regulations and the virtual closure of Calicut were affecting both.

The movement of spices through the Gulf and particularly the Red Sea to Egypt was more directly under threat. Portugal's rerouting of the pepper trade was already having a catastrophic effect on Mamluk revenues, while da Gama's treatment of Muslims, and of that great vessel from Jiddah in particular, had sent shockwaves through the Islamic world. As guardian of the holy cities of Mecca and Medina as well as the principal beneficiary of the spice traffic, Mamluk Egypt could ill afford to ignore the new challenge. Egged on by the Venetians, whose Christian allegiance invariably buckled under any threat to their trade – and perhaps assisted by them in the procurement of timber and artillery – the Cairo sultan began constructing a Red Sea fleet and calling to arms the maritime interests of the Muslim world.

Albeit tardily, Portugal's display of religious zealotry and commercial greed had prompted the concerted opposition that had hitherto been so conveniently lacking. To discourage attack from this new quarter, the Portuguese talked of a raid on Jiddah and even Mecca. (The Egyptian sultan responded by threatening Jerusalem's holy places with a similar fate.) Meanwhile the Portuguese extended their belligerent operations northward to the Arabian, Persian and Gujerati coasts. Opening a new sea-way had been only half the battle; interdicting the old was just as important. Like those cropped corpses sent ashore at Calicut, the spice route must be shorn of its Near Eastern fingers and pruned of all Muslim features.

In 1506 the island of Socotra was occupied. This was less for its output of aloes, whose laxative properties were in little demand among dysenteric *fidalgos*, than for its strategic location near the Bab el-Mandeb strait. It was not, however, near enough for a blockade of the strait, and the garrison was soon withdrawn. A better bet, and the original objective, was the rock-ringed harbour of Aden 'because from there we can see to it that no spices pass to the land of the Sultan [of Egypt]', as Almeida's instructions put it.[15] But in 1506 Aden's natural fortifications discouraged an assault, and in 1513 the city would put up such a stout defence that twenty Portuguese vessels and some two thousand attackers would make little impression. Although several Portuguese fleets would subsequently venture into the Red Sea, none mastered its tricky navigation, no *feitoria* was established there, and the Islamic Holy Land remained undefiled. With Aden still open for Muslim business, this vital trunk-route of the ancient spice trail would never be effectively closed, and during the course of the sixteenth century its trade would in fact stage an erratic recovery.

At the mouth of the Gulf, Aden's equivalent was Hormuz, the island-port at which the Polos had once panicked over the seaworthiness of Indo-Arab shipping. During Almeida's viceroyalty, a Portuguese flotilla fresh from the capture of Socotra and commanded by Affonso d'Albuquerque, the rising star of the Lusitanian marine, called at Hormuz, stayed several months, and called again in 1508. Albuquerque's six ships and five hundred men were inadequate for the city's outright capture but, when surrender was refused, its shipping was destroyed, its sea-front repeatedly bombarded, and a start made in the construction of a fortress to blockade it.

Almeida, unlike his eager subordinate Albuquerque, doubted the wisdom of acquiring landward responsibilities. More pressing concerns at sea occupied his viceroyalty. The Mamluk fleet, so long on the stocks, had sailed from Suez in 1507 and entered Indian waters in 1508. It headed for Chaul in the Gulf of Cambay where, in uneasy alliance with the Gujerati marine and abetted by the Zamorin's miraculously reconstituted forces, it fell upon a Portuguese flotilla. The Portuguese did not concede defeat, but the Egyptians claimed victory; and among the dead, in this unusual reversal of fortunes, was the Portuguese commander. He was also Almeida's son. Retribution was to be expected.

It came in the following year when Almeida himself, at the head of a veritable armada, stormed into the Gujerati port of Diu where the Egyptian fleet was moored. Despite heavy losses and utter confusion, Almeida destroyed the nascent Mamluk marine in what may rate as the most decisive engagement of the century. Portuguese supremacy in the Arabian Sea was thereby assured. Cairo's enthusiasm for naval encounters had been dented; Gujerat eventually sought an alliance with the Portuguese; and the Zamorin's Lazarus-like navy slunk back to Calicut. Almeida himself made for Cochin, advertising his victory *en passant* by bombarding the Konkan ports with shot and ball interspersed with heads, legs and any other body-parts of suitable bore that could be hacked from Egyptian corpses.

Almeida's reward for this Diu victory was to be replaced. It was a common fate in an age when news of Indian achievement could take eighteen months to win a nod of Portuguese approval. The outgoing governor was deemed too cautious; the incoming Albuquerque, then fresh from operations at Hormuz, was to make amends. His instructions specifically mentioned the acquisition of Goa as a more convenient and appropriate power-base than that afforded by guest-status at monsoon-lashed Cochin. Accordingly, after the by now standard assault on the raddled Zamorin's territory, in early 1510 Albuquerque sailed north.

Goa, then a petty fief within the domains of the Bijapur sultanate, possessed a secluded port with defensive potential but no actual defences worthy of the name. Wresting it from the Bijapuris was thus the easy part, especially since its mainly Hindu population welcomed the opportunity to throw off the Muslim yoke. Hanging on to it was a different matter. Within six months, a badly bloodied Albuquerque was running again for Cochin after heavy losses and nothing to show for them. He returned to Goa and recaptured it in November of the same year. This time a garrison was left behind. It was soon under siege from the resurgent Bijapuris. Not until 1512 and a third visitation by Albuquerque would Goa be finally secured and the flag raised above the future 'Lisbon of the East'. It would fly there without intermission for four and half centuries, so outlasting even British rule in the rest of India. With more churches and more church-goers than anywhere else in Asia, the city still proudly proclaims its Catholic credentials. It was Albuquerque's greatest memorial and, for a conqueror, a most fitting one; for if the Estado da India resembled a curtain-wall draped round the Asian coastline, Goa was its central bastion.

To east and west other bastions completed this structure. In 1515 the by then indisputably 'great Affonso d'Albuquerque' would return to Hormuz. This time the murder of the local sultan would be enough for the city to be transferred to the Portuguese crown. Hormuz would remain in Portuguese hands for over a century, commanding all traffic into and out of the Gulf. In 1507 it had jump-started the most illustrious career of any Portuguese pioneer; in 1515 it would prove the end of the road for the same career. Worn out, sick and superseded, Affonso d'Albuquerque would barely make it back to Goa before breathing his last.

As for the third bastion, the third great port-city from which the Portuguese would endeavour to control the Indian Ocean, it too was won by Albuquerque. In fact it was captured in 1511 during the yearlong interval between his second and third Goa visitations. Arguably this was his greatest achievement; certainly it was his most ambitious voyage and his most notable contribution to Portuguese control of the spice trade. For the place was Melaka at the tip of the Malayan peninsula, once Cheng-ho's operational base and now the wealthiest port in the East. Contemporaries vied with one another in extolling its merits. Barbosa hailed Melaka as both 'realm and city';[16] di Varthema, whose visit preceded Albuquerque's, noted 'more ships arriving than in any other place in the world';[17] and Tome Pires, who would reside there, thought it 'of such importance and profit that it seems to me it has no equal in the universe'.[18]

Quite apart from the attractions of the city itself, its location would open a whole new theatre of endeavour. In effect the Portuguese were about to take another giant stride that would carry them past India and into the clammier unknown that was south-east Asia and the Far East. Melaka promised mastery of the remaining sector of the spice route through its command of the Malacca Strait; it would bring them within striking range of the mysterious Spice Islands; and from pepper, Portuguese commercial appetites were about to diversify into the so-called 'fine', or high-value, spices of cinnamon, mace, nutmeg and cloves.

Pacific Approaches

MALACCA, see before where ye shall pitch
Your great Emporium, and your Magazins;
The Rendezvous of all that Ocean round
For Merchandizes rich that there abound.

Luis de Camoes, *Lusiads* x, 123–5[1]

FAMOUSLY CHRISTOPHER COLUMBUS, unlike da Gama, always disclaimed his greatest discovery. A 'new world', or even a 'lost' one, was emphatically not what he had found. On the contrary, attaining the 'old world', albeit from a new direction, had been his aim and that, he insisted, was what he had done. The Caribbean islands, through which he four times cruised, were in his reckoning outlying parts of Asia. Japan therefore lay in the vicinity of Texas; and the central American isthmus must be the Golden Chersonese. He would countenance no other construction. Vasco da Gama might have found a way to the pepper ports of India, but it was he who had first opened a route to those 7,459 islands in Marco Polo's 'Eastern Sea of Chin' whence came the cloves, nutmeg and mace.

So, roughly, said Columbus; but by the time he died in 1506, a year after Almeida arrived in India, contemporaries were becoming suspicious. His discoveries seemed a bit too convenient. Even on the basis of Ptolemy's underestimated circumference for the planet, any islands that could be reached from Spain in under a month's sailing were too near to be the Indies. They also seemed too big. The outflow from the lately discovered estuaries of the Orinoco and Amazon argued overwhelmingly for these rivers having extensive watersheds and so belonging to a land mass of continental rather than insular proportions.

More obviously, if all this was Asia, what had become of the great kingdom of Cathay reported by Polo, where were the fabled silks of Seres, where the giant junks, and where indeed the spices from the 7,459 islands?

In the first years of the sixteenth century rich beds of pearls near the Orinoco delta provided some compensation; later, Aztec gold and Inca silver would make Queen Isabella's investment in the Columbian enterprise the most rewarding ever. But in the second decade of the century a mineral bonanza was barely suspected. When, therefore, in 1513 Vasco Núñez de Balboa, having hacked his way across the Panama isthmus, saluted a new vista of mighty rollers and splashed out, sword aloft, into warm waters, his exultation was understandable. All was explained. It was this ocean, which, after the howling tempests of Patagonia, Magellan would consider 'pacific' – and so call it – that must be the island-studded 'Sea of Chin'. The Atlantic was revealed as just a breezy purgatory and the Americas as just a pearly gateway to the spicy paradise promised by the new horizon. In theatrically raising the standard of Castile while the surf pounded against his chain-mail, and in thus claiming for Spain this new westward-leading sea-way to the East, Balboa in effect reaffirmed Spanish interest in contesting not only control of the spice route but its whole trajectory.

The quest for the Indies was far from over. Spain was back in the spice race; and a young adventurer, whose return from India without fortune or further prospects coincided exactly with Balboa's discovery, was about to eclipse even Columbus and da Gama with the boldness of his vision. Fernão de Magalhaes to his Lisbon acquaintances, Fernando de Magallanes to his future employers, and 'Magellan' to an anglophonic posterity, he was also about to plunge the spiceries and the spice route into confusion.

King Manuel of Portugal (not to mention 'of the Algarves and of the Navigation and Conquest' of just about everywhere else) had followed the rise and fall of Spanish hopes with interest. The growing certainty that Columbus' discoveries were not the Spice Islands was encouraging; the Portuguese in India might in fact be nearer to them than were the Spanish in the Caribbean. But until the Spice Islands had actually been located there was no way of telling to whom they belonged. Even then it would not be obvious. The Tordesillas treaty said nothing definite about the line which divided the Portuguese and Spanish acquisitions in the Atlantic being applicable to the other side of the world; and the difficulty of calculating longitude, together with continuing uncertainty over the earth's circumference, would anyway make the positioning of such a line problematical. Meanwhile the danger of Spain reaching the Spice Islands first remained. If only to pre-empt a pre-emptive Spanish bid, they merited Portugal's urgent attention.

As early as 1506 a small Portuguese fleet commanded by Almeida's son, the one who would die at Chaul, had visited Sri Lanka. Like Dias at the Cape of Good Hope, young Lourenço Almeida made the first Portuguese passage beyond Cape Comorin by being storm-driven past it without a sighting. He then more or less collided with what the Portuguese, following Arab practice, called variously 'Serendib', 'Taprobane' or 'Ceilan'. The island was well known to be the source of the best cinnamon and, partly in the form of tribute, partly in trade, a cargo of the bark was obtained and an agreement reached with one of the island's kings. This would be followed by the establishment of a *feitoria* at Colombo in 1518, the ousting of Muslim rivals from the neighbourhood, and hence a largely undisputed access to as much cinnamon as Europe required.

'As regards cinnamon', writes C. R. Boxer, 'the Portuguese were able to exercise a more effective monopoly in this than in any other spice.'[2] But it was not a monopoly as the Dutch would come to understand the word. In the first half of the century no more than a third of the total crop reached Lisbon, the rest being siphoned off by smugglers and by Portuguese officials acting in a private capacity. Nor was any attempt made to subjugate the island. The Portuguese would notch up an impressive number of converts in Sri Lanka, but their managerial activities scarcely extended beyond reducing the caste of bark-peelers to a state of bondage and occasionally visiting the woods where, in a pinkish flush of shiny new leaf, the sprightly cinnamon trees flourished. Within easy reach of both Cochin and Goa, Sri Lanka's cinnamon exports would be commercially integrated with Malabar's pepper and ginger and would remain theoretically out of bounds to foreign competitors until the Dutch decided otherwise more than century later.

It was a different matter with the other 'fine spices' – cloves, nutmeg and mace. Da Gama and his immediate successors had remarked on the erratic availability of these commodities in India's ports and regretted that supply seemed to be beyond the control of India-based shipping. They had no clear idea of where the spices originated but were unanimous in reporting that they reached India exclusively from what da Gama called 'Malequa'. This was Melaka of the eponymous strait, the Mecca of eastern commerce and the gateway to the Moluccas. It was known to be ruled by a Muslim sultan, to be frequented by Arab, Gujerati, Malabari and Chinese merchants (among others), and to be a port of exceptional trade. For all of these reasons King Manuel had determined that it must quickly be 'discovered' and brought within the sphere of Portuguese operations.

A fleet was assembled in Lisbon and in 1509 assigned directly to Melaka. In an attempt to impose some order on his *estado*, the king had decided that Melaka, along with the Far East in general, should form a separate governorate, complementary to that of India (based on Cochin/Goa) but independent of it. A similar entity embracing the east African and Arabian coasts was also envisaged. But neither actually materialised. The would-be governor of the Arabian Sea died prematurely; meanwhile his Melaka counterpart had sailed into choppy waters.

Touching at Madagascar and then Cochin, Diogo Lopes de Sequeira had commandeered local pilots and breezed into the Malacca Strait in 1510. The procedure for foisting Portuguese supremacy on trade-dependent sultanates was now well rehearsed. Like da Gama on his first visit to Calicut, Sequeira displayed due deference, was cordially received by the sultan, and was graciously granted permission to establish a small *feitoria*.

More disconcertingly, the Calicut precedent then continued to repeat itself. Like the Zamorin, Melaka's sultan was dependent on a merchant community that was predominantly Muslim and understandably wary of Portuguese fire-power. He therefore had second thoughts. The *feitoria* came under assault, a few of its inmates were killed, and others, including its commander Ruy de Araujo, were arrested. Whether or not provoked, an attack on Sequeira's ships was also mounted. There were only four of them. After repelling the attackers, they administered a token bombardment of the city before beating a speedy, not to say ignominious, retreat. The sultan now had hostages in the persons of Araujo and his men; but in the detention of these same men the Portuguese had a pressing excuse for further action. With the honour of his sovereign at stake, Albuquerque rose to the occasion. Ignoring the putative division of the Estado da India, and deserting his hard-pressed settlement at Goa, he had sailed for Melaka in early 1511.

As well as information obtained from pilots and other local sea-farers, Albuquerque (and probably Sequeira) derived encouragement from a copy of a soon to be published itinerary by that shadowy gen-tleman of Bologna, Ludovico di Varthema. On whose behalf, if anyone's, Varthema had been spying out the East is not known. Nor is it certain that he visited all the places he claims to have visited. But even if he didn't, a short period in Portuguese employ, along with Albuquerque's possession of his unpublished *Travels*, strongly suggests that he was engaged in the sort of reconnaissance earlier undertaken by Pero de Covilha.

Arguably Varthema deserves recognition, alongside Jan Huyghen van Linschoten of later fame, as the century's most influential practi-tioner of commercial espionage. For besides visiting Mecca, sizing up India's peninsular politics and briefly serving at Cannanore as a Portuguese go-between, the Bolognese had cast his net much further afield. He had apparently visited most of the countries round the Bay of Bengal and had then – perhaps in 1505 – actually called at Melaka. 'The principal port of the main ocean', Melaka was situated, he reported, on the Malayan mainland, commanded the strait, and paid tribute to 'the king of Cini [China], who caused this place to be built about eighty years ago'.[3] Though it was now the most Muslim of Malay sultanates, Varthema had thus correctly noted Melaka's debt to the Cheng-ho voyages and its continued relationship with the Chinese empire. Either his sources were exceptionally well informed or his researches must indeed have been conducted on site.

Nor was this the extent of Varthema's intelligence. As well as linking Melaka with China and its legendary exports, he confirmed its pivotal role in the trade of the Indonesian archipelago, including that in nutmegs, mace and cloves. In fact it seemed that Varthema had actually visited the islands that produced these spices. Undefended and only two weeks' sailing away, they looked from his narrative to be there for the taking.

With such a mouth-watering report to hand, Albuquerque sailed for Melaka determined on nothing short of its submission. To his fleet of eighteen ships more were added as Gujerati, Coromandel and Javanese vessels were seized *en route*. 'It was the season [April] when the Moors navigate to the kingdoms...which lie to the east of Cape Comorin,' explains the official *Commentary*, which was probably written by Albuquerque's son; there was so much shipping about that 'they could have taken the largest prize that was ever beheld in those parts'.[4] When calling at the north Sumatran ports of Pasei and Pedir, they could also have secured that island's now considerable pepper trade. It seemed a shame to have to save their powder for Melaka.

As if to make amends, an almighty salute was fired from the entire squadron as, flags flying and trumpets blaring, Albuquerque sailed straight into Melaka's harbour. The demonstration seemed to have the desired effect; Sultan Mohamed agreed to release the prisoners and restore Portuguese property. But he wanted a guarantee of no further aggression; meanwhile the prisoners failed to appear. If intimidation was Albuquerque's preference, procrastination was evidently the sultan's.

Invincible at sea, on land the Portuguese enjoyed the advantages only of more disciplined troops and exceptional zealotry. Melaka was much the largest city they had yet assailed; and the sultan was known to have considerable forces plus a home-made artillery as good as any cast in Germany. A straightforward assault was out of the question. In a change of tactics, therefore, Albuquerque tried to sow dissent in the enemy ranks. The personnel of some Chinese junks were won over; one of the sultan's Javanese commanders promised neutrality; and his Gujerati clients were given to understand that, if they recommended caution, their property might be spared. But the sultan remained obdurate.

Albuquerque then ordered an attack on the harbour's shipping. The conflagration produced the release of Araujo and his companions but no agreement on compensation nor on the construction of a fort-ress/*feitoria*. On Araujo's advice, an assault on the long timber bridge

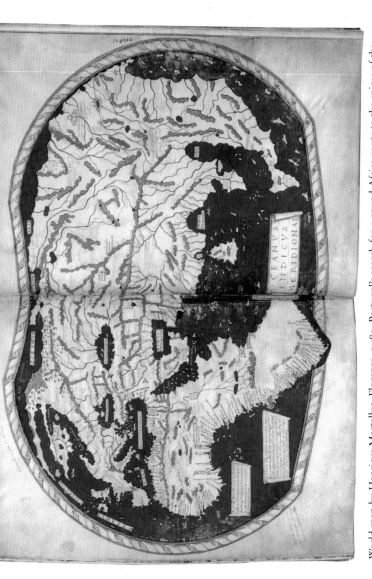

World map by Henricus Martellus, Florence, 1489. Portugal's search for a round-Africa route to the spices of the East was finally rewarded when Bartolomeu Dias passed the Cape of Good Hope in 1488. The news was instantly incorporated into maps produced by Europe's other trading nations

Vasco da Gama, by a Portuguese artist c.1600. Da Gama's first voyage (1497–9) pioneered the oceanic spice route to India; his second (1502–3) acquainted the East with the horrors of Christian zealotry

The pepper sought by Europeans was *Piper nigrum*, a vine that twisted itself around any handy tree, decorating its host with long clusters of berries

European imaginings about the pepper harvest in Quilon (Kollam) in Malabar. From a fifteenth-century French manuscript, *Livre des Merveilles*

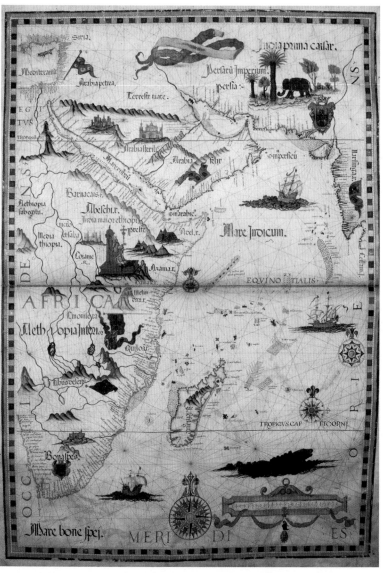

A map of the Indian Ocean by Diego Homem, 1558. Sixty years after da Gama reached India, Prester John remains enthroned in Ethiopia, testimony to Portugal's stubborn belief that large Christian populations dwelt in sub-Saharan Africa and Asia

Left: Affonso d'Albuquerque, Viceroy the Indies, by Lizuarte d'Abreu, *c.*1588–65. Albuquerque secured Portugal's Eastern empire by capturing Goa on the coast of India, Hormuz at the mouth of the Persian Gulf, and Melaka, the great spice entrepôt near t tip of the Malayan peninsula

Below: The city of Melaka, conquered the Portuguese in 1511. From the *Livr do Estado da India Oriental*, by Pedro Barretto de Resende, Portugal, *c.*1646

Opposite above: Celebration of the Portuguese fleet, from Book I of the *Leitura Nova* by Além-Douro, *c.*1513 The capture of Melaka was seen as a triumph for all Christendom and was celebrated as much in Rome as in Lisl

Opposite below: The Rhinoceros. Woodcut by Albrecht Dürer, 1515. Dürer's rhinoceros was a present from the ruler of Gujerat to Manuel I of Portugal. It reached Lisbon safely but was lost at sea when Manuel tried to forward it to the Pope

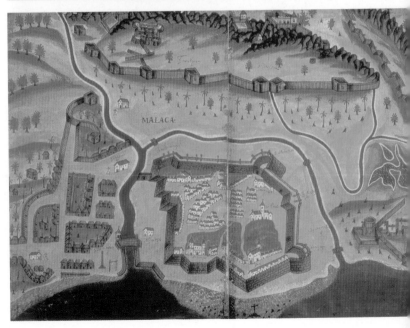

MALACA:

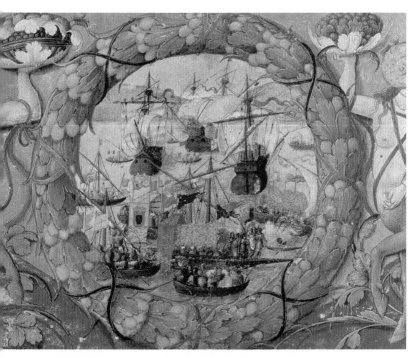

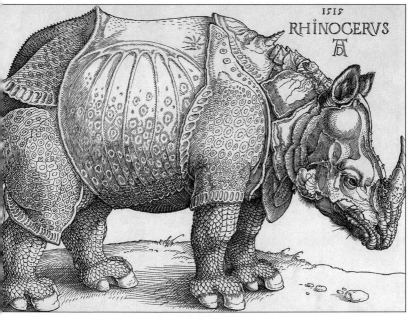

Above: A world map of *c.*1545 by the Genoese cartographer Battista Agnese incorporates the findings of the Magellan d'Elcano circumnavigation of 1519–22. Magellan's confirmation of a trans-Pacific route to the Spice Islands would induce Sir Francis Drake to repeat the feat in 1577–80

Left: Two circumnavigators and a pioneering slaver: Thomas Cavendish, Sir Francis Drake, and Sir John Hawkins, by an unknown artist, seventeenth century. Thanks to their voyages, by the end of the sixteenth century both the Dutch and the English were actively contesting the Portuguese monopoly of the spice route

above: The shipbuilding yards and warehouse of the
Dutch East India Company in Amsterdam, by a Dutch
artist, seventeenth century. The Dutch company quickly
dwarfed its English counterpart as it successfully ousted
the Portuguese from the spice-producing Moluccas

right: Jan Pieterzoon Coen (1587–1629). Oil painting
by Jacob Waben, 1625. Officially the Governor of the
Dutch East India Company's affairs in the East Indies,
Coen was known to the English as 'King Coen' and the
'Butcher of Banda'

below: The Dutch capture of Loki on Ceram in 1652,
by an unknown artist, c.1665. Loki was the centre of a
protracted rebellion against Dutch attempts to
monopolise clove production

The American chilli colonises India: women walk through a chilli-drying field in Bundi, Rajasthan. The decline in the importance of the spice trade owed something to the transplantion of spice seedlings, much to the introduction of native American spices (like t chilli) but perhaps most to the trade boom in other stimulants (like coffee, sugar and tea)

An early London coffee house, by an English artist, 1668. Coffee subsequently lost its soc distinction when it became widely available thanks to commercial plantations established the Dutch in Java

that linked the city to its main mosque and suburbs was then attempted. In some of the fiercest fighting they had ever experienced, the Portuguese gained the bridge but were unable to hold it.

By now the weeks were slipping away and the westward sailing season was approaching. With dissent as loud in his own ranks as in those of the enemy, Albuquerque delivered an impassioned plea. There was now, he told his men, no alternative to storming the city. Other options had been exhausted; and those who thought differently must think again. He gave two reasons, they bring precisely those that had brought the Portuguese to the East in the first place. Religion and trade – 'Christians and spices' – were still inseparable.

'The first [reason] is the great service which we shall perform to Our Lord in casting the Moors out of this country…if we can achieve this, it will result in the Moors resigning India [i.e. the East] altogether to our rule, for the greater part of them live upon the trade of this country and are become great and rich and lords of extensive territory…

And the other reason is the additional service which we shall render to King Dom Manuel in taking this city, because it is the headquarters of all the spiceries and drugs which the Moors carry every year to the Straits [of Bab el-Mandeb into the Red Sea] without our being able to prevent them from doing so; but if we deprive them of this ancient market here, there does not remain for them a single port…where they can carry on their trade…if we take this trade of Melaka away from them, Cairo and Mecca are entirely ruined, and to Venice no spiceries will be conveyed except that which her merchants go and buy in Portugal.'[5]

This fighting talk brought from his men a vote of confidence and, as soon as the tide permitted, a full-blooded attack. The bridge was again stormed, and this time retained and fortified; an elephant corps was routed, counter-attacks repelled. The bombards bombarded, the cannons cannonaded, the sultan fled, and the city fell.

Then it was sacked. 'Of the Moors, women and children, there died by the sword an infinite number, for no quarter was given to any of them,' says the eye-witness author of the *Commentary*.[6] The mosque was torn down and its stone used in the construction of a fort; treasure and merchandise of incalculable value were piled aboard Albuquerque's flagship, the *Flor del Mar*. In desperation the now fugitive sultan appealed to the Chinese emperor. It was a waste of time: Beijing was still indifferent to maritime trade. Instead of tall junks there came from China only fair words; and by the time they arrived, the sultan was dead and Albuquerque long gone.

Leaving Araujo in command of troops to hold the fortress and of ships to police the strait, Albuquerque had sailed back to India. Goa urgently needed relieving and, in the Gulf, Hormuz had yet to be secured. But neither would pose an insuperable challenge thanks to the fearsome reputation that now everywhere preceded Melaka's victor.

In what had instantly become a classic of Portuguese conquest, the only setback of note was the loss of the *Flor del Mar*. She was wrecked on a reef off the coast of Sumatra during the return voyage. With her disappeared 'the richest spoils that ever were seen since India was first discovered'. The disaster also cheated King Manuel's queen of an entire shop-floor of 'highly skilled' embroiderers – all female, they had presumably been in the sultan's service – as well as 'many young girls and youths of noble family' representing all the countries east of India; in effect hostages, they too were drowned. Albuquerque himself was one of the few survivors. Having pulled rank to commandeer the only raft, he had been fished aboard a sister ship like one of Captain Buzurg's heroes.

The disaster could have been worse. 'Had not Our Lord succoured them [the survivors] with [the capture of] two large Moorish ships... laden with pepper and silk, sandalwood and aloes-wood', the men might have starved; worse still, the expedition might have shown a loss. But providence had prevailed, and not even shipwreck could tarnish an otherwise crowning achievement. In less than a decade first Almeida had disposed of the only serious threat to the Estado da India and now Albuquerque had anchored it to the furthest of the great landward bastions from which it would withstand all challenges for a century. Echoing the 'great Affonso', Tome Pires, who reached Melaka in the following year, declared the city 'made for merchandise, fitter than any other in the world, the end of the [Indian] monsoon and the beginning of another'.

Whoever is lord of Melaka has his hand on the throat of Venice. [For] from Melaka, and from Melaka to China, and from China to the

Moluccas, and from the Moluccas to Java, and from Java back to
Sumatra and Melaka, [all] is in our power. And whoever understands
this will exalt Melaka, for in Melaka they prize garlic and onions above
musk, benzoin [benjamin, a rare Sumatran incense-resin] and all other
precious things.[7]

The last sentence was probably intended for Venetian readers; they
were to judge Melaka's prosperity from the news that the exotica
which Venice held priceless were there rated less than shallots. No
wonder King Manuel was soon crowing the glad tidings throughout
Christendom. Quite apart from the value of the place, he was desperate to win further papal endorsement. For Melaka's capture had
prompted Spain to renew its claims to the Spice Islands and to
announce an imminent initiative. Luckily Pope Leo X, a hard-headed
Medici, valued the Portuguese bird in the hand above the Spanish bird
in the bush. A public thanksgiving for the capture of Melaka was held
in the Holy City in 1512, and in 1514 it was followed by a magnifi-
cent parade of orientalia. Recalling the spectacles of the Roman
Empire, Indian slaves marched with leopards, panthers and parrots. An
elephant curtseyed to His Holiness, then sprayed the crowds with
water. Only the rhinoceros was absent, having expired in transit.

Naturally Rome's response came in the form of papal bulls. Those
of 1514 confirmed Portugal's exclusive privileges in 'Africa and in all
other places beyond the sea', including 'all places unfrequented [by
Christians, whether] recovered, discovered, found, acquired... in any
place or region whatsoever, even though perchance unknown to us at
present'.[8] The whole world and all within it now looked to be
Portugal's happy hunting ground. Yet the westward limits of Spain's
hemisphere remained undefined and so, potentially, just as extensive.
King Manuel would probably have swapped any number of 'whatso-
evers' and 'perchances' for a little more precision and a few proper
names – like 'Melaka', like 'Spice Islands'.

Before leaving Melaka, Albuquerque had also found time to initiate
future Portuguese policy in respect of the Far East. Save for one
exception, it was to be quite different from that pursued elsewhere.
Portuguese resources were inadequate for the heavy-handed regula-
tion of another trading arena, especially one that was probably busier

and bigger than any in the world. Moreover religious zealotry could be counter-productive in a region where Islam itself was a comparative newcomer and religion in general less contentious. 'Christians and spices' were not here complementary, nor even compatible; a choice had to be made.

The Portuguese in the Far East chose spices. According to one modern authority, 'in the Atlantic they were explorers, in the Indian Ocean they were conquerors, and in the Far East they were business-men.'[9] Melaka's prosperity depended on its being open to all-comers regardless of faith or nationality; the key to success therefore lay in accommodation; and with this in mind Albuquerque had sought to reassure Melaka's neighbours. Ambassadors were sent in response to overtures from Mataram (in Java) and Campar (in southern Sumatra); another embassy was despatched to the Thai capital of Ayuthia. And as soon as news of Melaka's fall reached Lisbon, King Manuel would set his heart on the 'discovery' of China, sending Tome Pires, author of much the most authoritative account of the Far East, to Canton.

The one exception was the Spice Islands; they were not to be 'discovered' but, as Albuquerque had urged, 'explored', a term which in the context of Portuguese empire was indistinguishable from 'exploited'. To this end Albuquerque had in late 1511 sent from Melaka a fleet of three ships plus a supply-junk under the command of Antonio d'Abreu.

The inspiration for the voyage seems again to have come from Ludovico di Varthema's narrative. Whether or not the Bolognese traveller had actually been to the Spice Islands, his was the only credible account of them. It was recent, and it marked a major advance on the vague notions of previous travellers like Polo, Ibn Batuta and de Conti. Admittedly Varthema's reason for visiting the Spice Islands was not the best that a master spice-spy could have come up with. It was all, he says, thanks to his travelling companion. Finding themselves in Sumatra and 'brought where the spices grow', this man had taken it into his head to see as many other spice islands as possible. He and Varthema had made enquiries, learnt that 'nutmeg and mace grew in an island which was distant 300 miles', and so, hiring boats and crews, had set off into the sunrise.

'We took aboard many articles of food, especially the best fruits I ever tasted, and thus took our way towards the island of Bandan.' The voyage had lasted 'fifteen days'. Like the '300 miles', this was probably a deliberate understatement; the distance was more like 1,000 miles (1,600 km) and the sailing time a month; making the Spice Islands sound nearer Melaka than they were would discourage Spanish interest. *En route* they had passed 'about twenty' other islands, some inhabited, some not. Then came 'Bandan'. It turned out to be 'very ugly and gloomy…about 100 miles in circumference'. The terrain was 'very low and flat' and the people 'very weak of intellect' and 'living like beasts'. A further twelve days' sailing to the north brought them to the Moluccas. There the ground was sandy 'but not sand', the air 'a little bit cooler', and the people even 'more vile and worthless'.[10] In effect, Varthema's Spice Islands had nothing to recommend them but their yield and bore absolutely no relation to today's archipelagic scatter of palm-fringed and coral-girt perfection.

Only his notes on the spices themselves carry conviction. Here for the first time, cloves were exclusively awarded to the Moluccas and nutmegs and mace to the Bandas. The botanical connection between the nut and its covering mace was correctly described; and some reliable observations on harvesting and prices were included. If Varthema never went there, he must again have had excellent sources. Albuquerque, when despatching his 'explorers', thus knew as much about the Spice Islands as Almeida had about Sri Lanka when sending his son there.

Primed on Varthema's itinerary, Antonio d'Abreu and his three ships made first for Banda. Albuquerque had chosen Abreu for the command as a way of rewarding him; during the final assault on Melaka, Abreu had been shot in the mouth yet had fought on minus the side of his face and a sizeable section of tongue. His companions were also Melaka veterans and included Francisco Serrão in command of the only ship that was lost on the outward voyage to the Spice Islands. Serrão survived and his ship was replaced by purchasing another junk.

Contrary to later tradition, Serrão's best friend, Fernão de Magalhaes (or Magellan), probably did not command Abreu's third vessel. Like Serrão, Magellan had certainly fought at Melaka as a member of both Sequeiro's and Albuquerque's expeditions, but he then seems to have returned with Albuquerque to India and sailed home via east Africa. With him he took as a manservant a slave purchased in Melaka. This was a common practice and tells us nothing about Magellan or the probably Malay 'Enrique'. Yet it may have had a notable sequel; for Enrique would accompany his master on his later voyage and would outlive him when disaster overtook them in the Philippines. If, as seems probable, Enrique then found his way back to Melaka, it was he – and not any of Magellan's Iberian followers – who was the first member of the human race to have completed a circumnavigation of the planet. The feat, unauthenticated at the time, has gone uncelebrated ever since because his fate, like that of the vast majority of those who sailed the spice route, was to be disqualified on the grounds that he was neither literate enough nor white enough.

Under strict instructions from Albuquerque to take no prizes on the voyage to Spice Islands and never to go ashore except for the purchase of spices, Abreu and his men were at a narrational disadvantage as they neared their destination. It would have been appropriate to record a tumultuous landfall at the Banda Islands even if an actual landing was forbidden. As the climax of a two-thousand-year quest for the most mysterious and mythologised of destinations, there should at least have been a sense of occasion, a hoisting of ensigns, a blaring of trumpets, thunderous salutes, well chosen words. Later arrivals would supply these, and not implausibly later writers have assumed them on Abreu's behalf; but the records remain mute on the matter.

The Bandanese did apparently welcome the newcomers. They welcomed anyone with goods to exchange for their only exportable commodity, and they particularly welcomed men who seemed otherwise allergic to dry land. Abreu possibly stayed a month while he loaded nutmegs and mace along with some cloves that had been forwarded from the Moluccas. Then he proceeded to the Moluccas themselves and an equally unremarkable reception. The islanders seemed to be quite unaware that they were at last face to face with those who considered themselves their oldest and remotest customers; nor is there any evidence of Abreu making the historical connection for them. What should have been one of the world's more momentous encounters looks to have passed off without acknowledgement. The dawning of the new spice age is obscured by a leaden sky of silence. If the disfigured Abreu did ever venture ashore, his small step onto a beach in the Bandas went unhailed as the giant leap for mankind that history had every right to expect.

The most that can be said of the Abreu expedition is that it confirmed Varthema's poor opinion of the islands and their peoples and heightened his sense of outrage over their undeserved abundance of spices. This discrepancy between the worthless islanders and their priceless produce would become axiomatic among the Portuguese and would often arouse in them a vehement blend of horror and lust. According to de Barros, the Moluccas were 'the dwelling place of all evil and have no merit save for cloves'.[11] He supposed that, since God made them, 'we have to call them good'; and in the light of subsequent events, they did remind him of the Garden of Eden, but only in so far as the cloves rivalled Eve's 'apple of discord' as a source of friction and enduring shame. Garcia da Orta, the Goa-based botanist and apothecary, would echo these sentiments in respect of the nutmeg isles. 'This Banda is very unhealthy,' he says. 'Many go there and few come back; yet people are always eager to go there because there is much profit.'[12]

After what amounted to no more than a commercial reconnaissance, Abreu turned to Ambon, a sheltered port in a deep inlet on an island of the same name. Adjacent to the larger island of Ceram, Ambon was handily positioned just short of midway between the Bandas and the Moluccas, and though without spices of its own, was destined to loom large in the grisly tale that would unfold over the next century. Making a note of its strategic potential, Abreu sailed west again back to Melaka.

No attempt had been made to establish a *feitoria* or to leave any form of Portuguese representation in the Spice Islands. But it so happened that about 150 miles (200km) out of Ambon, Francisco Serrão's junk became detached from Abreu's other vessels, struck a reef, and sank. Serrão, his nine companions and their assorted crew were lucky. They managed to scramble onto a deserted atoll and from there to decoy a passing *prahu*. Whether this boat contained well-intentioned rescuers or piratically minded predators is unclear. Either way, its complement was overpowered, the boat was commandeered, and Serrão put back to sea in it. He made for Ambon but overshot the main inlet and landed in the north of that island. Thence word of his military prowess in a local squabble with Ceram reached the north Moluccas. A prince of Ternate, the largest of the clove-producing islands, sped to claim the castaways; and thus it was in Ternate that Francisco Serrão would settle, marry a Javanese lady, father several children and rise to high rank in the sultan's employ. Despite their evil reputation, the Spice Islanders were perhaps the only nation to have welcomed their first Portuguese resident; and entirely by chance, Lisbon had obtained representation in the Spice Islands. Unnoted at the time, Magellan had also acquired an interest in the islands in that his old friend Serrão would prove a keen and inspirational correspondent.

It was thanks to this same string of maritime mishaps that the sweet-scented clove islands of the north Moluccas would become the focus of Portuguese attention while the nutmeg-musky Bandas 'enjoyed the enormous benefit of their neglect'.[13] Both island groups owed their profile to still active volcanoes and their celebrity to particular spices. But otherwise they differed. The north Moluccas (confusingly the Indonesian Republic's Maluku/Molucca province now includes the Bandas, which are known as the 'South Moluccas') comprised half a dozen clove-producing islands and others that did not produce cloves. Each of the more important islands had its own volcano and its own sultan; but only the sultans of Ternate and Tidore aspired to lord it over the other islands and over each other. The clove islands thus simmered with dynastic rivalries that were liable to erupt as unexpectedly as their volcanoes. This chronic discord invited exploitation as much as the clove harvest itself; and despite Portugal's claim to prior occupation, Spain's belated appearance would not therefore be in itself a handicap.

The Bandas, on the other hand, a more disciplined trickle of smaller islands, radiated out from a single volcano. They were enveloped in dense forest (the nutmeg trees did best beneath a high canopy), and were run by innumerable *orang kaya*. These 'rich men', or village chiefs, acknowledged no overlord or sultan. The Bandanese might, then, be described as republicans; and it was thus appropriate that their islands would be spared the overspill of Catholic Iberia's essentially dynastic squabbles. But it was only a reprieve until more suitable claimants materialised. Within a century the commonality of the Bandas would experience the bloody squabbles of Europe's Protestant powers, namely the republican Dutch and the constitutionally minded English. With delicious symmetry, the final rounds in the long drawn-out contest for control of the spice route would be fought out almost exclusively within the smouldering compass of the Spice Islands themselves.

Marooned in Ternate from late 1511, Francisco Serrão found ample time for correspondence. He probably communicated with Melaka via the Javanese and Makassarese shipping that traditionally uplifted the island's cloves; and a whole batch of his letters was collected from Ambon when the next Portuguese visitors called there in 1514. On the basis of this firsthand information, Tome Pires, when completing his *Suma Oriental* in Melaka in 1515, presented an unusually favourable picture of Ternate. The sultan was 'a man of good judgement', according to Pires/Serrão. Despite a harem of four hundred ('all daughters of men of good standing'), he 'would be glad to welcome Christian priests'. His island was 'healthy' and its air, if one excluded the sulphurous fumes from its volcano, 'good'. His men, of whom there were about two thousand, ranked as 'knights among those of the Moluccas'; about ten per cent had espoused Islam but they still enjoyed 'wines of their kind'. Besides the annual yield of 30 tons of cloves, the island produced 'abundant foodstuffs' including exotic fruits and seafood.[14] Ternate, in short, had all that a man could want and certainly all that Francisco Serrão could want; the castaway was evidently enjoying himself, and though he would happily promote Portuguese interests and assist Portuguese shipping, he was not in a hurry to be relieved.

The fleet that collected his letters from Ambon in 1514 had been to the Bandas for nutmegs; it did not call at Ternate and the north Moluccas. In the following year a couple of junks under Portuguese command did pay a visit. Serrão helped them to obtain a cargo of cloves but himself stayed put. His conduct had been censured in Melaka yet he was too well entrenched in Ternatean society to be extracted. Thereafter a Portuguese flotilla called annually for Ternate's cloves, and Serrão continued to be helpful. He was still there in 1519 when Magellan set forth to join him; and he may have been partly responsible for his friend sailing under new colours and approaching from a new quarter.

Serrão's letter, or letters, to Magellan have not survived. It is known, however, that a correspondence existed, and it is likely that it was influential in Magellan's decision. Neither man felt under any great obligation to the Portuguese crown. Serrão in his Ternatean retreat had effectively rejected Lisbon's authority, while Magellan in Portugal had become increasingly disillusioned. After his return from the East, Magellan had served in one of King Manuel's continuing 'crusades' against the Moors in Morocco. In doing so, he hoped to ingratiate himself with the king and so win promotion and the command of an expedition to the Moluccas. The campaign went well, but he returned only with a bad limp, the result of a war wound, and an impending indictment for embezzlement. Though the charge, which was almost certainly false, was eventually rejected, so was his application for an expeditionary command. In disgust he turned increasingly to the study of geographical knowledge, to the company of other disaffected *fidalgos*, and to the possibility of seeking his fortune elsewhere.

Spain had already raised the question of whether, under the terms of Tordesillas, the Moluccas could rightfully be claimed by Portugal. Serrão's letters probably posed the same question; and Magellan certainly studied the matter and secretly discussed it with others. If the dividing line in the Atlantic fell at roughly 46 degrees west, it followed that on the other side of the world it should, if continued over the poles, fall at 134 degrees east. In the light of Balboa's discovery of the Pacific shoreline, this was clearly well beyond the Americas; and given existing ideas of the earth's circumference, plus the immense eastward distances already covered by the Portuguese, the line of demarcation looked likely to fall near, or even on, the Asian mainland. Portugal might well find the Moluccas being lopped off its *estado*.

In deserting his Portuguese allegiance and swearing fealty to Charles I of Spain, Magellan could claim, and probably did, that clarification of the Tordesillas division meant upholding the authority of the papacy, an institution that transcended all mere monarchies. This did not reassure the Portuguese, who portrayed his defection as treason, nor the Spanish, who remained suspicious of his motives and critical of his preference for Portuguese officers. Had sensitive geographical data been the main objective of his proposed expedition, King Charles would surely have selected a Spanish navigator. Magellan's trump card was his friendship with Serrão and its promise of cloves. So far as can be established, his talk of spices and his estimate of profits was what most impressed King Charles and his advisers.

According to Pires, who was again indebted to Serrão for his information, merchandise (usually textiles, utensils and trinkets) bought in Melaka for 500 *reis* could be exchanged for a *bahar* (around 600 ponds/270 kg) of cloves in the Moluccas; the same *bahar* of cloves could then be sold back in Melaka, for 9–12 *cruzados*. At the then rate of 400 *reis* to the *cruzado*, that was 3,600–4,800 *reis*; in other words the value of the cloves had appreciated nearly ten times, five thousand per cent, on just the first leg of the usually three-stage voyage to Lisbon. By the time they reached India the value of the cloves may have increased another sixfold, 70 cruzados a *bahar* being the price paid in Chaul in the 1520s. Hereabouts bulk cargoes were broken up; India and its neighbours still consumed far more spices of every description than did Europe. Here also, for that part of the Moluccan cargo that continued west, the price trail becomes harder to follow. With every transaction the variables multiplied, exchange rates, units of measurement and seasonal factors being especially fickle. They could confound even contemporary calculation. But from India to Europe, a further appreciation of around ten times may be taken as an average. Thus from just over one *cruzado* in the Moluccas the wholesale price paid for a *bahar* of cloves had risen to 700 *cruzados* by the time it reached Lisbon.

Obviously this was not all profit. Freight charges, shipping losses, duties and a variety of other imposts had to be taken into account. Prices were never stable. At source, they rapidly escalated during the early sixteenth century, the consequence not of an increase in demand resulting from Portuguese access but of a decrease in shipping resulting from the Portuguese clamp-down on local carriers. But whatever the costs and however volatile the prices, on this notional appreciation of thirty-five thousand per cent in respect of cloves, wondrous profits were undoubtedly normal.

Not surprisingly, private Spanish backers were as keen to fund Magellan's proposed voyage as was King Charles; in fact their interest may have clinched matters with the royal council. When it came to the terms of Magellan's employment, commercial concerns topped the list, with the allocation of the expected profits being a contentious item. Spices were still the most exciting commodities in world trade; and just as they had provided the main incentive for Columbus' westward voyage, so they did for Magellan's. In undertaking to sail round the Americas and on to the East, Magellan's accepted objective was the rerouting of the spice trade.

He sailed from Seville in August 1519 with about 250 men in five ships. The ships were small. The largest displaced about 145 tons, and a Portuguese intelligence agent described them all as 'very old... patched up...[and] rotten...I would be ill-inclined to sail in them even to the Canaries.' This may have been sour grapes, or perhaps it was intended to discourage other would-be Portuguese defectors. Certainly one of the vessels, the *Victoria*, would prove durable enough, completing not only the circumnavigation but then crossing the Pacific for a second time.

The men were more of a problem. The suspicions and jealousies that had dogged the preparations for the voyage did not abate at sea, and flared afresh whenever adversity threatened, fanned by the discontent of motley crews increasingly anxious for their survival. Disappointed of a channel into the Pacific via what turned out to be the river Plate estuary, the fleet overwintered on the Atlantic coast of Argentina. A ship was lost on the rocks and the first of several mutinies was barely contained. A second vessel deserted in the vicinity of the strait between Patagonia and Tierra del Fuego. Named for Magellan, through it the three remaining vessels wriggled into the Pacific fifteen months after they had left Spain.

It was encouraging that ahead lay open sea, light winds and warmer climes; Magellan's men sniffed the breeze; the cloves could not be far. A salute was fired and a *Te Deum* sung. Had anyone realised that the new ocean in fact extended to a third of the world's entire circumference, a *Miserere* might have been preferred.

Ninety-eight days and two uninhabited atolls later, having recrossed the equator and steered by the stars for longer even than da

Gama, they sighted land again, albeit another island. By then scurvy had claimed nineteen lives, thirty of the survivors were suffering severely from other maladies, and all were starving. The leather that was wrapped round the main-yard to stop it chafing had been cooked and eaten. The ship's biscuit was more worm than crumb and stank of rats' urine – which was exactly how the now yellow drinking water tasted. Mimicking the rats, the men too had gnawed at the timbers and chewed on sawdust. As for rats-as-meat, 'they sold for half a ducat if we could catch any'.

The new landfall was Guam, but receiving a hostile reception, they continued west to the islands that would later be christened the Philippines. Here, though there were no spices, the people immediately recognised the spice samples that Magellan, like other navigators, presented for inspection. There was ceramic evidence of contact with China. Moreover Enrique, Magellan's manservant, found some fellow Malay-speakers and was able to act as interpreter. Clearly this was indeed Asia; the Spice Islands must be close at hand. But the relief seems to have made Magellan and his men light-headed. Weakened and possibly deranged by their sufferings, instead of hastening south to the Moluccas, they stayed on in Zzubu (Cebu) to oversee the mass conversion of the islanders. Crosses were erected, idols destroyed, instruction given, and masses said. The baptismal waters flowed.

Magellan insisted that the conversions must be spontaneous and the confessions of faith sincere. Only one village was burnt; the guns were not to be fired in anger. But that did not preclude offering assistance to Zzubu's now Christian king in a feud with his still pagan neighbour. With as many of his men as could fight, Magellan sailed to the offending island and waded ashore. In the ensuing battle, the enemy aimed their fire at Iberian legs, these being unencased in armour because of the wading. Twice hit in this extensive Achilles' heel, Magellan became separated from his men and finally fell face down in the water. 'On this, all at once rushed upon him with lances of iron and bamboo and with...javelins,' says the loyal Antonio Pigafetta, 'so that they slew our mirror, our light, our comfort, and our true guide'.

Among his other virtues, this most valiant and noble captain was more constant in a very high hazard and great affair than ever was any other.

He endured hunger better than any of the others. He was a navigator and made sea charts. And that that is true was seen openly, for no other had so much wit, boldness or knowledge to sail once around the world.[15]

The greatest of navigators according to Pigafetta, Magellan was yet no conquistador. The battle, a mischievous and entirely gratuitous distraction, was lost; so were eight of his men. Spanish imperialism in Asia had got off to a disastrous start; and Christian values, already discredited, were about to be further tarnished. Without Magellan, his captains fell to quarrelling again. In a confused struggle the Spanish among them, in league with the now disaffected king of Zzubu, deserted and probably betrayed Magellan's Portuguese following. This meant that when in May 1520 the fleet finally sailed away, there were not enough men to man all three ships. One was therefore burnt. Out of the five ships there now remained only the flagship *Trinidad* and the *Victoria*.

An excursion of doubtful purpose to Brunei in Borneo yielded more strife and some encouragement. They found camphor and a diminutive kind of cinnamon; porcelain tableware and 'bark-rigged' junks confirmed the proximity of China; and pilots who knew the Moluccas were secured. Meanwhile a Basque officer, Sebastiano d'Elcano (del Cano, Delcano), somehow won the confidence of his now overwhelmingly Spanish comrades and emerged as a worthy successor to Magellan. It was under d'Elcano's command that on 6 November 1521 they sighted four islands which the pilot declared to be the long sought Moluccas. 'Wherefore we gave thanks to God and for our great joy discharged all our artillery. It is no wonder that we should be so joyful, for we had suffered travails and perils for the space of twenty-five months less two days in the search for the Moluccas.'[16]

By sad coincidence Francisco Serrão had died, probably of poison, at about the same time as Magellan had been slaughtered in the Philippines. There would be no reunion of old friends in Ternate. The expedition was now unequivocally Spanish, while Ternate was seen as a Portuguese, and so hostile, dependency. Anxiety over Magellan's venture had already prompted Lisbon to order the building of a fort there; and the installation of a Portuguese 'governor' was imminent.

D'Elcano and the Spaniards therefore made for the neighbouring island of Tidore. The sultan of Tidore being both a relative and rival of the Ternate sultan, he appreciated the value of foreign guns and know-how. The newcomers, with their contempt for Portuguese pretensions, seemed like a God-sent counterweight. D'Elcano was therefore warmly welcomed. The sultan declared himself a vassal of Spain; the Spanish were to treat his island as their home; indeed it *was* their home, for had he not just renamed it 'Castile'? Cloves sufficient to load both ships were provided, and the foundations for a lasting Hispano-Tidorean – or 'pan-Castilian' – alliance were laid.

Though the location of the Moluccas in terms of longitude remained unclear, Portugal's eastward progress had finally been overlapped by Spain's westward progress. A line of collision, if not of demarcation, had been established; and it passed straight through the Spice Islands. Lisbon now had a rival for the most valued of spices. And da Gama's round-Africa route faced a challenge from Magellan's round-America route.

12

Blue Water

> Being young, and living idlelye in my native Countrie, some-
> times applying myself to the reading of Histories and straunge
> adventures wherein I tooke no small delight, I found myself so
> much addicted to see and travaile into straunge countries,
> thereby to seeke some adventure, that in the end I determined
> to satisfy myself and…to take the matter upon me, trusting in
> God that he would further my intent.
>
> Jan Huyghen van Linschoten's Itinerary, 1595[1]

ON 18 DECEMBER 1521 the remnants of Magellan's expedition –
perhaps half of the original 250 men – paid fond farewells to
their Moluccan hosts and prepared to sail. The *Victoria* stood out into
deep water and awaited the *Trinidad* before hoisting sail. She waited,
then waited some more. Both of the Spanish vessels were so loaded
with cloves that their timbers visibly bulged, and in the case of the
Trinidad this had caused the anchor to foul the hull and puncture it.
The hole was below the water-line. 'We heard the water entering it
as if through a pipe, but we could not find the place where it entered,'
says Pigafetta.[2] In some embarassment Captain d'Elcano ordered a
return to port and a hasty revision of plans.

Originally both vessels were to have continued west across the
Indian Ocean and round the Cape of Good Hope to Spain, so completing the circumnavigation. Now, with the *Trinidad* needing extensive carpentry and with the archipelago's short-lived westerlies about
to give way to its prevailing easterlies, this would not be possible.
Instead it was decided that the *Victoria* should depart immediately and
complete the world's circuit alone; the *Trinidad*, once seaworthy, could

avail herself of the change of wind and sail back by the Pacific. It was accepted that she could not withstand another wintry buffeting in the Magellan Strait. She was therefore to keep to the warmer climes and gentler breezes along the equator and make for Darien on the Panama isthmus. There transshipment of her cargo to the Gulf of Mexico and the hold of a homeward-bound vessel could be arranged for what would be the first spices ever to reach Europe from the west.

But this plan also failed, the winds of the equatorial Pacific proving consistently adverse. The easterlies quickly died and, as food and water ran low, the *Trinidad*'s scorbutic crew found themselves tacking extravagantly and getting nowhere in the middle of a briny nothing. Magellan, sailing east to west, had been well served by the north-east trades; crossing the Pacific from Asia to America was a very different matter and virtually impossible in such latitudes. Only in the 1560s, after much trial and error, would the problem be overcome by making a loop high into the northern hemisphere.

The *Trinidad*, denied a westward escape and now an eastward one, headed sadly back to Tidore. By then seven months had elapsed, and in the interim Portuguese claims to the Spice Islands had acquired some substance. A new governor was ensconced in Ternate where, hard by the royal township of Gammalamma, a fortified *feitoria*, or 'castle', was under construction. Tidore was in nominal submission to Ternate, and the few Spaniards left there by d'Elcano had been rounded up and sent for trial in Goa. A similar fate now awaited those who had survived the *Trinidad*'s latest Pacific outing. Of her perhaps sixty men, only two would ever reach Europe; the ship herself was a write-off.

King Charles of Spain, who in 1519 had become the Holy Roman Emperor Charles V, would not be discouraged by the news. With an imperial inheritance that stretched somewhat patchily from Sicily to Holland, he had other concerns; and anyway d'Elcano had just brought the *Victoria* safely home to Seville. Half of Christendom celebrated this sensational proof of the earth's sphericity; even the other half was impressed, with Lisbon registering a strong protest while it awaited confirmation of the Moluccan episode from its governor in Ternate. When this finally came in 1524, João III, who had succeeded King Manuel three years earlier, moved quickly to the negotiating table.

The table chosen was in fact a bridge between two small towns (hence the 'Badajoz–Elvas' negotiations), one on each side of the Spain–Portugal border. In the alfresco setting, the discussions took the form of a diplomatic tournament wherein honour was staunchly upheld but accord proved elusive. This was despite some distinguished players. For Spain there sallied forth to Badajoz Ferdinand Columbus, the explorer's son; Sebastian Cabot, formerly resident in England but of Genoese descent and now in Spanish employ; and Sebastiano d'Elcano of the Magellan expedition. For Portugal, Diogo Lopes de Sequeira of the first Melaka expedition put in an appearance. All shed lustre on the proceedings but little light; so did Ptolemy, who received a generous airing. And to cap it all, in what must rank as one of the most far-fetched suggestions in the history of procrastination, the Spanish proposed adjournment to the west Pacific for an on-site demarcation. It was that sort of occasion, a meeting not just of anxious adversaries but of ancient and modern, of the practical and the pre-posterous, in which science was invited to clarify medieval conceits while mystified circumnavigators thumbed classical texts looking for oceans that were not there. Though historically interesting, Badajoz–Elvas changed nothing. Basically neither side was willing to abandon its claim to the clove-rich Moluccas until their location in terms of the Tordesillas division had been convincingly established.

Nonetheless, following Charles's 1526 marriage to the Portuguese infanta, relations warmed, and in 1529 an agreement of sorts was duly signed at Saragossa (Zaragoza). Under its terms Spain accepted 350,000 ducats for ceding all claims to the Moluccas. That much was clear. But whether this was in perpetuity or merely until such time as science could pronounce on the matter is uncertain. 'The exact meaning of the Treaty of Saragossa is hard to determine,' writes Donald Lach.[3] Since the ducats were to be refunded if Portugal's rights were upheld, it might be supposed that, if Spain's rights were upheld, the whole controversy would be reopened. The Spanish claim to the Moluccas had seemingly been pawned, not sold; the possibility of its redemption therefore remained. Mercifully, this option was never taken up, for science would indeed find for Portugal. But the 1580 union of the two Iberian crowns would dispose of the refund question; and anyway Spanish retention of the Philippines, which lie north and slightly west of the Moluccas, would render the whole notion of a clean-cut demarcation along a straight line of longitude impossible.

Meanwhile back in Seville the cargo of the *Victoria*, the sole survivor of Magellan's expedition, had long since been sold. The profits realised from her single loading of about 26 tons of cloves covered all the costs (including the three lost ships) of the entire Magellan expedition and left a modest surplus to be divided among the investors. The finest spices might be the furthest and the fewest, but they were also the most rewarding. Despite determined Portuguese opposition, a heavy loss of ships, and a flagrant breach of the Saragossa agreement to do nothing of the sort, Spanish fleets would continue to make sporadic visits to the clove islands and would still be a factor to reckon with when the English and Dutch arrived on the scene eighty years later.

Less noticed at the time, there was also a navigational dividend from the last leg of the Magellan expedition. Arguably d'Elcano's return voyage had pioneered a whole new spice route. For just as da Gama had outflanked the Red Sea–Mediterranean route by opening a passage round Africa, so d'Elcano had outflanked the Melaka–Goa–Africa route by pioneering a southern passage across the Indian Ocean. Once tightly tied to trans-isthmian portages, then loosely looped between peninsular entrepôts, the spice route was finally breaking free of all landward support and going blue-water.

Admittedly the new route was relevant only to spice shipments from Indonesia and would not be much used until some time later. The Portuguese preferred to operate to and from Goa and to use Melaka as their entrepôt for the Moluccas; they ventured south of the equator only when they had to – like rounding the Cape. Meanwhile vessels of other nations remained barred from the Indian Ocean by those papal bulls awarding the navigation and conquest of the eastern hemisphere exclusively to Portugal. The bulls, however unsatisfactory their wording, would remain uncontested until papal authority was itself roundly rejected by the cash-strapped and pro-Reformation English monarchy and by the more maritime and Calvinist of the Dutch provinces.

The magnitude of d'Elcano's discovery also went uncelebrated because it was not matched by much public detail. Antonio Pigafetta, the Venetian whose devotion to Magellan resulted in a popular narrative of the voyage that is second to none, seems to have lost interest in bold deeds and uncharted waters soon after the *Victoria*'s departure from the Moluccas. From Tidore, Pigafetta was to have sailed home in the *Trinidad* but was permitted to transfer to the *Victoria* after the incident with the anchor; he ought therefore to have been grateful. Yet he portrays the return voyage as a formality and gives d'Elcano not a mention, as if his name were unworthy to share quill and vellum with 'our mirror, our light, our comfort'. Instead of the usually acute and enlightened observations of peoples and places for which he is revered, the Italian belies his Renaissance credentials with a jumble of extravagant hearsay that would not have been out of place in the *Book* of his fellow citizen Marco Polo.

D'Elcano's two main concerns on leaving Tidore had been to evade detection by the Portuguese and to make the speediest possible return voyage; the first precluded using the Malacca Strait or entering Indian waters, while the second posed the question of whether a sub-equatorial routing direct from the Indonesian islands to the Atlantic was feasible. To men who had just crossed the Pacific it was. Empty seas were their element and the Southern Cross was their friend. The *Victoria* therefore headed south, recrossed the equator keeping the Banda Islands well to the east, and via the Alor Strait cut through the long island arc of eastern Indonesia to Timor. Except for possibly grazing the coast of north-west Australia – an eventuality that, had it occurred, might have had interesting repercussions – there now lay nothing but open ocean between them and the Cape.

Faced with a probably landless voyage of unknown duration, they provisioned and watered the ship in Timor. Pigafetta gathered some dubious information on the cutting of sandalwood, but none of the fragrant timber was loaded; the hold was already full of Tidore's cloves. Besides, they dare not tarry. Here, as on the west coast of India, the 'Frankish disease' was rife; and where there was syphilis, there too were Europeans, presumably Portuguese.

> On Tuesday night drawing toward Wednesday the eleventh day of February, one thousand five hundred and twenty-two, having departed from the island of Timor, we entered the great sea called Laut Chidol ['South Sea'], and laying course between west and southwest we left

on our right hand towards the north (for fear of the king of Portugal) the island of Zamatra [Sumatra]...In order to round the Cape of Good Hope we went as far south as forty-two degrees towards the Antarctic Pole. We remained near the Cape for seven weeks with sails furled because of the north and northwest wind on our bow, and in a very great storm.[4]

This is all Pigafetta has to say of the first recorded sub-equatorial crossing of the Indian Ocean. He does not even mention how long it took. Instead, both before and within this extract, he regales his readers with a selection of those voyeuristic yarns, as old as the spice route itself, of freakish peoples and improbable fauna. Here again is the Amazon island where the women become pregnant by the wind and kill all males, whether offspring or outsiders; here too are the pygmies and the cannibals and the little people with ears so big 'that of one they make the bed and with the other they cover themselves'. In his story of the giant bird that can lift an elephant there is an echo of Herodotus' account of the Arabian vultures and the cinnamon sticks, not to mention the accounts by Sindbad and Marco Polo of the colossal roc. Pigafetta's birds inhabit a colossal tree whose fruit they likewise distribute throughout adjacent lands by casually dropping it on handy beaches. In the interests of science he gives the Malay name for the tree in question and describes the fruit as 'bigger than a cucumber'. A respected observer who has occasionally been dubbed one of the founding fathers of anthropology, Pigafetta makes one other concession to the times: the more improbable yarns are, he concedes, 'what the pilot says'. No doubt it was from just such informants that Marco Polo and his ilk obtained their material.

After seven weeks battling the gales off the Cape of the Good Hope, the *Victoria* was in a sorry state. Many argued for putting ashore at Mozambique and throwing themselves on the mercies of its Portuguese *feitoria*; 'but others, more mindful of their honour than their own life, determined to go for Spain dead or alive.' They scorned the shore and pressed on.

Another twenty-one died before they reached the Cape Verde Islands; the rest were now starving. Though the islands were Portuguese, honour here yielded to exigency. A boat was sent ashore to obtain rice and, going back for a second load, its thirteen-man crew was arrested. It was thus that only eighteen of the sixty men who had left Tidore nine months earlier brought the *Victoria* to anchor off the Seville river. But the unlucky thirteen in the Cape Verde Islands were eventually released; and with the two from the *Trinidad* plus those who had turned back at the Magellan Strait, about eighty of the 250 who had originally set forth with Magellan returned to Spain.

Pigafetta claims to have kept up his diary throughout their three years (less a month) away. He was therefore puzzled when, landing at the Cape Verde Islands on a Wednesday, the Portuguese insisted that it was Thursday. 'We knew not how we had fallen into error.' Only subsequently was he relieved to learn that 'there had been no mistake'. The explanation, as he understood it, was that 'we had always made our voyage westward and had returned to the same place of departure as the sun, wherefore the long voyage had brought the gain of twenty-four hours, as is clearly seen.'[5] Pigafetta was impressed by this theft of a day. Clearly seen or not, the calendar as well as the map was beginning to look more manageable. Time, like distance, was susceptible to human enquiry; the plod of history, like the sprawl of geography, beckoned the impatient.

The Magellan/d'Elcano circumnavigation of the world would not be repeated for over fifty years. Spanish ships reaching the Moluccas usually did so from the Philippines or Mexico and returned to the Americas, if they returned at all, by way of the Pacific. A trickle of cloves made its way to the New World by this route and even on to Europe. But all other spices continued to flow west, and for most of the sixteenth century Portugal's control of the westward spice route remained uncontested by other European powers.

This supremacy did not, however, confer control of the spice trade. Contrary to early Portuguese conceits and to much popular history ever since, Lisbon never controlled the trade. The Portuguese crown claimed a monopoly of the maritime traffic in spices, but this was little respected after the early years of the sixteenth century and was rarely effective for more than a few monsoons at a time. Asian shipping quickly found ways of eluding the *cartaz* regime, often with the collusion of Portuguese officials either trading on their own behalf or covertly peddling exemptions. Whoever held Melaka did not, as

Tome Pires had forecast, find his hand on the throat of Venice; much of the time he barely had his hand on the Malacca Strait. Nor were Cairo and Mecca 'entirely ruined' by Melaka's capture, as supposed by Albuquerque. On the contrary, once the initial shock of the Portuguese presence in the Indian Ocean had worn off, trade via the Red Sea route to Mecca, Cairo, Alexandria and Venice revived. Venetian merchants were largely spared the indignity of having to repair to Lisbon for the purchase of spices, and their republic continued to bask in its fading glories throughout the sixteenth century. The Doge's Palace was substantially rebuilt in 1574–5 following a fire; the Rialto Bridge as we know it today was not constructed until 1590.

Writing in 1560, the Portuguese ambassador to the papal court had it on good authority that 'there come to Alexandria each year forty thousand quintals of spices, being pepper for the most part'. All came via the Red Sea which, following the Ottoman conquest of Egypt and then Aden, was now a Turkish lake. Moreover forty thousand quintals, the equivalent of about 2,000 tonnes, equalled Alexandria's spice imports in the pre-Portuguese 1490s and slightly exceeded the level of Lisbon's current imports. Da Gama must have been turning in his grave. As the ambassador put it, 'there being so much which comes to the dominion of the Turks, it is no wonder so little comes to Lisbon'.[6] The Estado da India, while it appeared to be gorging itself on spices, was haemorrhaging them just as copiously.

This is not to say that Portugal's impact on the trade, and on its rerouting of it, was insignificant. Scholars warn that the 1560s may have been the short-lived peak of an otherwise unsensational revival in the Red Sea–Levant route.[7] Spices passing through Alexandria were not all destined for Europe; several thousand quintals may have been consigned to the Ottoman lands. And the quantity may not have reflected their value. Prices tended to soar when Portuguese control was most effective but to tumble when it was most lax; if, as seems to be the case, the Portuguese increasingly concentrated on the finer high-value spices, Alexandria's forty thousand quintals of 'pepper for the most part' may have been worth only a fraction of Lisbon's trade.

One thing was clear though: the European demand for most spices was escalating. There were exceptions. Arabian and Somali incense now commanded only an ecclesiastical sale and, thanks to the

Reformation, would lose much of that. The perfumer's requirement for nards, balsams and gum-resins was also limited. Similarly that bewildering range of exotica sought by the druggist and the apothecary could make no great impact on a trade expressed in *bahars* (600 pounds/270 kg), quintals (hundredweights) and tonnes. Spices might retain their supposedly medicinal properties but pharmacology's requirements were better served by specialist retailers. This estrangement from the bulk trade in spices would be marked in London by the 1617 breakaway of the Apothecaries Society from the Grossers' (or Grocers') Company. Originally the Pepperers' Company, the Grossers' had been renamed in the fifteenth century to reflect both the City's growing trade in spices and the Livery Company's role in their 'grossing', or wholesaling. In England 'grossery' then diversified into related commodities, like sugar, and so into general provisioning. It also opted for the alternative spelling of 'grocery'. A similar development occurred in France, although there grocers retained their original designation as spicers – *épiciers*; hence the still familiar *épicerie*.

Dyes, like brazil-wood and indigo, a vetch-like plant from north India, came to feature more prominently in import manifests, but it was the edible spices that proved much the most susceptible to rising demand. For all practical purposes, spices now meant just vegetable condiments and alimentary additives, among which in terms of quantity, pepper (and to a lesser extent ginger), and in terms of value, cinnamon, cloves, nutmeg and mace dwarfed all others. For these demand rose steadily throughout the fifteenth and sixteenth centuries, thanks in part to the growth in Europe's population and in part to the growth in disposable wealth and to its wider distribution. Then in the early seventeenth century it soared dramatically thanks to the increased supply and falling prices occasioned by Dutch and English shipments.

This would prove a mixed blessing. As pepper-pots assumed their place at the centre of even humble tables, *piper nigrum* began its fall from grace. Sprinkled on everything from porter to porridge, it lost its air of distinction and became an unexciting domestic staple. By ancient association it would remain a spice, but the term 'spice' would itself thereby be devalued. A commodity of such well-known provenance, unsubtle properties, bulk supply and increasingly affordable price could no longer lay claim to any romance. As is the way, mass demand demeaned.

This explosion in pepper use presupposed an elasticity in production that was by no means true of all spices. Cloves and cinnamon were still largely gathered from the wild; the trees took years to get established and the idea of managing their cultivation or transplanting seedlings elsewhere was as yet a novelty. Nutmeg trees, which produced their heaviest yield as mature specimens of alder-size, were almost never cultivated. The finer spices therefore remained firmly rooted to their native localities and supply could only gradually be increased by more extensive harvesting. Pepper was different. Easily transplanted given favourable conditions, it obligingly twined itself up any host, whether tree or post, bore berries within a couple of years and continued to do so for another twelve years. During the fifteenth and sixteenth centuries more pepper gardens were established in the Malabar hills and production there certainly increased, although by no means all of it found its way down to the coast to meet the foreign demand.

Much more important in meeting this growing demand, and so in determining the future of the spice route, was the rapidly increasing pepper yield of Sumatra and western Java. As noted, black pepper had first made its appearance in Sumatra in the thirteenth century. From the few gardens in the hills behind the north Sumatran ports of Pasei and Pidie (Pedir) as reported by Cheng-ho, cultivation had gradually spread to the whole of what is now Aceh province, then right down the island's long west coast and across the Sunda Strait to Java.

In the course of the sixteenth century the sultanate of Aceh rose to supremacy throughout northern Sumatra on this tide of pepper. Cause and effect are hard to disentangle; probably pepper-based prosperity both enticed the Acehnese advance and sustained it. Pasei and Pedir were subjugated, then the vast Minangkabau region that stretches above the west coast. New pepper ports were opened and Aceh's sultans grew both rich and powerful. From Melaka the Portuguese looked askance at the rise of this Muslim power on their doorstep but failed to assemble the forces necessary to challenge it. Rather did the Acehnese fleet repeatedly threaten Melaka and harass Portuguese shipping in the Malacca Strait.

It was this Sumatran pepper, rather than that of Malabar, that was mainly responsible for the revival of the Red Sea trade. By 1565, according to a Venetian source, 'about fifty ships a year' were sailing from 'Assi' (presumably Aceh) to the Red Sea;[8] and by the end of the century the Acehnese 'were exporting much more pepper to Jiddah than the Portuguese were taking round the Cape to Lisbon'.[9] The ships working this route were mostly owned by Gujerati Muslims but did not necessarily call at Gujerati ports. To give the Portuguese in Sri Lanka and Malabar the widest possible berth, they sailed from Aceh to the Maldive Islands and thence direct to Aden. A new Islamic axis across the Indian Ocean developed, and along it close religious and military ties were forged between Aceh, Arabia and Ottoman Egypt. The Sumatran sultanate thereby acquired a formidable arsenal of cannon, some Turkish troops and much diplomatic encouragement. Far from Asian competitors being eliminated, at least one major rival was successfully using the proceeds of the spice trade to challenge Portuguese hegemony.

Where an Asian power could prosper, so too could European inter-lopers. Goa's failure to deal with the Acehnese reflected the weakness of the Portuguese position throughout the East and especially in the archipelago. Sumatran pepper, like the ill-secured cloves of the Moluccas, positively invited the attentions of European enemies. And of these, in the second half of the sixteenth century, there were many.

In a Christendom sundered by the Reformation, those who believed the pope to be the anti-Christ needed no excuse for contesting rights of 'navigation, conquest' and so on based on papal authority, nor for challenging the Catholic powers who enjoyed them. Spain, the oppressor of the Protestant cause in the Netherlands, was a prime target; Portugal, particularly after its dynastic union with Spain in 1580, was another. In the Atlantic, the Caribbean and then the Pacific and the East, the ravenous sea-dogs of Elizabeth's England and of the about-to-be United Provinces of the Netherlands enjoyed good hunting and rich pickings. War and peace made little difference. Yesterday's admiral became today's privateer. The royal standard was lowered yet royal approval was still needed and the sovereign usually took a cut of the profits; doctrinal differences did the rest, sanctioning, even sanctifying, outrages that would today be accounted acts of the most contemptible terrorism and that then, as now, elicited out-raged cries for vengeance.

State-sponsored and Church-blessed, the perpetrators needed no excuse, just a navy; and in this respect the insurgent Dutch provinces and an assertive Tudor England were well placed. Both possessed modern merchant marines and much navigational experience gained from trade and fishing on the Atlantic seaboard and from exploration directed towards the discovery of a northern passage. Equivalent to the new-found routes round Africa and South America, a north-west passage round Canada or a north-east one round Russia would reward God-fearing Protestants with their own sea-way to the spicy Orient. Sheer symmetry, a concept still beloved of geographers, along with the growing conviction that every land mass must be an island, posi-tively demanded the existence of these northern passages. But wooden ships and leather buskins being no match for polar seas and icy winters, the passages eluded discovery. Frobisher and Davis got no further than Labrador, Willoughby, Chancellor and Barents no further than Novaya Zemlaya and the Kara Sea. The search went on; but for many, including John Davis and Jan Huyghen van Linschoten, the existing routes to the East offered an easier option.

The first to try them was Francis Drake. Following in the trans-Pacific wake of Magellan and d'Elcano, the *Golden Hind* blew into the Moluccas for a one-week stay in late 1579. Unlike Magellan's circum-navigation, Drake's contributed little to geographical knowledge and was prompted neither by trade nor spices. The attraction was Spain's bonanza of gold and silver in the Americas, and an Englishman's only trade there was piracy. On rounding Patagonia, Drake had quibbled with Magellan's naming of the Pacific. 'Called by some *mare pacificum* but proving to us to be more *mare furiosum*', it had greeted its first English visitors with an 'eccliptical' tempest that scattered his fleet and left the *Golden Hind* to fend for herself. Thereafter the fury was entirely of Drake's own making. By the time his men sighted the Moluccas, there lay behind them a trail of smouldering ports and bat-tered galleons that stretched from Chile to California and the Philippines. The ship was already awash with Mexican gold, Peruvian silver and Chilean wine. Any Moluccan spices loaded on top of this loot would be as icing on the cake. 'There are foure high piked Ilands', says the author of *The World Encompassed*, who was probably Drake himself; 'their names Terenate, Tidore, Matchan, Batchan, all of them very fruitfull and yeelding abundance of cloves, whereof wee furnished our selves of as much as we desired at a very cheape rate.'[10]

Presumably on information gleaned from Pigafetta, Drake had headed for Tidore rather than risk an encounter with the Portuguese on Ternate. But his progress towards it had been arrested by a 'canow' paddled out with fresher news: apparently the Portuguese had been ejected from Ternate and were now holed up in Tidore. Tweedledee had become Tweedledum, and for this detail Drake was deeply indebted, resolving, as he put it, 'to run with Terenate'. In the course of glittering receptions and gratifying exchanges, he was handsomely rewarded. As well as the cloves, he received from Sultan Baab a signet-ring together with what the English would regard as a binding pledge that Ternate's 'traffique and commodities' would henceforth be 'sequestered from others, especially from his [the sultan's] enemies the Portugals' and 'reserved to the intercourse of our Nation, if we would embrace it'.[11] This 'treaty', says one authority, 'was regarded as an achievement surpassing the capture of Spanish treasure'.[12]

Time had clearly done the Portuguese no favours. Fifty years of sporadic warfare with the Moluccan islanders, of continuous intrigue, suicidal in-fighting and casual oppression had left this extremity of the *estado* hanging by a thread. For much of the time Gammalamma Castle had been under siege; in 1575 it had been surrendered; and now it was occupied by the affable Sultan Baab and his innumerable dependants. Meanwhile the Portuguese and a few stranded Spaniards were barely able to hang on to little Tidore. Drake's visit spoke for itself: the Portuguese presence in the Moluccas was negligible, cloves 'cheape', and the islands' leading sultan eager for English trade.

From the Moluccas, Drake, like d'Elcano, steered for the open waters of the Indian Ocean. His route is not entirely clear but at first ran close to Sulawesi, where a near-disaster on a reef occasioned frantic sermonising and much subsequent repair-work. The *Golden Hind* then passed into the Indian Ocean, probably through the Lombok Strait east of Bali. Water and provisions were loaded on the south coast of Java. There Drake's musicians gave several performances and were joined by a gamelan ensemble. No Portuguese encounters are reported in *The World Encompassed*. Vessels plying between Melaka and the Spice Islands usually passed north of the island and occasionally called at ports on that coast. But Java's south coast was unknown to the Portuguese, who still imagined the island to be not string-like but square. Some even supposed it not an island at all but an extremity of Ptolemy's southern continent, 'which shoulde reach from that place to the Cape [of Good Hope]'.[13] In which case d'Elcano and now Drake would have been trapped.

Drake's voyage ended back at Plymouth on 26 September 1580 (or the 27th 'in the just and ordinary reckoning of those who had stayed at home in one place'). Its sensational success, not to mention his personal enrichment and knighthood, inspired imitation. In 1582 Edward Fenton sailed for the Moluccas on what should have been England's first west–east voyage to the Indies. But Fenton never even reached the Cape of Good Hope. His colleagues preferred the richer pickings to be found along the South American coast; the exploration of the spice route was aborted.

Drake likewise resumed his depredations in the Atlantic. In 1587, fresh from a bonfire of Spanish shipping in Cadiz with the smell of singed beard still in his nostrils, he overpowered a Portuguese Indiaman in the Azores. As a 'carrack', the name given to the now 1,000-ton-plus *naus*, the ease of her taking was as much a revelation as her cargo, which, mostly pepper and other spices, was valued at £140,000. As the richest prize on record, it served as a timely reminder that spices in quantity could be as rewarding as Spanish gold. Richard Hakluyt, the contemporary chronicler, marvelled more that English ships were now a match for any; 'carracks were no such bugs that [they] might be taken,' he wrote.[14] But bug-hunting carried risks, not least that of so troubling the hive as to provoke a swarm. The Spanish fleet, long abuzz, duly streamed forth, 130 strong, in the summer of 1588.

News of the Spanish Armada and of its defeat by the unfancied English caused an international sensation and was known even in the Moluccas within eighteen months. It also rather obscured another achievement. Only weeks after the English triumph, while the English Channel was still littered with Spanish wrecks, the world's third circumnavigator narrowly missed the returning Spanish flagship and slipped quietly into Plymouth. This was Thomas Cavendish, whose 'compassing' of the world had been inspired by Drake's feat and whose routing and exploits had closely mirrored it.

> I have either discovered or brought certaine intelligence of all the rich places of the world that ever were knowne...I burnt and sunk nine-teene sayles of ships small and great. All the villages and townes that ever I landed at, I burnt and spoyled...I sayled along the Islands of the Malucos, where among some of the heathen people I was well entreated, [and] where our countreymen may have trade as freely as the Portugals, if they will. From thence I passed by the Cape [of Good Hope], and found out by the way homeward the Island of S. Helena, where the Portugals relieve themselves.[15]

To avoid Melaka, Cavendish had cut through the Indonesian archipelago by the Sunda Strait between Sumatra and Java. He too had then provisioned on the south coast of Java and had there been accosted by two Portuguese anxious to relieve themselves – not in this case of dire want but of some highly treasonable thoughts. When Philip II of Spain had inherited the Portuguese crown, a rival claimant called Dom Antonio had fled to England and then France. Half-hearted attempts to use Dom Antonio's claim as a diversionary tactic against the Spanish had failed, but the pretender enjoyed some support in far-flung corners of the Portuguese *estado*, including apparently the extreme East. Indeed, according to Cavendish's informants, 'if Dom Antonio would come unto them', he might have at his command 'the Malucos, China, Sangles [Japan?] and the Isles of the Philippinas'. To anyone of adventurous mind, the news of potential allies awaiting their Portuguese pretender provided further reason for a trial of the spice route.

Perhaps so encouraged, a year after Cavendish's return petitioners sought from Queen Elizabeth permission for another voyage into Asian waters by the Cape route. The ships to be used belonged to London merchants engaged in the trade with the Levant. Spices were their business; and because of falling Portuguese imports – no pepper at all would reach Lisbon in 1591 because of shipping losses – prices were currently high enough to make at least a reconnaissance desirable. The royal permission was given and the fleet left in 1591.

It experienced nothing but disaster. Of its three ships not one would certainly complete the voyage and of its 198 men barely fifty would survive. Most of these were aboard a ship sent back from the Cape crammed with invalids; scurvy had overtaken them as they lay becalmed in the Atlantic. The next vessel was lost with all hands in a storm somewhere off Madagascar. And the last, though she did reach the Malacca Strait – albeit minus half her crew after a battle with the Comoros Islanders – was lost when she drifted from her moorings in the West Indies during the return voyage. No trade had been attempted. The only gains were ill-gotten ones, mostly at the expense of Indian and Burmese shipping; and even these had probably been lost when the final vessel drifted out of reach. (Whether she eventually sank, was taken by the French, or was 'worked home from Newfoundland' by 'five men and a boy' is unclear.[16])

Another voyage, in 1596, was even more disastrous; no one at all returned. That made three consecutive catastrophes. The first English attempts to reach the East could well have been the last. Spices, though theoretically profitable, were occasioning only heavy losses; investors shied away, and mariners turned again to happier hunting grounds across the Atlantic. But James Lancaster, the skipper of the vessel that had reached the West Indies, remained bullish. Five years later it would be he who commanded the first fleet to be despatched by the English East India Company. And for that momentous venture the inspiration would be provided not by London's requiems for its lost fleets but by Amsterdam's hallelujahs for their more profitable Dutch counterparts.

How a few seafaring but semi-submerged provinces of the northern Netherlands found the resources to explore and capture the spice trade beggars easy understanding. At the time Holland, Zeeland and their neighbours were in the midst of an eighty-year life-and-death struggle for secession from the Hapsburg–Spanish empire. This struggle contained elements of both a religious war and a republican revolution, yet its projectors lacked even the cohesion of a shared nationhood. The southern provinces were buckling under the Spanish assault; the northern ones were too jealous of their independence to form more than a loose federation. Commandeering the most remote and demanding of all long-distance freight routes ought not to have been a high priority. Nor would it seem to have been a practical proposition.

Historians address this conundrum with gusto. The Dutch economy is said to have been unique. Up to a point it mimicked those of the Italian city-states in being highly responsive and flexible, the result of relying more on the quicksilver of exchange than on the entrenched instincts of a well-landed gentry. The commercial revolution pioneered in Venice was imitated in Amsterdam. There too practices and institutions were adopted to manage the risks and speed the transactions inherent in commerce; stock issues, insurance, reinsurance, various banking services and, inevitably, 'double-entry bookkeeping' are cited. Yet the Dutch economy was different in that it was run by an expanding bourgeoisie that included manufacturers and tradesmen as well as commercial and financial interests.

As for its overseas dimension, the merchant fleets of Holland and Zeeland already dominated trade from the Baltic to the Mediterranean. Their ships, especially the sailing barges known as *fluits* or 'flytes', were easy to build and economic to operate; and as major distributors of Lisbon's imports, the Dutch ports had experience of the spice trade second only to that of Venice. As for the loss of the southern provinces of the Netherlands, it was actually a bonus; from especially Antwerp the exodus of merchants, bankers and capital elevated Amsterdam into the business hub of northern Europe and created a nexus of Dutch trading-houses throughout Europe. Conversely the diaspora of Iberia's Jews prompted by the Inquisition brought to the independent Netherlands a dynamic community of scholars, artisans and scientists.

History manages well without such things as the agency of personality, the attribution of national character, or the action of capricious fate. But in the case of the spice trade, these unfashionable considerations should not be discounted. If method and purpose may be taken as characteristic of the emerging Dutch state, a decisive factor behind its participation in the spice trade was the return to Holland in 1592 of Jan Huyghen van Linschoten and the 1595 publication of his three-part *Itinerary*.

At the time Portuguese paranoia about information on its Estado da India falling into foreign hands had somewhat abated. Tome Pires' great tome *The Suma Oriental* remained under lock and key; but either in abbreviated form or *in toto*, the works of Barbosa, Correa, Camoes, de Barros, da Orta and others were now available. From these the curious might learn something of the geography, history and productions of the East and much about the heroism of Portugal's pioneers. But what were still not generally available were the navigational *roteiros* (sailing instructions) and the charts compiled and used by Portuguese mariners. Nor was there any work that depicted the sorry condition to which corruption, inadequate resources and an ineffective administration had reduced the *estado*.

It was these which van Linschoten made public. Sallying forth from Enkhuisen on the Zuider Zee, the teenage van Linschoten had gone to Spain, then Portugal, and had there taken ship to Goa in the employ of its incumbent Archbishop of the Indies. There was nothing underhand in this. Van Linschoten was a Catholic and, while Europeans of many nationalities served in the Portuguese Indies, he probably saw rather less of the East than most. For six years (1583–9) he scarcely moved from Goa. His avowed thirst for 'travaile into straunge countries' and 'adventure' can scarcely have been satisfied. But in Goa he did have access to written materials and to informants beyond the reach of most travellers. He also made copious notes of all he read, saw and heard. To suppose that he did so purely for personal interest would be naive. Like Ludovico di Varthema, Jan Huyghen van Linschoten was well aware of the value of his observations. He too was in the business of espionage.

The first Dutch fleet to the Indies sailed under the command of Cornelis de Houten in 1595. This was a year after James Lancaster's return made the failure of the second English expedition public and a year before the publication of van Linschoten's complete *Itinerary*. But while Lancaster's experience offered no encouragement, van Linschoten's information and advocacy were critical. By 1595 he had been back in Holland for two years. His brains had been picked, his reports heeded, and his great work was probably written. Certainly the two of its three parts that dealt with routes and navigation were familiar to de Houten. Likewise were the maps which would be incorporated in the book. Combining a wide range of sources, they would be a revelation to all but map-makers and depicted especially the Indonesian archipelago 'more acurately and in greater detail than any other printed map'.[17] Whether in person, in manuscript, or in print, van Linschoten had already lifted the veil of secrecy from Portugal's sea-routes, and his great work was well on its way to becoming 'the navigator's *vade mecum* for Eastern seas'.[18]

More specifically, van Linschoten drew attention to the western end of the island of Java. The area was highly productive, especially of pepper which was apparently of better quality and in greater quantity than that of Malabar. Moreover 'the Portingales come not thether'. Instead, the Javanese usually transported the pepper to Melaka themselves. Anyone attaining west Java's principal port of Sunda Kelapa would be able to buy at a better price and without Portuguese interference. Nor would it be necessary to run the gauntlet of the Malacca Strait. For as van Linschoten reminded his readers, 'Thomas Candish [Cavendish], an Inglish captaine', had found a way round this obstacle by passing into the Indian Ocean via the 'Sunda straighte' between Java and Sumatra.[19]

Here, then, was a plausible proposal backed by navigational directions and with a specific objective. Unlike earlier English voyages, van Linschoten's suggestion did not rely on chance prize-taking and might therefore evade Portuguese retaliation. Less an adventure than a business proposition, it appealed to investors and especially to a consortium of Amsterdam merchants who, for this one voyage, called themselves 'The Company for Far Distant Lands'.

De Houten, the fleet's designated commander, followed van Linschoten's directions religiously, if somewhat aggressively. Scurvy took its usual toll in the Atlantic, but after recuperating at the Cape and in Madagascar, de Houten's four ships shaped their course straight for Sunda and arrived safely at the Javanese port of Bantam. This was west of Sunda Kelapa and may have been preferred because it handled pepper from the neighbouring regions of Sumatra as well as from Java itself. Not without opposition from his unruly men, from Portuguese trouble-makers and from the dismayed Javanese, de Houten obtained both a cargo and an agreement about future trade. He cruised along the south coast of Java, so finally obtaining a clear idea of its dimensions, then sailed for home. One vessel had been abandoned and about two-thirds of his men had been lost. But the voyage returned a modest profit and was accounted a success.

A veritable armada of Dutch fleets, each independently financed, then took to the high seas. Within four years (1597–1601) at least sixty-five ships in fourteen fleets sailed from the Netherlands to the East. Some fetched up as far afield as Japan; factories were established at Bantam, in the Bandas, in the Moluccas and elsewhere; two fleets attempted the Pacific route, from where Oliver van Noort returned as the fourth man to command a circumnavigation; and in July 1599 Jakob van Neck brought home from Bantam the four ships laden with spices, mostly pepper, that the artist Hendrick Vroom portrayed in *Return of the Second Dutch Expedition to the East Indies*. This voyage enjoyed instant celebrity and, like the painting, set a high standard for imitators. Profits accruing to its backers in the Oude Compagnie of Amsterdam were estimated at four hundred per cent. Like the Venetian diarist Girolamo Priuli bemoaning the success of da Gama's voyage, a representative of London's Levant Company noted that van Neck's voyage had 'clean overthrown' the trade with the eastern Mediterranean.[20]

Consumed with envy, London could only follow suit. Six weeks after the news arrived from Amsterdam, a consortium of English merchants presented a petition to the queen's privy council. Many of the petitioners were from the Levant Company and already familiar with the spice trade. In proposing the formation of an English East India Company they implicitly recognised that the spice route had changed and that to remain competitive they must imitate the Dutch and develop direct maritime links with the spice-producing countries. The queen hesitated; diplomatic overtures with Spain/Portugal were afoot. But Dutch attempts to hire English ships and poach English navigators (John Davis was already serving as pilot on de Houten's second voyage) decided the matter. On the last day of the year 1600, a charter for 'the Company of Merchants of London trading into the East Indies' received the royal seal.

The London, or English, East India Company despatched its first fleet under James Lancaster's command two months later. A year after that, the numerous Dutch companies were bullied into amalgamation as the Vereenigde Oost-Indische Compagnie, otherwise the VOC or

Dutch 'United East India Company'. Protestant allies in Europe, but soon deadly commercial rivals throughout the East, the two great companies of England and the Netherlands would contest the spice route only briefly. But in doing so they would determine the political fate of the region for three centuries and strip the spice trade of a mystique that had lasted for as many millennia.

13

Infected by Spices

Hence the Warre, so portentuous in the midst of peace, not betwixt the two Nations, their Princes and States (which hold confederacie and amitie), but betwixt our Merchants and theirs, our Mariners and theirs, our Sea-Commanders and theirs; the two Companies in those parts, as it were growing fierce with infection of those fiercer [Eastern] Nations, changing their conditions more than their complexions, putting off with their warmer clothes in that hotter climate their solid vertues, putting on Heathenish qualities with their commerce, putting up fiery ferity with their hot Spices, putting out in great part humanitie, civilitie, Christianitie, in those various Currents and diversified Seas, Shoalds, Ilands.[1]

Revd Samuel Purchas, 1625

NO SHIPS PLIED the spice route loaded only with spices. East–west trade always included a variety of other goods, some of high value like silks, gems and bullion, others of high density like timbers, molasses, metals and minerals. Goods in the latter category, quite apart from their resale potential, were useful in the stowage of the spices, which might otherwise become damaged or contaminate one another, and in the handling of the ship, which might otherwise capsize. How many ships were lost through displacement of the cargo is not known, but complaints of goods being spoiled in transit are common. Whether Asian, Portuguese, English or Dutch, ships needed as much care in the loading as they did in the sailing.

The subject is little discussed in contemporary chronicles, but light has been shed into the hold of one Dutch East Indiaman by the Danish scholar Kristof Glamann, working from documentation in the Colonial Archives of the VOC.[2] At about 300 tons 'burthen', the

Ceulen was smaller than the average vessel engaged in the inter-oceanic trade at the period. She carried forty guns, and when she sailed from Batavia (Jakarta) for Holland in January 1697, her crew numbered 105, to which were added thirty soldiers, five artificers and ten invalids. In-board accommodation for the invalids and officers may have been adequate but everyone else was merely on board, clambering round the vessel like monkeys.

Working from the bottom upwards, the hold of the *Ceulen* contained eight big cast-iron anchors wedged between four hundred chests of Japanese copper, 134 pieces of Siamese tin, 50,000 *ponds* (a *pond* was half a kilogram, slightly more than today's pound) of sappan-wood (brazil-wood), and a hefty 580,000 *ponds* of loose black pepper (which was about the same weight as the ship itself). This was just the ballast. On top came the *Ceulen*'s dunnage (packing or padding) consisting of fourteen hundred bags of saltpetre (used in the manufacture of gunpowder), some more Siamese tin, thirty-two 'whole ahms' (casks?) of ginger and sixteen of nutmeg, six thousand *ponds* of 'tainted nutmegs' and, isolated behind a specially erected bulkhead, 312 bags of cloves and twenty of cardamom.

So much for the dunnage. On top of that was spread the cargo proper in six deep layers that extended fore and aft of the mainmast. The first layer included seventy-five chests of chinaware, seventy-two bags of white pepper, fifty-two chests of benzoin (benjamin) and forty-seven parcels of cottons, also some silk yarn and 'various chests and bags of drugs'. The second and third levels contained much the same but with more textiles; the fourth, fifth and sixth consisted almost entirely of baled cinnamon.

Ballast (except the black pepper), dunnage and cargo were all securely roped to prevent any movement, then the hold was covered and padlocked. But that was not the whole story, for the cabins too were crammed with goods, some or all presumably being the personal investment of individual officers. One cabin held seventeen thousand *ponds* of the best nutmegs, another silks and eleven cases of indigo, another 'a chest of nutmeg cakes, 2 small cases of birds' nests, 1 pot of civet and 15 bales of Chinese tea'. (Civet, used in perfumery, came from the anal gland of a Javanese wild cat; birds' nests, as in the Chinese soup, were those of a cave-loving swiftlet found mostly in Borneo and the Philippines.)

'The cargo of the *Ceulen*,' says Glamann, was 'typical of a large number of the returning ships'. She had not presumably been to the Spice Islands or there would have been more cloves and some mace; and the small quantities of Chinese produce were peculiar to the late seventeenth century, a time at which tea, in particular, was still a novelty, poised between experimental status and its post–1720s emergence as a staple. Otherwise, the *Ceulen*'s loading may be taken as representative of the seventeenth century as a whole.

This mix of goods is confirmed by a chatty entry of earlier date in the diary of Samuel Pepys. As Surveyor-General of Victualling for the English fleet, Pepys had access to prizes taken in battle and seems to have expected a share in them. Rarely, then, can the job have been so congenial as on 16 November 1665 when he descended into the hold of a Dutch Indiaman lately captured by the Earl of Sandwich. There in the half-light, rummaged by the confusion of battle, lay what he reckoned 'the greatest wealth...that a man can see in the world... Pepper [was so] scattered through every chink you trod on it; and in cloves and nutmegs I walked above the knees, whole rooms full. And silk in bales and boxes of copper-plate, one of which I opened.'[3] Pepys was so impressed, he repeated himself: 'as noble a sight as ever I saw in my life.' Like the equally gossipy Ibn Batuta when he first saw peppercorns being weighed by the bushel, the diarist seems to have been impressed by the sheer quantity of the stuff. Normally sold by the ounce, the most precious spices here filled the room-size sections of the hold, while loose pepper lay so deep that you had to scrunch through it.

The spice trade was still buoyant and would continue so throughout the seventeenth century. Steadily rising consumption was not always matched by steadily rising prices, yet profit levels on most spices remained substantial. A crucial change however, was under way: by the 1660s the value of the spice trade relative to that in other eastern imports, especially textiles, was falling dramatically. Between then and the end of the century, although the quantity of spice imports continued to rise, their value fell from being half of the VOC's total import bill to a quarter; and the same was true of the London Company's trade. Pepys was slavering over a declining stock. Spices, once the essence of eastern trade, were being marginalised by other commodities. Cottons and silks were pushing even the finer spices deeper into the hold, where tea, coffee and sugar would eventually swamp them.

It was the inevitable consequence of more shipping being available. In the early 1590s an average of perhaps four Portuguese vessels had returned from the East every year. By 1620 around ten Dutch and English Indiamen, plus whatever the Portuguese could manage, were annually homeward bound; and this upward trend in the available tonnage would continue, with occasional set-backs, throughout the century. The greater availability of hold-space meant that bulkier commodities with a lower value-to-weight ratio were becoming commercially attractive. Conversely, the higher value-to-weight ratio that in the days of restricted transport had made spices such a perfect cargo was no longer so relevant.

How much difference a few extra pepper shipments could make may be judged from the effect of the first voyage of the newly chartered English East India Company in 1601. With four 'tall ships', £27,000 in coin and merchandise, and the hopes of the Company's subscribers, not to mention the entire English nation, riding on the venture, James Lancaster sailed again for the East in 1601. Stopping to provision at the Cape and in Madagascar, he set a course for Aceh at the tip of Sumatra.

John Davis, the Arctic explorer, had been to Aceh in 1599 as pilot on de Houten's second voyage. He found the place awash with pepper and the Portuguese in Melaka too ill supplied with shipping to interfere. Returning to the Netherlands and then England in 1600, Davis had therefore recommended the Sumatran sultanate to prospective members of the English East India Company. The unhappy fact that de Houten and sixty-eight of his men had been treacherously slaughtered by the Acehnese might have been considered discouraging, but Davis insisted otherwise. Aceh's sultan detested only the Dutch. He had been devoted to the English ever since he heard of their victory over the Spanish armada, and much to de Houten's annoyance, had flaunted this preference by consorting exclusively with Davis. 'Excessive eating and drinking was our entertainement,' says Davis.[4] As a final gesture of friendship the sultan had made sure that the Englishman's life was spared in the massacre.

This partiality, along with the news that pepper in Aceh could be bought for less than a penny ha'penny a pound, had proved decisive; Aceh was designated Lancaster's first port of call and in due course all four of his ships had safely reached the sultan's seaside kingdom. A sandier, healthier place than much of Sumatra, it disappointed only in respect of the pepper, which cost nearly threepence a pound. Otherwise Sultan Ala-uddin Shah could not have been more oblig-ing. His entertainment lived up to the most alcoholic expectations, and with his approval and assistance, Lancaster augmented the value of his trading capital by seizing a Portuguese carrack laden with Indian textiles at the mouth of the Malacca Strait. Though careful to disguise this act of piracy as the work of Aceh's corsairs, the English 'general' rejoiced; for God, as he put it, had not only provided sufficient capital to load all his four ships with spices 'but has given me as much as will lade as many more ships if I had them to lade'.[5]

Despatching one spice-laden vessel for home, and with another to follow after loading more pepper on the Sumatran coast, Lancaster doubled back to Aceh and, with fond farewells to the sultan, sailed down the island's west coast and through the Sunda Strait to Bantam in Java. There, beside a foetid anchorage that has since been invaded by mangroves, the Dutch had already set up shop on ground of appro-priately dike-able potential wrested from the local ruler. Lancaster fol-lowed suit, so establishing the English Company's first 'factory' in the East. A handful of 'factors' were left to guard unsold goods and buy spices in expectation of the next fleet from London, while Lancaster, with his two remaining ships now laden with yet more pepper, set sail for home.

Not without a heavy loss in manpower and a near-disaster off the Cape, all four ships made it back to London during the year 1603. Given past disappointments, it was a notable achievement. Lancaster was knighted, and investors toasted his health while in the Thames something like a million pounds (0.5 million kg) of pepper were triumphantly unloaded. At the time this represented about a quarter of Europe's entire annual consumption. In the same year Dutch ship-ping brought home about 3 million pounds (1.5 million kg), so making up the remaining three-quarters and leaving whatever the Portuguese and Venetians had been able to import as surplus.

The effect was predictable. The price per pound in London, which in the previous decade had soared to eight shillings, plummeted to 1s. 2d.[6] Even at that rate, there were no buyers; the king (James VI of Scotland had just succeeded as James I of England) had placed an embargo on all pepper sales until he could off-load his own stocks, presumably obtained from another captured prize. Investors were obliged to wait, then to accept a dividend in kind and dispose of it when, and as best, they could. They would not have been comforted to learn that peppercorns had anciently served as currency both in the East and in Europe. Though apparently profitable on paper, stocks of pepper from the first voyage were still reported as unsold 'six or seven years after'.

Not every successful voyage would have quite such a disastrous impact. As of 1609, rival sellers – like the king – were bought off by the Company's agreeing to pay a tax on its pepper imports in return for a monopoly of the home market. More crucially, the re-export of spices to elsewhere in Europe, which would eventually account for four-fifths of the English Company's pepper imports and still more of the Dutch Company's, would be better organised to handle sudden gluts. And the fall in prices did have the advantage of effectively ending any competition in pepper from the Red Sea trade. Indeed by 1615 London's Levant Company, instead of importing pepper from the eastern Mediterranean, was exporting it to the eastern Mediterranean. Additionally, the risk of over-supply could to some extent be managed by engaging in the great Asian market for spices. With trading posts dotted throughout the East from the Persian Gulf to China and Japan, the Dutch in particular would actively contest the Asian market.

But in Europe that apparent contradiction between the rising demand for spices and the declining importance of the trade had begun. Eastern trade was now only a branch of world trade; the spice trade represented only a diminishing percentage of eastern trade; and while the quantity of spice imports went on rising, prices were liable to fall. This was particularly true of black pepper. Still much the most heavily traded of all spices, it was also much the most difficult to regulate. To meet the growing demand, cultivation was being extended up the Malabar coast towards Goa, across the water to Sri Lanka and

Malaya, and throughout the interior regions of Sumatra and western Java. No nation could hope to police so many outlets, and although the VOC would make a half-hearted attempt, no company could expect to engross so extensive a trade. *Piper nigrum* had ceased to conform to the enticing commercial profile of a spice and became just another inessential bulk commodity. Pepper 'mountains' accumulated in the warehouses of the European companies. In the last years of Cromwellian London, the price slumped to as little as 7*d.* a pound. In Amsterdam pepper was occasionally sold at a loss.

One solution, perceived as early as 1603 when Lancaster flooded the London pepper market, was to concentrate on the higher-value 'fine spices'. The Dutch had already reached the same conclusion. It meant confounding Portuguese claims to a monopoly of all spice shipments, which was evidently no great challenge. And it meant wresting from the Portuguese their pre-eminent position in the Spice Islands and Sri Lanka, after which, the English supposed, the trade might be open to all.

But the Dutch had no such illusions. To the Herren XVII – the 'Seventeen Gentlemen' who ran the VOC – the great attraction of the spice trade was its particularity. Though the mystery of where cloves and nutmeg came from had been dispelled, the miracle of their being reserved to a handful of minuscule and eminently monopolis-able islands remained. Competition under such circumstances could be disastrous; either prices would get out of hand or spice seedlings would be purloined and planted elsewhere – probably both. Not unreasonably, therefore, the Dutch would insist on exclusive access. And since, as the Portuguese had discovered, controlling the spice trade by policing the movement of spices was expensive and not always effective, the obvious answer lay in controlling production. The tussle for control of the spice route was about to be carried into the spice groves themselves.

The first Dutch vessels to reach the Spice Islands had been a detach-ment from van Neck's fleet of 1598–9 – otherwise the highly success-ful 'Second Dutch Expedition to the East Indies'. Calling at both the mace-and-nutmeg Banda Islands and at clove-producing Ternate, the Dutch announced that they had come to end Portuguese pretensions and were accordingly welcomed by the islanders. Banda's *orang kaya* (leading citizens or village chiefs) had provided a cargo. Ternate's Sultan Said had had himself paddled out from Gammalamma Castle to greet the strangers in a royal fleet of gaily bedecked *kora-kora* (long canoes with up to a hundred paddlers ranged in two banks); once aboard the Dutch flagship, the sultan took such an interest in its facilities that it seemed, says the voyage's chronicler, 'he had a mind to buy her'; hours were spent with the pilot poring over 'Jan Huyghen [van Linschoten]'s *Travels* and…the maps and figures that were in his book'.[7]

The Hispano-Portuguese garrison in nearby Tidore was too small to offer other than verbal objections. Thirty years earlier the Portuguese had removed their headquarters in the Spice Islands to the sheltered inlet formed by the horseshoe-shaped island of Ambon (Amboyna, Amboina) 300 miles (500km) to the south. There, courtesy of one of St Francis Xavier's spectacular mass conversions in the 1540s, Christianity had gained a precarious purchase on what was still the leading edge of an advancing Islam. The Christian presence had presented the *estado* with both an obligation and an opportunity. Aided by their co-religionists, the Portuguese hastily constructed the gloomy (and today much rebuilt) Castle Victoria; and by way of employment for their co-religionists, they managed to establish clove culture in Ambon.

This seems to have involved the transplantation of seedlings from Tidore as well as the improvement of wild stock indigenous to the dense forests of Ceram, the large but little explored island that all but engulfs Ambon. In a feat barely noticed at the time but of much future significance, cloves had thus performed their first island-hop; European initiative had ended the north Moluccan monopoly of one of the most valuable spices; and Ambon, together with the few districts of Ceram that were not entirely impenetrable, had joined the select company of the Spice Islands.

A second Dutch visit to the Moluccas was made in 1601, and there were probably others. It was not until 1605 that the English belatedly, as was their way, followed suit. Amsterdam's claims to precedence over London's in the clove and nutmeg trade would therefore be well founded, though the English could, and would, recall that Drake had been to Ternate twenty years before the first Hollander. When Henry

Middleton, in command of the English Company's second voyage, finally entered Moluccan waters, Drake's 'treaty' with Sultan Baab, the father of Sultan Said, was deemed still operative. Indeed it represented Middleton's greatest asset. In all other respects he was hopelessly ill-prepared for what would turn out to be a decisive moment in the fate of the spice trade.

Coming from Bantam, where he had left two ships to load with pepper, Middleton had taken his other two vesssels to seek out the finer spices so desired by the Company's directors. All four ships were the same as had sailed under Lancaster; so were many of the men, including Henry Middleton. But on the two ships that in 1605 duly headed for Ambon, all was not well. Dysentery, otherwise the 'fluxe' or 'flixe', was running riot; scarcely an entry in the ship's log ended without a formulaic 'This day dyed of the flixe Mr so-and-so'. Far from contesting possession of the Spice Islands, Middleton's only ambition was to secure a cargo and get back to Bantam while he still had enough hands to man both ships.

In this determination he appeared at first to be succeeding. The Portuguese governor in Ambon's Castle Victoria was relieved 'to hear of the peace between England and Spaine' that had followed the death of Queen Elizabeth – an event of which Middleton submitted as proof a painting of King James wearing his crown together with samples 'of His Majestie's new coin'. Permission for the English to buy Ambon's cloves was promised. But on the very day that it was finally granted, '5 sayles of Hollanders were [reported] entered into the mouth of the harbour and turning up for the fort'. The five sails were soon joined by several more, this being a vast VOC fleet commanded by Steven van der Hagen, carrying over fifteen hundred men, and under orders to eject the Portuguese from all the Spice Islands.

In Ambon the size of this armada was enough; the Portuguese quietly capitulated. Castle Victoria thus passed from the Estado da India to the VOC without a shot being fired. Unwittingly it also inaugurated a sequence of more sensational transfers which, though rarely so peaceful, would within half a century include Melaka, Colombo and Cochin. Meanwhile the English, here in the person of Middleton, stood by, lacking orders to intervene and generally powerless to do so. Middleton's authorisation to trade had become redundant before he had had a chance to use it; for the Dutch, having taken the trouble to deprive the Portuguese of Ambon's cloves, were not disposed to share them with anyone else. Despite the plight of his crew, Middleton's only hope of a cargo now lay in forestalling the Dutch progress elsewhere. One ship, the *Ascension*, was accordingly sent post-haste to the Bandas; meanwhile Middleton in the *Red Dragon* made heavy weather *en route* to Ternate.

There events followed the pattern set in Ambon. Only a part-load of cloves had been hauled aboard the *Red Dragon* before the Dutch fleet, in uneasy alliance with Ternate's sultan, anchored before the Portuguese fort on Tidore. This time the Portuguese offered some spirited resistance. The bombardment lasted three days and the Dutch landing party was actually fleeing back to the ships when there was a series of explosions. All eyes turned to Tidore's presiding volcano; a serene wisp of steam clung to its flanks as usual. It was the fort that had erupted. Something – either a lucky shot, a treacherous arrow or an innocent cooking-fire asplutter with cloves – had ignited the powder magazine. Dutch and Ternateans returned to the fray. By nightfall the town itself was ablaze, the attackers victorious, and the Portuguese in chains. Middleton's chances of more cloves, let alone a factory, had gone up in the conflagration.

The Dutch, who suspected the English intruder of supplying the Portuguese with guns and powder, ordered his immediate departure. Reluctantly Sultan Said concurred, confessing himself unable to honour his father's promise to Drake, though according to Middleton's diarist, far from happy at the turn of events.

> He said the Hollanders did threaten...to establish a factory at Tydore if he did let the English tarry in the country...they saying we were theeves and robbers...that Holland was able to set out 20 ships for England's one, and that the King of Holland [presumably the Prince of Orange] was stronger by sea than all Christendome... This day dyed of the flixe Thomas Richmond.[8]

'If this frothy nation may have the trade of the Indians [i.e. the Indies] all to themselves (which is the thing they hope for), their pride and insolencie will be intollerable', huffed Middleton by way of a parting shot.

With the fall of both Ambon and the north Moluccas, the Dutch appeared to have cornered the clove trade. Though a Spanish expedition from Manila would drive them out of the north Moluccas in 1606, they would be back in Ternate by the end of that year. The Spanish would retain an outpost in Tidore until 1648, but the Dutch position was by far the stronger, enabling them to enjoy largely uncontested access to as much of the north Moluccan clove harvest as they required.

This would not be much, and would soon be none. As clove production in Ambon and Ceram prospered, the yield from Ternate, Tidore and their north Moluccan neighbours obligingly declined, and what they did produce came to be seen as unwelcome competition. From about 1630 Dutch visits to these islands, and to the unadministered parts of Ceram, were more often in the nature of punitive expeditions than purchasing exercises, with resident garrisons in the islands acting as informers and enforcers rather than protectors. Under a policy succinctly known as 'Extirpation', clove-farming villages were burnt, clove pickers hunted down by the hundred, and clove trees uprooted in their tens of thousands. Favoured villages, especially in Ambon, were forced to cultivate cloves and nothing else, so rendering them dependent on the Dutch for all foodstuffs. Less favoured villages, especially in the north Moluccas, were forbidden to cultivate cloves on pain of death and destruction.

The idea, of course, was to tailor supply to demand and so ensure high prices. In practice, the difficulty of matching the yield of tiny flower-buds from a slow maturing tree to the fluctuating fortunes of a luxury market scattered round the world meant an endless production cycle of surplus and shortage. Designated clove growers, no less than undesignated ones, found themselves under permanent pressure and increasingly in debt; their situation was little better than that of bonded labourers. It is not even certain that the system was of great benefit to the Dutch. As an early attempt at a plantation economy, it brought rich dividends to the VOC's investors and was therefore accounted a success. But the cost of enforcement was heavy and, though unquantified, would seem crippling when prices fell.

★

While Middleton had nursed the crew of the *Red Dragon* through difficult days in the north Moluccas, her sister ship the *Ascension* hung about the Banda Islands. There she too was soon joined by part of van der Hagen's fleet. The Bandas being only a day and a half's sailing from now Dutch Ambon, and considerably smaller than the clove islands, they looked a much more manageable proposition for would-be monopolists. The Portuguese, let alone the Spanish, had never established themselves there; so evil was the reputation of the islanders, and so difficult was it to deal with the innumerable *orang kaya*, that the Portuguese had ventured ashore only to trade. No nutmeg seedlings had been smuggled off the islands, and no more than makeshift shop premises had been built there.

Nor had the inconvenient Drake left any conflicting claim. In the Bandas the Dutch had indisputably pipped the English, first arriving in 1598, and by 1605 they had obtained Bandanese signatures on a series of agreements that promised them exclusive rights to the islands' – and so the world's – entire nutmeg and mace production. These documents were, however, of questionable legality. Apart from doubts over whether the Bandanese understood what they signed, there was no recognised body of *orang kaya* that could speak for all of the little archipelago's scattered communities. Republicanism had its drawbacks, as citizens of the fiercely independent Dutch provinces appreciated better than most. Heedless of paperwork, the Bandanese continued to sell to all-comers, some being traditional trading partners from Java and Makassar (a Sulawesi port-city renowned for its *cartaz*-busting impertinence) and others being representatives of the English East India Company.

Though in derisory numbers, the English had managed to retain a toe-hold on the two most distant of the Banda islands since 1601. A party of those left behind at Bantam by Lancaster had sailed east for nutmegs and had established a token presence on Pulo Ai (Ay, Wai, Weh etc.) and Pulo Run (Roon), respectively 5 and 10 miles (8 and 16km) west of the other Banda islands. Thence mace and nutmegs were shipped back to Bantam, mostly by hired junk and *prahu* and often via Makassar. Only rarely did a vessel flying the East India Company's flag, like the *Ascension*, put in an appearance. Rather the English relied for protection on the growing Bandanese dislike of the

Dutch and on the considerable difficulty of effecting a landing on either Ai or Run, both being steep-sided, densely forested, hemmed about by coral reefs and unapproachable during the monsoon months.

The Dutch tolerated this situation until such time as they could redress it. Meanwhile the *Ascension* in 1605, then the *Hector* in 1609 and the *Expedition* in 1610 cruised with impunity about the islands, sometimes chased by indignant Dutch skippers and sometimes welcomed by their doleful colleagues for some mutual commiseration over the unhappy lot of the exile. Like the Portuguese, both the Dutch and the English formed a poor opinion of the Bandanese. According to instructions issued by the London Company to one of its captains, they were 'peevish, perverse, diffident and perfidious...apt to take a disgust upon small occasions, and being moved, are more cumbersome than wasps'.[9]

Matters took a turn for the worse when in 1609 a Dutch expeditionary force, having encountered objections from the Bandanese to the construction of a fort, went ahead with it anyway. Seven hundred and fifty shovel-wielding soldiers trooped ashore, at which the islanders were certainly 'moved'; in fact they moved out, deserting Banda Naira (Neira) where the fort was to be built. Naira was one in a cluster of three islands that formed the central nucleus of the Bandas and afforded shelter to visiting ships; of the other two islands in this cluster, Great Banda (or Lonthor) comprised a long shaggy ridge blanketed in nutmeg trees, and Gunung Api was just a volcano – it evinced its own disapproval of the invasion by showering the fort-builders with volcanic ash. The Dutch chose another site, and Fort Nassau began to take shape. The Bandanese then asked for more talks. When the Dutch admiral, Pieter Verhoef (Verhoeven), rashly agreed to attend without his escort, he and twenty-nine of his compatriots were smartly slaughtered.

Known as 'the Verhoeven Massacre', or 'the Vile Bandanese Treachery of 1609', this ended Dutch complacency, and because the English presence had encouraged the Bandanese, also ended any chance of an Anglo-Dutch accommodation in the islands. Though at home allied in faith against the Catholic powers, and though elsewhere in the East often combining commercially against the Portuguese, in the archipelago the Dutch and the English now fought one another whenever occasion offered. What the Reverend Samuel Purchas, a contemporary editor of far-flung voyages, called this 'warre so portentuous in the midst of peace' would rumble on in vicious fits and spiteful starts for the next twelve years.

In 1609, after reprisals, more losses and the founding of a second fort (Fort Belgica), the Dutch presented to those *orang kaya* who would sign it another treaty. As usual it included a clause providing for exclusive Dutch trade – which was probably being infringed even as the Bandanese made their mark – and added another to the effect that Naira was now to be regarded as under Dutch sovereignty. The United Provinces thus gained their second Eastern possession, Ambon being the first (and Bantam being technically leased).

The English, as ever, could do no better than follow suit. In 1616, by when Pulo Ai had been overrun by the Dutch but Pulo Run still resisted, they probably orchestrated, certainly drafted, and then triumphantly entertained an offer of allegiance from the *orang kaya* of Run and Ai (the latter being now refugees). It was accompanied by the sincerest pledge that a Bandanese could make, namely a bunch of leafy nutmeg seedlings, each of them well rooted in its own bowl of earth (the records are silent about any attempt to grow them on in foreign soil). Thus did England too, and hence the future British Empire, gain its first possession in the East. In an eloquent document signifying the hand-over, King James was duly if contentiously styled as 'by the grace of God, king of England, Scotland, Ireland, France, Puloway and Pularoone'.[10]

Sovereignty imposed new responsibilities even when it applied only to a remote island whose under 2 square miles (5 sq. m) of pristine woodland even today betray no glimmer of civilisation. Taking command of Run in 1616, Nathaniel Courthope of the London East India Company was under instructions simply to sit tight. He did so for four long and often fraught years. Abandoning the place would have been treason, but having lost his only ship, just obtaining food and water from the other islands – the nearest 5 miles (8 km) away and all patrolled by the Dutch – taxed the ingenuity of his men and their Bandanese allies. At one point relief in the form of an English fleet got within waving distance before being chased away. Other English vessels were taken by the Dutch and their crews imprisoned on Naira.

By 1618, two years into his life as a castaway, Courthope was getting anxious. 'I have but thirtie eight men against [the Hollanders'] force and tyranny, our wants extreme: neither have we victuals or drinke but only Rice and water. They have at present eight ships here and two Gallies, and to my knowledge all fitted to come against us. I look daily and howerly for them.'[11] A year later the situation was desperate. 'We have rubbed off the skin alreadie, and if we rub any longer, shall rub to the bone,' wrote Courthope in what would turn out to be his last communication. In 1620, while returning from one of the neighbouring islands at dead of night, his boat was ambushed. What became of Courthope is not clear. He may have been killed or he may have been drowned while swimming to safety. All that is sure is that his body was later washed up on Pulo Ai.

This affair attracted some attention at the time (and more since[12]) partly because, eighteen months earlier but still unknown in the Bandas, the two Companies had officially suspended hostilities. Under pressure from their respective governments, they had signed an agreement that made them now partners in the spice trade and allies in a bid to put paid to Portuguese claims. Courthope's stand had not been in vain; and had he but known of the new state of affairs, he need never have risked his life by venturing forth under cover of darkness.

Larger ructions had produced this turn-round, mostly in Java, where in 1611 the Dutch had relocated their headquarters from malarial Bantam to Jacatra (Batavia, Jakarta). The English, of course, had followed suit; and having a strong fleet to hand, they had spied a chance of redressing numerous grievances by besieging the new but still unfortified Dutch factory. The arrival of an even larger Dutch fleet drove them off with heavy losses, and for a few months the ships of both sides opened fire whenever they met. In this bellicose climate the Herren XVII had appointed Jan Pieterszoon Coen as governor of their affairs in the Indies.

The scowling 'King Coen' (this being much the nicest of the many epithets coined for him by the English) had always made his intentions perfectly clear. In the archipelago he sought a Dutch monopoly of the spice trade, and against English competition and Bandanese treachery he was quite prepared to use any means. The news of the accord between the two Companies, which arrived just after he had worsted the English off Java, did not deter him. On the contrary, it freed his hands. So did the timely removal of Courthope. In early 1621, just weeks after Courthope's death, he sailed for the Bandas to supervise their 'final solution'.

Great Banda was first. After some preliminary goading, a supposed call to arms by the Bandanese became the signal for the Dutch assault. Villages were razed, possessions burnt, and the entire population – men, women and children – either rounded up or dispersed. A few escaped to the other islands, some died in the hills, some were mown down in the forests, and some jumped to their death from the cliffs. Most were deported and then sold into slavery in Java. 'Of the original population of perhaps fifteen thousand persons, no more than a thousand seem to have survived within the [Bandas] archipelago,' says Willard Hanna, an indefatigable and much respected champion of the Moluccan peoples. The survivors fled to Run and Ai 'where the English presence provided not active protection but some meagre deterrence to atrocities'.[13] Of Great Banda's *orang kaya*, forty-four were tortured – the technical term was 'tried' – and then marched in chains to a circular enclosure, there to be neatly carved into quarters and beheaded by a team of samurai executioners recruited by the Dutch factory in Japan.

The islanders of Ai, some of whom had already been deported, suffered a similar fate. On Run the small English contingent, though understandably horrified, did no more than move aside; now allies of the Dutch, they too were implicated. Later they abandoned the island altogether; as a reward for its years of staunch resistance, it would be de-nutmegged as well as depopulated.

Coen was secretly castigated by some of his own officers and would later be mildly censured by his superiors, but he was never brought to justice. Rather he was reappointed. This recognised his good work in the second phase of his final solution for the Bandas. To provide the VOC with nutmegs and mace in reliable quantities and at fixed prices, the now empty islands were divided into sixty-eight *perken*, or plots, each *perk* being leased to a *perkenier*, or plot-holder, along with twenty-five slaves to work it. The slaves were imported, mostly from the jungles of Ceram, New Guinea and other unadministered islands; the *perkeniers*, also incomers, were largely ex-employees of the VOC who, often for reasons best unscrutinised, had chosen not to return to the Netherlands.

Both slaves and *perkeniers* proved unruly and necessitated a draconian penal code. A German who spent five years in the islands in the 1630s witnessed twenty-five assorted executions – by decapitation (nine), by hanging (nine), by garotting (three), by incineration (two), by breaking on the wheel (one) and by arquebus (one); judicial floggings (seventeen) and mutilations (fifty-two) were routine;[14] and this amongst a population of under four thousand. In one of the most idyllic locations imaginable, where the pigeons boomed and the palm fronds stirred and all nature conspired to reproduce that balmy paradise from which spices had been supposed to come, life for most was nasty, extraordinarily brutish and often short.

But spice production picked up. The monopoly was moderately effective, the VOC sold in Amsterdam at around twelve thousand per cent of the price paid in the Bandas, and in the kitchens of Europe a comforting hint of nutmeg found its way into ever more baked cakes, white sauces, warmed wines and candied confections.

According to the Reverend Samuel Purchas, the mayhem in the Bandas and the Moluccas could best be attributed to the pernicious abandon induced by equatorial temperatures; decent men, Dutch and English, shed their 'solid vertues' with their thick European clothes, became excited by the 'fiery ferity' of their own spices, and surrendered themselves to the 'heathenish qualities' of their swarthy associates. It was as good an explanation as any, and it appeared to be confirmed by an otherwise inexplicable outrage that occurred just as Purchas put down his pen. Coming two years after Coen's reign of terror in the Bandas, 'the Amboina Massacre' would be a far greater scandal and the final straw so far as the London Company's participation in the spice trade was concerned.

Herman van Speult, the Dutch governor of Ambon, was one of Coen's scruple-free disciples; having weathered several insurrections and mutinies, the VOC in Ambon was understandably paranoid; and there as in the Bandas, the English only made things worse. They declined to co-operate with their new partners, reneged on financial and military commitments made under the 1619 accord, and openly derided the 'frothy' endeavours of those they called 'butter-boxes', 'horse-turds' and worse.

The Dutch, for their part, likened their situation to that of being saddled with a spendthrift wife who consorted behind their back with native paramours. Yet by 1623 the agony was almost over; a separation had already been mutually agreed. The London Company, unable to bear either the burden or the ignominy of further association, had decided to withdraw from the Spice Islands; and this was evidently known in Ambon. But perhaps Governor van Speult did not accept it; or perhaps the English became more insufferable as the hour of their release drew near.

Assuming the governor to have been of sound mind, he must have believed that he was serving the VOC's cause when he made his move. Without warning, he arrested a group of fourteen Englishmen and ten Japanese on charges of planning to make a grab for Castle Victoria. The Japanese, as Dutch mercenaries, were deemed mutineers and, as Asiatics, of little account; their supposed part in the affair seems to have been simply to implicate the Englishmen, after which they were executed. Ten of the English were also executed. Confined within the fort's dank dungeons, they were tortured till they confessed, then convicted and beheaded. One of them, Gabriel Towerson, was the chief factor in Ambon; the other nine included senior figures of the London Company's local establishment. They, certainly, were of account; such deaths could not be glossed over.

Explanations were sought from the Dutch in both Batavia (as Jacatra had now become) and Amsterdam, but to no avail. Van Speult was ordered home but died before he arrived. King James promised action but did nothing. All of which only increased public discontent in England. 'This crying business of Amboina', as it was called, stirred national sentiment and produced a spate of tracts and pamphlets; modelled on Foxe's *Book of Martyrs*, some contained stark woodcuts illustrating the various tortures for the benefit of the illiterate. John Dryden would write a play about the affair; and the governor of the East India Company would announce that, because of government inaction, the Company must 'give over the trade of the Indies'. The exaggeration was understandable. Apart from the confessions extracted under torture, there was no evidence that the men had plotted to seize the fort, no chance of their succeeding in such a venture, and no discernible reason for their attempting it.

Like Courthope's protracted resistance and like the loss of Pulo Run, the Amboina Massacre joined the growing list of English grievances against the Dutch. Written up and dusted down, all featured prominently when Cromwell went to war with the United Provinces in 1652–4 and when Charles II did likewise in 1665–7. Mainly naval affairs fought in the North Sea, the first Anglo–Dutch war ended with some compensation for the families of the 'Amboina martyrs', while the second, that which took Samuel Pepys into the hold of a Dutch East Indiaman, produced an extensive trade-off between the two countries of largely redundant colonial assets. Among other concessions in this Peace of Breda, the Dutch relinquished various claims in north America, including that to New Amsterdam and its island of Manhattan, while the English relinquished all their rights in the Spice Islands, including those to now depopulated Pulo Run. Run was not exchanged for New York, as New Amsterdam now became; its transfer just happened to be part of the same settlement.

As for the spice trade, the English Company had been as good as its word, withdrawing from the Moluccas (including the Bandas) in 1624, retracing its move from Batavia to Bantam in 1628 and eventually being forced out of Java altogether in 1683. This steady westward retraction from the archipelago mirrored the Company's declining interest in nutmegs and cloves but did not amount to a complete renunciation. Spices from the Moluccas, 'smuggled', as the Dutch would have it, by *prahu* and pinnace to Makassar and Borneo, still found their way in limited quantities into English holds. And pepper, even after the loss of Bantam, still justified an East India Company factory at Bengkulu (Benkulen) at the south-west end of Sumatra – which was where much of Bantam's stock came from anyway.

Bengkulu, also known as Fort York (after the duke who became James II) and then Fort Marlborough (after the general who became a duke), would prove a place of little profit and exceptional ill repute. Though the settlement lingered on throughout the eighteenth century, it would be easily overlooked at a time when the English East India Company, putting aside the spicy dreams of its infancy, was discovering its true vocation in the cottons of Gujerat, Tamil Nadu and

Bengal, together with Persian silks, indigo and saltpetre, all from the south Asian mainland. Madras (Chennai) was acquired and fortified in 1640, Bombay (Mumbai) in 1668, and Calcutta (Kolkata) in 1689. The seeds of England's empire of trade took root not in insular but in continental Asia. During the eighteenth century they would sprout sensationally. British arms overwhelmed the challenge of Bourbon France throughout the Indian subcontinent, tea from China came to exceed all the Company's other Oriental imports, and opium from India provided the means to pay for it. In retrospect the Dutch, by effectively expelling the English from Indonesia and the spice trade, seemed to have done them a favour.

It would be wrong, though, to suppose that there was some India-for-Indonesia equivalent of the Breda trade-off. No more than the English Company relinquished the spice trade to concentrate on India did the VOC stand aside in India to concentrate on Indonesia's spices. Until the mid-eighteenth century, the VOC was a major participant in the India trade, its representation in Gujerat, Malabar, Tamil Nadu and Bengal being in no way inferior to that of the London Company. Likewise in east Asia, where Dutch trade with Japan was, while it lasted, the most lucrative in the VOC's entire portfolio.

Rather was it the erosion of Portugal's Estado da India that determined the pattern of Anglo-Dutch colonial development. In the Arabian Sea fortune favoured the English. Hormuz, the *estado*'s western bastion at the mouth of the Persian Gulf, fell to a joint Anglo-Persian attack in 1621; two decades later an Anglo-Portuguese alliance was signed to deter Dutch encroachment in India; and two decades after that, Bombay passed peacefully to the English as part of the dowry of Charles II's bride, Catherine of Braganza.

But on the other side of India, it was a different story. There Melaka, the third of Albuquerque's great bastions and still a major entrepôt for spices, especially those destined for China, was taken by the Dutch in 1641. Melaka's second fall to a European power was almost as significant as its first. Again it signalled a transfer of control over the spice route, the only difference being that this time the port's fame was not celebrated but terminated. Its trade was largely diverted to Batavia, which city then grew into a 'Queen of the Indies' worthy of being the VOC's headquarters. From Batavia the VOC at last exercised uncontested control of the Malacca Strait into the Indian Ocean; and through the strait, over the next two decades, VOC fleets from Batavia poured forth to relieve the Portuguese of their *estado* in Sri Lanka, the Coromandel coast of Tamil Nadu and the Malabar coast of Kerala.

Sri Lanka had been visited by some of the earliest Dutch voyages; but the opportunity of engrossing its famous cinnamon yield did not arise until after the English and the Portuguese had been seen off in the Spice Islands. Heavy fighting in the 1630s between the Portuguese and the kingdom of Kandy left the Portuguese enfeebled and Kandy anxious for an ally. The Dutch were happy to oblige, expelling the Portuguese from Batticaloa on the west coast in 1638 and then exploiting the weakness of both parties to extract ever more concessions and territory. Colombo fell after a long siege in 1656; a year later Admiral Johan Maetsuycker declared the VOC to be 'complete masters of the whole island of Ceylon as far as it had been occupied by the Portuguese'.[15]

The Coromandel ports of Tuticorin and Negapatnam were taken a year later, those of Malabar – Quilon, Cannanore and Cochin – in 1661–2. Indian pepper as well as Sri Lankan cinnamon was thus added to the VOC's portfolio of spices, though over neither was it able to exercise anything like as effective a monopoly as over cloves, nutmeg and mace. Meanwhile, to service the volume of shipping passing round the tip of Africa, the Dutch established the first European settlement at the Cape in 1652.

Direct sailings between Amsterdam and Batavia were often quicker via the Sunda Strait between Java and Sumatra than via the Malacca Strait. But control of Melaka had reopened the routing from the archipelago round the Malay Peninsula to India that had been the essence and axis of the ancient spice route. History had come full circle; as the Dutch increasingly strove to supply Asia as well as Europe with spices, shipments of cloves, nutmegs and mace again passed through the Malacca Strait to India, much as they had in the days of Marco Polo. The path of Dutch colonial expansion had followed the old spice route west so faithfully that it might have been reinstating it.

There would be no further development of the spice route. The isthmus-crossings had been eliminated, the peninsulas rounded, the straits secured. Save for the addition of a few new ports, like Singapore, spices would continue to travel west along the sea-lanes pioneered by Hippalos, da Gama, Dias and d'Elcano. But as of about 1800 they did so inconspicuously. Like sealing wax and sailing ships, their day had passed. Spices had served their purpose, titillating palates and tantalising pioneers long enough to draw them to the ends of the earth and turn them into monsters. Now the glamour was gone, the glory won; blood had been spilled, greed assuaged. The cellophane sachets of a supermarket limbo awaited.

Epilogue: Outsold and Outsourced

The demise of spices as a significant commodity in East–West trade was a protracted process. Knowledge of whence they came had dispelled their mystique, and dependable supply had somewhat dissipated their air of distinction; but tastes were slow to change, and even as courtiers tired of peppered game-pies and scented ales, palates less jaded relished them. The golden age of the Netherlands' spice empire lasted from the 1630s until the 1730s, during which time demand if anything rose, while thanks to continuing 'extirpations' in the Spice Islands and the occasional bonfire of unsold stocks in Amsterdam, prices held reasonably steady.

Where spices disappointed was in their inability to keep pace with the expanding world economy. The soaring expectations of the VOC's investors, the rising costs of monopoly enforcement, and the explosion in world trade left them for dead. In business terms, spices failed to perform. A dull stock lost its glitter, and this contributed to their declining popularity with the moneyed consumer. Instead of withering away, the spice trade was being smothered by the lusher growth of other commodities while its own growth was inhibited by a range of factors, all of them extraneous and so easily ignored in Eurocentric accounts of the trade's history, this one included.

Asian demand was one such factor. Having established a near monopoly over the production of the finer spices, the Dutch naturally endeavoured to exploit the vast market in Asia as well as that in Europe. A thriving traffic in cloves, cinnamon and nutmeg (and pepper where applicable) from Batavia to China, Japan and especially India resulted; but it was very price-sensitive. Too high a valuation left cargoes unsold, while too low a valuation tempted Asian merchants to buy on behalf of rival shippers – English, Portuguese, Danish and

French – for re-export to Europe. The Dutch pared overheads to a minimum and often entrusted inter-Asian freight to Asian carriers. But it was not easy to strike the right balance; and it meant that in Europe, too, prices had to be held below the levels at which sensational profits might be realised in order to discourage other importers. The global market had its attractions, but without a monopoly of shipping such as the Portuguese had briefly boasted, it could seem a liability.

Another inhibition stemmed from the Americas. 'I believe I have found rhubarb and cinnamon,' Columbus had reported after his first voyage; nutmeg he also thought likely, though it had been the wrong time of year for nuts; and there was definitely some kind of pepper. Back in Spain his samples of these spices had been rubbished as nothing of the sort, yet the native Americans did indeed have their own spices. Vanilla, allspice and the great tribe of capsicums were found only in the Americas. Columbus' gleanings may have included variants of these; and as the Spanish penetrated the mainland, they further explored such natural productions.

Vanilla quickly proved a popular novelty. The beans in pod were imported as a drug during the sixteenth century; in England, Queen Elizabeth's personal apothecary first recommended them as a flavouring; and thereafter they challenged cinnamon for the attention of bakers and confectioners. Allspice had but to live up to its name. Combining a hint of pepper, cloves, nutmeg and cinnamon all in a single spice, it could be used as a four-in-one curry powder. But capsicums, especially *Capsicum annuum*, or the chilli, turned the spice trade on its head. Here was a culinary 'pepper' of good flavour, attractive hue, agreeable consistency and sometimes incendiary effect that needed neither to be traded nor transported. It travelled as seed and it germinated as sowed, wherever its modest requirements of sunshine and soil were met. By the end of the sixteenth century it was well established in the milder parts of Europe and, thanks to the Portuguese, was spreading throughout the East. India would eventually become the world's largest producer. Though black pepper retained a market share, long pepper was almost edged out of cultivation by the invader.

Technically the chilli is a fruit; yet it may be eaten green like a herb, may be commercially classed as a vegetable, and today rates as a spice, indeed the definitive spice without which no sauce can pass as tabasco nor *masala* call itself *garam*. The New World had a way of confounding existing categories, and none more so than those of botany. Potatoes and tomatoes came from closely related plants, but of the former it was the tuber that was edible – and hence it was a vegetable – while of the latter it was the fruit – as to whose classification there is still no consensus. Chocolate beans, or cacao, were used as currency in the West Indies; in noting this, Columbus had called them 'almonds'. Their function as a beverage had to be learned from the Aztecs and was introduced into Europe at much the same time as coffee. By way of a morning pick-me-up, Pepys tried both; and as Aztec practice had suggested, tobacco went well with either. Its smoke so filled the new beverage houses of Europe's capitals that non-smokers received a lung-full for nothing. Produced by ignition, inviting inhalation, and promising relaxation, tobacco smoke recalled the myrrh-fumes that once wafted through senatorial halls. It was the new incense.

A shrewd merchant like Pegolotti would have classed all these productions as spices; and when introduced, some did directly compete with existing spices. But not necessarily in the kitchen. Like spices in the ancient world, their great virtue lay in their exotic origins and their supposed properties. As status symbols as well as stimulants they challenged the whole spectrum of conventional spices and postulated a new level of indulgence. Either they gratified the palate more, delivered a more heady effect, or simply proclaimed the more adventurous and sophisticated life-style of those who consumed them.

They were also new, and at a time when novelty and spices scarcely went together, this enhanced their allure. Physical as well as mental stimulation was readily credited to nearly all introductions. Shakespeare thought even the potato an aphrodisiac, and from names like *pomme d'amour* and *pomodoro* it would seem that the French and Italians thought the same of the tomato. Society flocked to the coffee-house, and fashion endorsed the teapot. Contemporaries took careful note of such changing social habits – and social historians take note of these notes. It would be wrong, though, to assume from Pepys that in the third quarter of the seventeenth century coffee and chocolate, let alone tea, challenged the hegemony of spices or played any major part in world trade. That would take another fifty years. Coffee in the 1660s came only from southern Arabia. Although small quantities were shipped from the port of Mocha by both English and Dutch East India Companies, most of what reached Europe did so via the Levant. Rare and novel, as well as flavoursome, coffee, tea and chocolate had won a few devoted drinkers but not a nation of them.

The breakthrough came when the Dutch managed to establish coffee cultivation in Malabar and then Java. The first bushes were planted in the Preanger uplands of west Java in 1696 and the first sale of 900 *ponds* was made in 1711. A decade later deliveries of Java coffee were running at over a million *ponds* a year, and a decade after that at about six million *ponds*. In quantity, they now exceeded those of black pepper, and their value was more than double. It was a sign of the times that in Ambon an attempt was made to replace clove trees with coffee bushes, while in the Bandas coffee-drinkers were sought among the gin-swilling burghers who held the nutmeg *perks*. Meanwhile pepper in Java became an endangered species. By the mid-eighteenth century the island's coffee exports were worth ten times its pepper exports, and only by insisting that every delivery of coffee beans was accompanied by a few *ponds* of peppercorns was pepper cultivation saved. In the space of a generation the VOC's spice empire had turned into a coffee colony.

Tea's triumph in the trading manifests of the English East India Company was just as remarkable. Sample quantities of green tea from China were imported by both companies in the 1660s, but at about 1 pound for £1 the directors of the English Company were still in the 1680s requesting only sufficient 'to make presents therein to our great friends at court'. By concentrating on the cheaper and blacker Bohea tea, in 1720 the price dropped to 7s. a pound on an import of 200,000 pounds. Canton was now one of the Company's busier trading ports, and tea was entering mass reckoning. Matching the VOC's coffee imports, it passed the million-pounds-a-year mark a decade later and by 1770 was up to £9 million. By now the value of the China trade exceeded that of all the English Company's India establishments put together. The single most important commodity in its commercial portfolio, tea contributed one-tenth of the home government's entire revenue receipts in the form of import duties. And this was only the official trade. As with coffee, tea was being shipped in perhaps equal quantity by interlopers and foreigners, much of it being then smuggled into Britain.

A society largely unacquainted with hot drinks would perhaps have welcomed any sort of beverage, but what made these brown infusions so palatable and popular was the simultaneous surfeit of an increasingly refined sugar. Sugars in various forms had once been classed as spices. Supply remained limited until cane-sugar, a native of south Asia, began its travels courtesy of the spice route. It had spread fitfully through Asia and to the Mediterranean and the Canary Islands before Columbus took a few canes to the West Indies. There, thanks to a congenial climate, rapacious colonists and an enslaved labour-force, production took off in the late seventeenth century. The same thing happened in Java, where sugar came to rival coffee as a cash crop, so further marginalising traditional spices. But whereas much of Java's sugar found ready markets in Asia, that of the West Indies came substantially to Europe.

By a happy coincidence the New World thus brought to Europe's table the brimming sugar-bowl just as the Old World delivered the steaming teapot or some version of the dribbling cafetière. Few people consciously forswore, say, nutmeg for chocolate; but a day punctuated by sweet brown drinks, accompanied perhaps with a sugary biscuit or a smoke, scarcely prepared the palate for a bombardment of subtle flavours at the dinner-table. As stimulants and comforters, spices by the mid-eighteenth century were being both outperformed and undercut. And it is against this background of an Oriental trade beset by static prices, limited demand, strong competition and waning economic relevance that the exploits of the spice-hunters should be seen.

The idea of subverting the Moluccan monopoly of cloves and nutmegs by naturalising these spices elsewhere had occurred to many. The Spanish had tried and failed to establish cloves in the Philippines. The Portuguese had succeeded with cloves in Ambon and its adjacent islands, and they had attempted to do the same with nutmegs in Timor. Ambon had acquired its own nutmegs thanks to the Dutch in the seventeenth century. And as of the 1690s the English at Bengkulu in Sumatra seem to have experimented with both cloves and nutmeg, the seedlings presumably being obtained through local smugglers. Success eluded most of these efforts. On the other hand the remarkable results being obtained from the naturalisation and exploitation of sugar, coffee and other exotics provided encouragement.

In the 1750s the challenge was taken up by the French adventurer Pierre Poivre. Whether his name ('Peter Pepper', 'Peter *Piper*') in any way inspired his mission – or the popular tongue-twister – is not known. Scholar, patriot and amateur botanist, he combined an incorrigible optimism with the enlightened sentiments of his age and a deep sense of vocation. In China and Vietnam he had worked on behalf of the French Catholic missions but he was not ordained. He lost an arm when his vessel was taken by the British near the Malacca Strait, spent some time in Batavia as a prisoner of the Dutch, and there taking an interest in botany, conceived the idea of obtaining for France a share of the trade in tropical produce. Not Christians, just spices, would be his vocation.

France being a late-comer to Eastern waters, the Compagnie des Indes had often had to settle for second best. From the south-east (Coromandel) coast, Joseph Dupleix was staging an ambitious bid for French dominion on the Indian subcontinent, but in the Indian Ocean France was represented only by the newly acquired Ile de France (later Mauritius) and Ile de Bourbon (later Réunion). These islands provided vital facilities for French naval activity in the East but were otherwise a heavy expense. Poivre's mission would be to redeem their fortunes by making them spice islands.

With official support, in 1751 he reached the Philippines and from there tried to obtain clove and nutmeg seedlings. Two years of frustration resulted in just nine nutmeg seedlings, four of which drooped and died on the way back to Mauritius. He set off again for the Moluccas in 1754; during his absence the surviving five seedlings also died. But after further exploits both rash and improbable, he secured eleven more little nutmeg trees plus some some clove seeds. These too seem not to have survived long enough for propagation purposes, possibly because Poivre himself was again unable to lavish his attention on them. He had returned to France to report on the venture, had there married, and was happily establishing a botanical garden in Lyon when in 1776 he was reassigned to Mauritius and Réunion.

This time he went out as *intendant*, or civil governor, with instructions to reform the islands' ailing agricultural economy. He built a house, laid out a garden where all manner of tropical products were naturalised, and of course revived his designs on the spices of the Moluccas. The designs bore fruit in 1770. His two vessels found a disenchanted Dutchman on Ceram who directed them to some disaffected islanders nearby. Hundreds of nutmeg and clove seedlings and thousands of seeds and untreated nutmegs (the Dutch habitually sterilised exportable nuts with lime) were loaded; both ships then returned safely to Mauritius.

Poivre now had the means to realise his dream. Not without difficulty the trees were successfully raised, and the islands became a spice nursery. Although their modest export of dried spices made little impression on the overall trade, their export of healthy young seedlings finally ended the Moluccan monopoly. By the 1790s cultivation was spreading north to Madagascar and then Zanzibar (still the world's major clove producer) and west to Martinique in the Caribbean and then Grenada (still the major producer of nutmegs and mace). Production continued in Ambon and the Bandas, and it still does. Yet Indonesia is today a net importer of cloves, consuming more than any other market in the world. A few are eaten; the vast majority are smoked. Once a medicine, then a culinary additive, the *clou de girofle* is now a smokey aroma. Blended with tobacco and smoked without restraint, the clove-sweet *kretek* scents the entire archipelago. The Spice Islands still smell of spices, but they come from Zanzibar and are inhaled in cigarettes.

Hard on Poivre's heels, the British during the Napoleonic wars twice occupied the Moluccas and lifted more spice seedlings. Thomas Stamford Raffles, during his governorship of Bengkulu in 1815–20, found both cloves and nutmegs already there. Like Poivre, he encouraged further plantings in the hope of rescuing the otherwise ailing settlement by cashing in on what was now a decidedly niche market. But this Sumatran experiment was not a success. Like the introduction of pepper to Penang, which island had in 1796 become the first British settlement in Malaya, the difficulty of establishing spice gardens proved less formidable than that of finding a profitable market for their yield. In the 1890s the most successful arm of the spice trade was a cut-price operation involving Aceh's pepper and American vessels. With minimal crews and no overheads, the swift-sailing New England ships carried Sumatran pepper to Boston, often reshipped it to Europe and even the Levant, and still managed to undercut the Dutch.

Raffles's 1819 seizure of Singapore, and its rapid development as the commercial hub of the region in succession to Melaka and Batavia, might have given the British a hand on the throat of Amsterdam as grasping as Albuquerque's on the throat of Venice. Spice gardens were established on the Malay peninsula, and Singapore did indeed become the world's major spice market and entrepôt. It still is. But as a percentage of its total trade, spices were, and are, negligible.

Perhaps it was inevitable that as the definition of what consituted a spice became narrower, so their importance would contract. *Species* had been getting more specific ever since Pegolotti produced his list of 289. By the seventeenth century, drugs, dyes, incenses and perfumes had been progressively excluded. Only culinary additives still qualified; and only four or five of these were traded in sufficient quantity to merit commercial attention. New contenders, like tea and coffee, did not count; nor did sugar and opium, both of which were included in Pegolotti's listing. Nor did tobacco.

Oddly, the modern notion of spicy food being exclusively Asian or Mexican may be about to reverse this trend. A jar of *garam masala* plucked at random from a supermarket shelf lists only two recognised spices among its ingredients – ginger and cloves. Pepper – either black or chilli – is absent, an unaccountable omission which should disqualify the mix as *garam*. And the other components in this 'authentic blend of aromatic Indian spices' are all dried herbs or vegetables – coriander, fennel, dill and celery. The herbal invasion of the spice shelf seems to be gathering momentum with paprika, rose-petals, lemon grass and the seeds of poppy, fenugreek, sesame and mustard all represented. The heavy debt owed by the spice trade, and the spice route, to the vagaries of common usage and dictionary definition continues.

Notes

Chapter 1: Before the Fall

1. Pires, vol. II, p. 204.
2. Orta, p. 273.
3. Wallace, p. 297.
4. Herodotus, iii, III, quoted in Dalby, p. 37.
5. Maundevile, pp. 167–9.
6. Wheatley, pp. 282–305.
7. Yule and Burnell, p. 529.
8. Quoted in Chau Ju-Kua, p. 63.
9. Ibid, p. 62.
10. Strabo, II. 5.32, XV. 1.

Chapter 2: On the Origin of *Species*

1. Beeton, p. 216.
2. Pliny, XII. 3. 6.
3. Davidson, p. 744.
4. Pliny, XII. 33. 59.
5. Castanheda, Fernão Lopez de, *Historia do descobrimento e conquista da India*, quoted in Yule and Burnell, p. 284.
6. Lopez and Irving, p. 108; Pegolotti's list, pp. 109–14.
7. Quoted in Dalby, p. 70.
8. Maundevile, p. 56.
9. Pliny, XII. 54. 111.
10. John XII, 3.
11. Parry, p. 36.

12. Beeton, p. 183.
13. Rosengarten, p. 7.
14. Davidson, p. 745.
15. Pliny, XIII. 2. 18.
16. Ibid., XIII. 4. 22.
17. Ibid., XIII. 4. 25.

Chapter 3: Frankincense and Cinnamon

1. Pliny, XIII. 1. 2.
2. Proverbs vii, 17–18.
3. Pliny, XIII. 1. 1.
4. Ibid., XII. 14. 29.
5. Groom, pp. 22–4.
6. I Kings, 9–10.
7. Groom, p. 52.
8. Miller, pp. 153–172 and *passim*.
9. Pliny, XII. 42. 86–8.
10. Miller, p. 157.
11. Strabo, II. i. 17.
12. Ibid., II. 1. 14.
13. Miller, p. 10.
14. Agatharchides v. 52b.
15. Herodotus, III. 107.
16. Groom, pp. 160–1.
17. Browning, pp. 47–8.
18. See Crone, *passim*.
19. Agatharchides v. 99b.
20. Ibid., v. 101–1a.
21. Ibid., v. 105a.

Chapter 4: Hippalos and the Passage Across

1. Anon., *The Periplus of the Erythraean Sea*, p. 54.
2. Ibid., p. 52.
3. Strabo, XV. 1. 71.
4. Anon., *Periplus* p. 32.
5. Strabo, 111, p. 210.

6. Anon., *Periplus*, p. 35.
7. Ibid., p. 36.
8. Lionel Casson, 'Ancient Naval Technology and the Route to India', in Begley and de Puma, p. 10.
9. Anon., *Periplus*, pp. 41–2.
10. Ibid., pp. 42–3.
11. De Puma, 'The Roman Bronzes from Kolhapur', in Begley and de Puma, pp. 82–5.
12. Anon., *Periplus*, p. 50.
13. Pliny, XII. 60. 129.
14. Anon., *Periplus*, p. 54.
15. Ibid., p. 163.
16. Wheeler, pp. 137–50.
17. Anon., *Periplus*, p. 56.
18. Warmington, p. 189.

Chapter 5: Land of the Luminous Carbuncle

1. Lionel Casson, 'Ancient Naval Technology and the Route to India', in Begley and de Puma, p. 10.
2. E.g. in Miller, pp. 26–8.
3. Pliny, XII. 41. 84.
4. Miller, p. 11.
5. Pliny, XV. 31. 105.
6. Miller, p. 11.
7. Quoted in Dalby, p. 88.
8. Quoted ibid., p. 131.
9. Pliny, XII. 15. 30.
10. Wheeler, pp. 133–4.
11. Ibid., p. 139.
12. Wheatley, p. 138.
13. Quoted ibid., p. 139.
14. McCrindle, pp. 239–41.
15. Ibid., pp. 247–53.
16. Warmington, p. 140.
17. Cosmas Indicopleustes, p. 322 and *passim*.
18. Ibid., p. 365.
19. Ibid., p. 373.

Chapter 6: Insects on Splinters

1. Ferrand, vol. 1, pp. 101–2.
2. Quoted in Hourani, pp. 118–20.
3. Yule and Burnell, pp. 563–4.
4. Quoted in Hourani, pp. 54–5.
5. Quoted ibid., p. 66.
6. Edouard Chavannes, quoted in Ferrand, vol. 1, p. 633.
7. Quoted in Ferrard, vol. 1, p. 26.
8. Ibid., p. 28.
9. Ibid., p. 566.
10. Ibid., p. 31.
11. Hourani, pp. 76–7.
12. Ibid., pp. 75–6.
13. Buzurg, pp. 84–6.
14. Chaudhuri, p. 148.
15. Buzurg, pp. 49–52.

Chapter 7: The World Travellers

1. Goitein, vol. 1, pp. 215, 276.
2. Zakariya al-Kazwini, quoted in Mackintosh-Smith, p. 126.
3. Ferrand, vol. 11, pp. 300–15.
4. Pernoud, p. 104.
5. Ibid., pp. 108–9.
6. Rickert, pp. 87–8.
7. Chaucer, p. 90.
8. Maundevile, pp. 163, 196, 203, 223.
9. Ibid., pp. 187–8.
10. Ibid., p. 5.
11. Yule, vol. 1, p. 28.
12. Abu'l Ghazi Bahadur, khan of Khiva, quoted in Tucker, p. 224.
13. Yule, vol. 11, p. 293.
14. Polo, vol. 1, p. 108.
15. Ibn Batuta, vol. 11, p. 413.
16. Ibid., p. 361.
17. Polo, vol. 11, pp. 249–50.
18. Ibn Batuta, vol. 1V, pp. 813–14.
19. Polo, vol. 11, pp. 264–5.

20. Chau Ju-Kua, pp. 209–11.
21. Polo, vol. II, p. 284.
22. Ma Huan, pp. 108–9.

Chapter 8: East to West

1. Galvano, p. 57.
2. Paranavitana, pp. 331–41.
3. Ma Huan, p. 6.
4. Quoted in Wheatley, p. 89.
5. Ma Huan, pp. 91–2.
6. Ibid., p. 118.
7. See Levathes, pp. 114–17.
8. Ibid., pp. 195–203.
9. See Menzies.
10. Quoted in Wheatley, p. 89.
11. Conti, p. 17.
12. Ashtor, *Levant Trade*, p. 63.
13. Cadamosto, pp. 4–6.
14. Boxer, *The Portuguese Seaborne Empire*, p. 21.

Chapter 9: Christians and Spices

1. Camoes, vol. II, p. 11.
2. Cadamosto, pp. 36 ff.
3. Boxer, *The Portuguese Seaborne Empire*, p. 31.
4. Cadamosto, p. 108.
5. Ibid., pp. 46–7.
6. Ibid., p. 73.
7. Ibid., p. 91.
8. Ibid., pp. 108, 110, 124.
9. Galvano, p. 67.
10. João de Barros, quoted in Diffie and Winius, p. 176.
11. Osorius, quoted in Correa, pp. 38–9.
12. Gama pp. 3–5.
13. B. W. Diffie, in Diffie and Winius, p. 177.
14. Gama, p. 13.
15. Ibid., pp. 23–4.

16. De Barros, quoted in Correa, pp. 80–3.
17. Tibbetts, pp. 9–11.
18. Gama, p. 48.
19. Ibid., p. 77–8.
20. Ibid., p. 131.

Chapter 10: Peppered Ports and Curried Friar

1. Pires, vol. 1, p. 1.
2. Gama, pp. 87–93.
3. Ibid., pp. 113–14.
4. Ibid., pp. 115–16.
5. Ibid., p. 128.
6. 'Brazil-wood', in Yule and Burnell, p. 113.
7. Heyd, p. 519.
8. Lach, vol. 1, bk 1, pp. 104–5.
9. Correa, p. 381.
10. Ibid., pp. 299–302.
11. Ibid., p. 311.
12. Ibid., pp. 312–20.
13. Ibid., pp. 331–2.
14. Varthema, pp. 156, 178.
15. Correa, quoted in Diffie and Winius, p. 263.
16. Barbosa, vol. 11, p. 169.
17. Varthema, p. 224.
18. Pires, vol. 11, p. 285.

Chapter 11: Pacific Approaches

1. Camoes, trans. Fanshaw, quoted in Albuquerque, pp. 71–2.
2. Boxer, *The Portuguese Seaborne Empire*, pp. 62.
3. Varthema, pp. 223–4.
4. Albuquerque, vol. 111, p. 65.
5. Ibid., pp. 116–18.
6. Ibid., p. 127.
7. Pires, vol. 11, pp. 286–7.
8. Lach, vol. 1, bk 1, pp. 166–7.
9. Diffie and Winius, p. 360.

10. Varthema, pp. 243–7.
11. Quoted in Diffie and Winius, p. 361.
12. Orta, p. 273.
13. Hanna, p. 8.
14. Pires, vol. I, pp. 214–15.
15. Pigafetta, vol. I, p. 88.
16. Ibid., p. 113.

Chapter 12: Blue Water

1. Linschoten, vol. I, pp. 1–2.
2. Pigafetta, vol. I, p. 127.
3. Lach, vol. I, bk I, p. 118.
4. Pigafetta, vol. I, pp. 146–7.
5. Ibid., p. 148.
6. F. C. Lane 'The Mediterranean Spice Trade: Further Evidence of its Revival in the Sixteenth Century', in *American Historical Review*, vol. XLV, 1940, repr. in Pearson, p. 585.
7. See especially C. H. H. Wake, 'The Changing Pattern of Europe's Pepper and Spice Imports, *ca* 1400–1700', in *Journal of European Economic History*, vol. VIII, 1979, repr: in Pearson pp. 361–403.
8. Meilink-Roelofsz, p. 144.
9. C. R. Boxer, 'A Note on Portuguese Reactions to the Revival of the Red Sea Spice Trade and the Rise of Atjeh, 1540–1600', in *Journal of Southeast Asian History* vol. X, 1969, pp. 415–28.
10. Drake, p. 137.
11. Ibid., p. 138.
12. Williamson, p. 193.
13. Linschoten, vol. I, pp. 112–13.
14. Quoted in Keay, *Honourable Company*, p. 11.
15. Purchas, vol. II, p. 186.
16. See Furber, vol. II, p. 343.
17. Lach, vol. I bk I, pp. 225–6.
18. Penrose, p. 201.
19. Linschoten, vol. I, pp. 111–14.
20. Furber, vol. II, p. 12.

Chapter 13: Infected by Spices

1. Purchas, vol. v, p. 232.
2. Glamann, pp. 23–4.
3. Pepys, v, p. 146.
4. Purchas, vol. II, p. 315.
5. Lancaster, p. 108.
6. John Bastin, 'The Changing Balance of the Southeast Asian Pepper Trade', repr. in Pearson, pp. 284–5.
7. Quoted in Hanna and Des Alwi, pp. 118–9.
8. Middleton, p. 54.
9. Quoted in Hanna, p. 34.
10. Purchas, vol. v, p. 182.
11. Ibid., pp. 104–5.
12. See Hanna; Keay, *Honourable Company*; and Milton.
13. Hanna, p. 55.
14. J.S. Wurfbain, 'Fifj Jaren op Banda', ed. N. P. van den Berg, in *Tijdscrift van het Bataavisch Genootshap*, 1872, quoted in Hanna, pp. 66–7.
15. Quoted in Furber, p. 57.

Select Bibliography

Agatharchides of Cnidos, *On the Erythraean Sea*, trans. Stanley M. Burnstein, Hakluyt Society, London, 1989.

Albuquerque, Affonso de, *The Commentaries of the Great Afonzo Dalboquerque*, trans. and ed. W. de G. Birch, 4 vols, Hakluyt Society, London, 1880–4.

Anon, *The Periplus of the Erythraean Sea*, trans. G. W. B. Huntingford, Hakluyt Society, London, 1980

Ashtor, Eliyahu, *Levant Trade in the Later Middle Ages*, Princeton University Press, Princeton, 1983.

——, (ed.), *Studies on the Levantine Trade in the Middle Ages*, Variorum, London, 1978.

Ballard, G. A., *Rulers of the Indian Ocean*, London, 1926; repr. Asian Education Services, New Delhi, 1998.

Barbosa, Duarte, *The Book of Duarte Barbosa: an Account of the Countries Bordering on the Indian Ocean etc.*, ed. M. L. Dames, 2 vols, Hakluyt Society, London, 1918–21.

Beeton, Isabella, *Mrs Beeton's Book of Household Management*, Ward, Lock, London, 1915.

Begley, Vimala, and de Puma, R. D. (eds), *Rome and India: the Ancient Sea Route*, University of Wisconsin Press, Madison, 1991.

Boxer, C. R., *The Dutch Seaborne Empire 1600–1800*, Hutchinson, London, 1965.

——, *The Portuguese Seaborne Empire 1415–1825*, Hutchinson, London, 1969.

——, *Dutch Merchants and Mariners in Asia 1602–1795*, Variorum, London, 1988

Browning, Iain, *Petra*, Chatto and Windus, London, 1973.

Buzurg ibn Shahriyar of Ramhormus, *The Book of the Wonders of India*, ed. and trans. G. S. P. Freeman-Grenville, East-West, London, 1981.

Byrne, E. H., *Genoese Shipping in the Twelfth and Thirteenth Centuries*, Medieval Academy of America, Cambridge, Mass., 1930.

Cabral, Pedro Alvares, *The Voyage of Cabral*, trans. and ed. William Brooks Greenlee, Hakluyt Society, London, 1938.

Cadamosto, *The Voyages of Cadamosto and Other Documents*, trans. and ed. C. R. Crone, Hakluyt Society, London, 1937.

Camoes, Luis de, *Os Lusiadas*, trans. R. F. Burton, 2 vols, Quaritch, London, 1880.

Cary, M. and Warmington, E. H., *The Ancient Explorers*, Methuen, London, 1929.

Charlesworth, M. P., *Trade Routes and Commerce of the Roman Empire*, Cambridge University Press, Cambridge. 1926.

Chaucer, Geoffrey, 'The Tale of Sir Topas' *The Canterbury Tales*, in *The Works of Geoffrey Chaucer*, ed. A. W. Pollard, Macmillan, London, 1898.

Chaudhuri, K. N., *Trade and Civilization in the Indian Ocean: an Economic History from the Rise of Islam until 1750*, Cambridge University Press, Cambridge, 1985.

Chau Ju-Kua, *His Work on the Chinese and Arab Trade in the Twelfth and Thirteenth Centuries entitled* Chu-fan-shi, trans. F. Hirth and W. W. Rockhill, Imperial Academy of Sciences, St Petersburg, 1911.

Conti, Nicolo de, 'The Travels of Nicolo de Conti in the East' in *India in the Fifteenth Century*, ed. R. H. Major, Hakluyt Society, London, 1857.

Corn, Charles, *The Scents of Eden: a History of the Spice Trade*, Kodansha, New York, 1998.

Correa, Gaspar, *The Three Voyages of Vasco da Gama and his Viceroyalty*, trans. and ed. H. E. J. Stanley, Hakluyt Society, London, 1869.

Cosmas Indicopleustes, *The Christian Topography of Cosmas*, trans. and ed. J. W. MacCrindle, Hakluyt Society, London, 1897.

Crone, Patricia, *Meccan Trade and the Rise of Islam*, Blackwell, Oxford, 1987.

Cummins, John, *Francis Drake: the Lives of a Hero*, Weidenfeld and Nicolson, London, 1995.

Dalby, Andrew, *Dangerous Tastes: the Story of Spices*, British Museum, London, 2000.

Danvers, F. C., *The Portuguese in India*, W. H. Allen & Co., London, 1894.

Davidson, Alan, *The Oxford Companion to Food*, Oxford University Press, Oxford, 1999.

Davis, John, *The Works and Voyages of John Davis*, ed. A. H. Markham, Hakluyt Society, London, 1880.

Diffie, B. W. and Winius, G. D., *Foundations of the Portuguese Empire 1415–1580*, University of Minnesota Press, Minneapolis, 1977.

Disney, A. R., *Twilight of the Pepper Empire, Portuguese Trade in South West*

India in the Early Seventeenth Century, Harvard University Press, Cambridge, Mass., 1978.

Drake, Francis, *The World Encompassed*, ed. W. S. W. Vaux, Hakluyt Society, London, 1854.

Fels, Marthe, *Pierre Poivre ou l'Amour des Epices*, Hachette, Paris, 1968.

Ferrand, Gabriel (trans. and ed.), *Relations de Voyages et Textes Géographiques Arabes, Persans et Turks Relatifs à l'Extrême Orient du VIIIe à XVIIIe Siècles*, 2 vols, Leroux, Paris, 1913.

Furber, Holden, *Rival Empires of Trade in the Orient 1600–1800*, Oxford University Press, London, 1976.

Galvão, Antonio, *The Discoveries of the World from their First Original unto AD 1555*, ed. C. R. D. Bethune, Hakluyt Society, London, 1862.

Gama, Vasco da, *Journal of the First Voyage*, ed. E. G. Ravenstein, Hakluyt Society, London, 1898.

Glamann, Kristof, *Dutch Asiatic Trade 1620–1740*, Danish Science Press and Martinius Nijhoff, Copenhagen and The Hague, 1968.

Goitein, S. D., *A Mediterranean Society: the Jewish Communities of the Arab World as Portrayed in the Documents of Cairo Geniza*, 6 vols, University of California Press, Berkeley, 1967–93.

Groom, Nigel, *Frankincense and Myrrh*, Longman, London, 1981.

Hall, Richard, *Empires of the Monsoon: a History of the Indian Ocean and its Invaders*, HarperCollins, London, 1996.

Hanna, Willard A., *Indonesian Banda: Colonialism and its Aftermath in the Nutmeg Islands*, Institute for the Study of Human Issues, Philadelphia, 1978.

Hanna, Willard A and Des Alwi, *Turbulent Times Past in Ternate and Tidore*, Yayasan Warisan dan Budaya, Banda Naira, 1990.

Herodotus, *The Histories*, trans. Aubrey de Selincourt, Penguin, London, 1972.

Heyd, W., *Histoire de Commerce du Levant au Moyen Age*, 2 vols, Harrassowitz, Leipzig, 1923.

Hourani, G. F., *Arab Seafaring in the Indian Ocean in Ancient and Early Medieval Times*, Khayats, Beirut, 1963.

Jayne, C. K., *Vasco da Gama and His Successors, 1460–1580*, Methuen, London, 1910.

Ibn Batuta, *The Travels of Ibn Battuta*, trans. H. A. R. Gibb, 5 vols, Hakluyt Society, Cambridge, 1962.

Keay, John, *The Honourable Company: a History of the English East India Company*, HarperCollins, London, 1991.

——, *India: a History*, HarperCollins, London, 2000.

Lach, Donald, *Asia in the Making of Europe*, 6 vols, University of Chicago Press, Chicago, 1965–93.

Lancaster, James, *The Voyages of Sir James Lancaster to Brazil and the East Indies 1591–1603*, ed. William Foster, Hakluyt Society, London, 1940.

Lane, F. C., *Venetian Ships and Ship-building of the Renaissance*, Johns Hopkins Press, Baltimore, 1934.

Levathes, Louise, *When China Ruled the Seas*, Oxford University Press, Oxford, 1990.

Linschoten, Jan Huyghen van, *The Voyage of Jan Huyghen van Linschoten*, ed. and trans. A. C. Burnell and P. A. Tiele, 2 vols, Hakluyt Society, London, 1885.

Lopez, R. S. and Raymond, I. W., *Medieval Trade in the Mediterranean World: Illustrative Documents*, Oxford University Press, London, 1955.

Ma Huan, *Ying-Yai Shen-Yang, 'The Overall Survey of the Ocean's Shores'*, trans. J. V. G. Mills, Hakluyt Society, Cambridge, 1970.

McCrindle, J. W., *Ancient India as Described by Ptolemy*, Calcutta, 1885.

Mackintosh-Smith, Tim, *Travels with a Tangerine*, Murray, London, 2001.

Maundevile, Sir John, *The Voiage and Travaile*, ed. G. Halliwell, Reeves and Turner, London, 1883.

Meilink-Roelofsz, M. A. P., *Asian Trade and European Influence in the Indonesian Archipelago, 1500–1630*, Nijhoff, The Hague, 1962.

Menzies, Gavin, *1421: The Year China Discovered the World*, Bantam, London, 2002.

Middleton, Henry, *The Voyage of Sir Henry Middleton to the Moluccas 1604–06*, ed. William Foster, Hakluyt Society, London, 1943.

Miller, J. Innes, *The Spice Trade of the Roman Empire, 29 BC to AD 641*, Clarendon Press, Oxford, 1969.

Milton, Giles, *Nathaniel's Nutmeg*, Hodder, London, 1999.

Orta, Garcia da, *Colloquies on the Simples and Drugs of India*, trans. and ed. C. R. Markham, Henry Sotheran & Co., London, 1913.

Paranavitana, S., 'The Tamil Inscription on the Galle Trilingual Slab', in *Epigraphia Zeylanica*, no. 36, vol 3 (1928–33), OUP, London, 1933.

Parry, J. H., *Europe and a Wider World 1415–17*, Hutchinson, London, 1949.

Parsons, Edward Alexander, *The Alexandrian Library*, American Elsevier, New York, 1952.

Pearson, M. N. (ed.), *Spices in the Indian Ocean World*, Variorum, London, 1996.

Penrose, Boies, *Travel and Discovery in the Renaissance 1420–1620*, Harvard University Press, Cambridge, Mass., 1960.

Pepys, Samuel, *The Diary of Samuel Pepys*, ed. H. B. Wheatley, Geo Ben, London, 1895.

Pernoud, Regine, *The Crusades*, trans. Enid MacLeod, Secker and Warburg, London, 1962.

Pigafetta, Antonio, *Magellan's Voyage: a Narrative Account of the First Circumnavigation*, trans. and ed. R. A. Skelton, 2 vols, Yale University Press, New Haven, 1969.

Pires, Tome, *The Suma Oriental*, trans. and ed. A. Cortesao, 2 vols, Hakluyt Society, London, 1944.

Pliny, *Natural History*, trans. H. Rackham, 10 vols, Heineman, London, 1968.

Polo, Marco, *The Book of Ser Marco Polo*, trans. and ed. H. Yule and H. Cordier, 2 vols, Murray, London, 1921.

Ptolemy, *Ancient India as Described by Ptolemy*, ed. J. W. MacCrindle, Trubner, London, 1865.

Purchas, Samuel, *Hakluytus Posthumus or Purchas His Pilgrimes*, 20 vols, repr. Maclehose, Glasgow, 1905.

Rickert, E., *Chaucer's World*, Oxford University Press, London, 1948.

Rosengarten, Frederick, *A Book of Spices*, Livingston Publishing Co., Wynnewood, PA, 1969.

Schivelbusch, Wolfgang, *Tastes of Paradise*, Pantheon, New York, 1992.

Simkin, C. G. F., *The Traditional Trade of Asia*, Oxford University Press, London, 1968.

Strabo, *The Geography*, trans. H. C. Hamilton and W. Falconer, 3 vols, H. G. Bohn, London, 1854.

Theophrastus, *Enquiry into Plants* and *Concerning Odours*, trans. A. Hart, Loeb, London, 1916.

Tibbetts, G. R., *Arab Navigation in the Indian Ocean Before the Coming of the Portuguese*, Royal Asiatic Society and Luzac, London, 1971.

Tomalin, Claire, *Samuel Pepys: The Unequalled Self*, Viking, London, 2002.

Tucker, Jonathan, *The Silk Road: Art and History*, Philip Wilson, London, 2003.

Turner, Jack, *Spice: the History of a Temptation*, HarperCollins, London, 2004.

Unger, Richard W., *The Ship in the Medieval Economy 600–1600*, Croom Helm, London, 1980.

Valentijn, François, *Description of Ceylon*, trans. and ed. Sinnappan Arasaratnam, Hakluyt Society, London, 1978.

Varthema, Ludovico di, *Travels of Ludovico di Varthema*, trans. J.W. Jones and G. P. Badger, Hakluyt Society, London, 1863.

Wallace, A. R., *The Malay Archipelago*, 1869, repr. Oxford University Press, Singapore, 1986.

Warmington, E. H., *The Commerce Between the Roman Empire and India*, Cambridge University Press, Cambridge, 1928.

Wheatley, Paul, *The Golden Khersonese*, University of Malaya Press, Kuala Lumpur, 1961.

Wheeler, R. E. M., *Rome Beyond the Imperial Frontiers*, G. Bell & Sons, London, 1954.

Williamson, James A., *The Age of Drake*, A. and C. Black, London, 1938.

Wood, Frances, *The Silk Road*, Folio Society, London, 2002.

Yule, H., *Cathay and the Way Thither*, 2 vols, Hakluyt Society, London, 1866.

Yule, H. and Burnell, A. C., *Hobson-Jobson: a Glossary of Anglo-Indian Words etc.*, 1886, repr. Routledge and Kegan Paul, London, 1968.

Index

INDEX

Chancellor, Richard, 217
Chandragupta, Mauryan Emperor, 46, 65
Chang-lo, Fujian, 131
Charles I, King of Spain, 200
Charles II, King of England, 245–6
Charles V, Holy Roman Emperor
(Charles I, King of Spain), 200–1,
207–8
Chau Ju-Kua, 25; 'Description of the
Barbarous People', 11, 118
Chaucer, Geoffrey, 105, 111
Cheng-ho (Zheng He), Admiral, 88,
122, 127–8, 130–5, 143, 152, 163,
189, 215
chilli see pepper, chilli
China: Arab trade with, 100–3; Buddhist
pilgrims from, 90; curtails voyages,
134–5; and development of Melaka,
122, 131, 189; early use of spices,
33–4; foreign merchants in, 101;
imports costus, 26; Maundeville on,
112; Ming enterprise and voyages,
129–30, 133–5; monopolises spice
trade, 30; and overland spice route,
8–9; pepper imports, 13; in Periplus,
70, 81–2; Portuguese interest in, 194;
presence in Sri Lanka, 126–7; in
Ptolemy, 81–2; putative round-the-
world voyage, 134; ship design, 94–5,
101–4, 115–16, 128–30; silk from, xi,
70, 75, 87, 99; in spice trade from
Malaya and Indonesia, xi, 9–10, 76,
101; tea from, 246, 252; trans-
Himalayan trade, 71; volume of spice
trade, 122; and western trade, 89;
western travellers to, 114; withdraws
from Indian Ocean exploration, 128–9
chocolate (drink), 251, 253
Chola kingdom (Tamil Nadu), 120
Chou K'u-fei, 11
Christianity: adopted by Rome, 84; in
Ambon, 234; conflict with Islam,
106–7; in Kerala, 78–9, 170;
Portuguese voyagers proselytise, 144,
147; rise of, 80
Chryse see Sumatra

cinnabar (dragon's blood), 24, 61
cinnamon: from Americas, 250; in
ancient Egypt, 36; from Arabia, 100;
early trade routes, 41–3; early use in
China, 33; Herodotus on, 4–5, 10;
from India, 67, 170; price, 73,
214–15; sources, xiii, 5, 42–4, 58, 99,
137, 163, 187, 247; from Sri Lanka,
99, 137, 163, 187, 247
Claudius, Roman Emperor, 78
Cleopatra, Queen of Egypt, 14, 57
cloves: Aetius on, 84; in Ambon, 234,
236–7, 253; in ancient Rome, 76;
availability in India, 188; in Calicut,
163; as meat preservative, 27; as
modern ingredient, 256; from
Moluccas, 1, 4, 9, 13, 34, 76, 118,
137, 195, 197–9, 205, 234, 253;
prices, 201; sources, 100, 255; trade
routes, 41, 212, 247; transport, 13;
value, 214–15; in Zanzibar, 255
Clysma (Suez), 79
Cochin: Dutch occupy, 235, 247;
harbour, 133; and local pepper trade,
67; Portuguese in, 170, 178–9, 183
coconut, 86
Coelho, Nicolau, 157, 165, 167, 168
Coen, Jan Pieterszoon, 241–3
coffee, 230, 251–3
cogs (ships), 139
coins, Greek: in Barygaza, 64
coins, Roman: in India, 12, 70, 79; in
Sri Lanka, 83
coir, 102, 115
colocynth, 26
Colombo, Sri Lanka, 187, 235, 247
Columbus, Christopher: believes arrival
in Indies, 81, 185–6; discoveries,
153–4, 156; lands in Hispaniola, 109;
and Marco Polo's descriptions, 115;
misidentifies spices, 166, 250–1;
proposes westward voyage to Indies,
151–3; revisits Caribbean, 154–5; in
search for spices, ix, 6; ships, xiii;
takes sugar cane to West Indies, 253;
on voyage to Gold Coast, 151

274